CRISIS

40 STORIES REVEALING
THE PERSONAL, SOCIAL, AND RELIGIOUS
PAIN AND TRAUMA OF GROWING UP GAY IN AMERICA

EDITED BY
MITCHELL GOLD
WITH **MINDY DRUCKER**

GREENLEAF
BOOK GROUP PRESS

Published by Greenleaf Book Group Press
4425 South Mo Pac Expwy, Suite 600
Longhorn Building, 3rd Floor
Austin, TX 78735

Distributed by Greenleaf Book Group LLC

For ordering information or special discounts for bulk purchases, please contact Greenleaf Book Group LLC at 4425 South Mo Pac Expwy, Suite 600, Longhorn Building, 3rd Floor, Austin, TX 78735, (512) 891-6100.

Design and composition by Greenleaf Book Group LLC
Cover design by Greenleaf Book Group LLC

Publisher's Cataloging-in-Publication Data
(Prepared by The Donohue Group, Inc.)
Crisis : 40 stories revealing the personal, social, and religious pain and
  trauma of growing up gay in America / edited by Mitchell Gold with Mindy
  Drucker. -- 1st ed.
    p. ; cm.

  ISBN: 978-1-929774-10-4

1. Homosexuality--United States. 2. Gays--United States--Social conditions. 3. Gays--United States--Biography. 4. Gays--United States--Attitudes. 5. Homophobia--United States. I. Gold, Mitchell. II. Drucker, Mindy. III. Title.
HQ76.3.U6 C75 2008
306.76/6/0973   2008931128

Printed in the United States of America on recycled paper

Part of the Tree Neutral™ program that offsets the number of trees consumed in printing this book by taking proactive steps such as planting trees in direct proportion to the number of trees used. www.treeneutral.com

TreeNeutral

12 11 10 09 08   10 9 8 7 6 5 4 3 2 1

First Edition

DEDICATION

There are teenagers all over the world today in crisis mode because they fear what will happen if others discover their sexual orientation. They suffer debilitating depression, isolation, and possibly even suicidal thoughts. I dedicate this book to them in the hopes that not one more teenager will have to live the way I did in my teenage years.

And to news correspondent Scott Shepard. Our cup of coffee in the great hall of Washington's Union Station was the catalyst for me to put this book together. Sometimes asking a basic question leads to answers far beyond what we imagined.

CONTENTS

*Martina Navratilova in 1980, above,
and at Wimbledon in 2007, opposite*

FOREWORD
BY MARTINA NAVRATILOVA

While I don't share an American teen experience with the contributors to this book, I have been out in America since I got my U.S. citizenship in 1981, at age twenty-five. People have called me brave for living as an openly gay person in the public eye for so many years. But why should it require bravery simply to be who you are?

I want gay teenagers today to feel safe and accepted and comfortable coming out. I don't want them to be afraid. In my experience, being the best at something requires you to fully know yourself and to be able to be yourself with others: No wasting energy hiding something that is simply not wrong. No making choices to keep your "secret" rather than achieve your potential. No living a lie because you feel you must to be successful.

As a professional tennis player, when I came out, my focus wasn't on things like losing endorsements or handling the press or even sacrificing personal privacy. The biggest thing on my mind was being true to myself: I realized that I couldn't go on being a champion on the court if I was leaving half of myself off the court. I know some people felt I could have reached my potential without it; but now, looking back, I know I couldn't have.

That's my advice to every young person: Consider the cost of not being yourself. When you hide who you are, you come at life from such a negative angle that it makes you feel like you're not as good as the person next to you—you yourself feel less than. And that is no way to become a champion. It also affects you on a personal level: You need to love yourself before you can do the same for someone else.

One of the most important things anyone can do is to read and get educated. That's what helped my father come to terms with my being gay. I hadn't planned on telling my parents I was gay unless they asked. When I was twenty-five my father said, "You and your girlfriend live like man and wife." And I said, "Well, yes." And he immediately said, "What did we do wrong? Did you have a bad experience with your boyfriend?" I tried to tell him it didn't have anything to do with him and that the boyfriend had been just fine (though not brilliant . . .).

He was confused. He said some things that weren't very nice. But we never stopped talking. He decided to read some books to educate himself. I didn't give him any books; my father took it upon himself to get ones he felt were fair and impartial. And what he read helped him realize that neither he nor I had anything to do with it. It was unusual, but it was perfectly natural. Within a year, he came around to the point where what he cared about was me being happy, not that I was gay. Which is exactly how it should be.

That's why this book is so important. It will help educate and enlighten. And its editor, Mitchell Gold, is the right guide. When I first met Mitchell at a fundraiser for the Metropolitan Community Church, I knew I'd found a kindred spirit. One thing we have in common is our belief that prejudice of any sort, for any reason, is unacceptable. And each of us in our own way is committed to doing all we can to obliterate it—Mitchell with this book and his nonprofit organization, Faith in America, and me with the Rainbow Endowment, a philanthropic group that supports gay causes.

When Mitchell told me he was putting together "an exposé of a mental health crisis in this country that can easily be solved"—the pain, depression, isolation, and fear gay teens past and present have experienced—I couldn't have agreed more about the need for a book like this. I, too, believe this crisis can be solved with simple human compassion, respect, acceptance, and understanding. This is a problem being created by prejudiced people looking to cause drama and to foment hate. It's really no different from the Ku Klux Klan.

If you are heterosexual, I ask you to read this book with an open mind and have compassion for the unnecessary pain gay teens go through. Please know that your support can make a huge difference in the lives of your gay family members, friends, neighbors, and coworkers. When I first came out, the public support I received from Chris Evert, my on-court rival and long-time friend, made such a difference to me. Her acceptance made other people's prejudices easier to bear.

If you are a member of the gay community, please share this book with your family and friends. The stories it contains will encourage them to work with you to create lasting change.

To the parents, educators, and clergy of gay teens, please give gay kids the acceptance and support they need. To politicians, when you legislate, remember that the lives of these young Americans are in your hands. And to the members of the media, many of whom I've come to know over the years, please take the time to ask the tough questions of people in power so they don't get away with denying other people their rights because of religion-based bigotry once again.

It is astonishing to see the negativity that comes out of the supposedly loving environment of the church. Religion plays such a divisive role—which is so sad because it is supposed to bring people together. Lately, it is being used to separate people more and more. As if we didn't have enough problems in our world today . . .

Thank you for trying to understand and doing your part in ridding our world of all prejudices.

—Martina Navratilova, September 2008

Preface
WHY THIS BOOK?

L ast year someone accused me of being anti-religion. I am not, of course. Actually, over the past several years I have gained a greater appreciation for religion from clergy including the Reverends Jimmy Creech, Mel White, Stephen Shoemaker, Jeff Miner, Pat Bumgardner, Larry Keene, Gene Robinson, and Nancy Wilson—and through the nonprofit organization I founded three years ago, Faith in America, which gives voice to people of deep faith. This misconception may have occurred because I often talk about how religion has been, and continues to be, misused by so many people to hurt other people. The misguided and ill-informed preachings of some cause great harm to gay people—from severe emotional pain to increasing the likelihood of being victims of physical violence and even leading some to feel they have no alternative but suicide. I'm not sure people know this, and so I've compiled this book in the hopes that it will encourage everyone to take a serious look at the effects of religious intolerance on their gay, lesbian, bisexual, and transgender children, family, friends, and neighbors.

I know how religious teachings can lead to prejudice. As a Jewish boy growing up in New Jersey in the 1960s, I experienced it firsthand. One day in particular stands out: I was ten years old, and like most days, headed across the street to see if Jimmy B. could come out to play. As I approached his house, Jimmy came running out, screaming for me to stop. He called me a "dirty Jew" and said he didn't want me on his property. He was frantic. I was shocked. I had no idea what he was talking about. His mother, one of the nicest people I can remember, appeared behind him, also in shock. She asked him why he had spoken to me that way. Jimmy explained that the nun at school (he attended the local parochial school) had taught them that the Jews killed Jesus and that they were sinners.

I can't remember exactly what Mrs. B. told him, but she calmed him down and somehow explained that although this was part of history as Catholics saw it, it was not a reason to hate me. It left me very confused.

Around the same time I also began to see that not everything I was learning about my own religion could be taken at face value. In religious school, we were taught that the Jews were "the chosen people." I can't remember exactly how our teachers explained what that meant, but the impression we kids got was that we were better than non-Jews because of it. When I tried asking my parents about it, the way they frowned at the idea that Jews, or anybody, could be better than anybody else, made me realize that not all of what I heard at synagogue was to be taken literally. This was my first loss of youthful innocence in the face of religion, and it made me aware that there was more than one way to interpret religious doctrine.

I got two other very vivid childhood lessons about prejudice and discrimination from my parents. Those lessons have shaped me into the person I am today.

When I was in junior high, my father owned a grocery store. One of his employees, an older black woman, became ill, and after a long recovery, she stopped in to tell us she'd be back to work the following week. She was so happy to be well! My father, who was very fond of her, gave her a big hug—to my surprise. But when she tried to hug me, I pulled away. At school many kids said blacks were inferior—they often talked about how it said so in the Bible. I wasn't going to hug a colored woman . . .

My father was furious. I can still see the embarrassment and disappointment on his face. He pulled me into the back of the store, where I got a long lesson in respect—which I believe was his way of saying equality—one I never forgot.

Via our black-and-white television, the words of Alabama governor George Wallace's 1963 inaugural address penetrated our Northern suburban bubble: "Segregation now, segregation tomorrow, segregation forever!" I can also recall how Wallace—along with many Southern religious institutions—misused religion to justify his bigotry and his opposition to the Civil Rights Act of 1964. It was my mother who explained to me that not all religious people felt that way. One of the many things I cherish about my parents is that they taught me not just that prejudice is wrong, but how very destructive it is.

I became interested in history and learned that abolitionism and women's suffrage had their roots in religious communities like the Quakers and Congregationalists. Some people, it seemed, used their religious beliefs to look for ways to love instead of hate. I remember feeling delight as I realized this.

I thought about that a lot when I moved to Hickory, the small North Carolina town where I've lived for almost twenty years. Coming from New York City in the late 1980s, I had expected the South to be far less accepting of homosexuality, of course. Still, I was taken aback by how ingrained some of the prejudice was. The local fundamentalist churches, which say they interpret their Bible literally, look at being gay as a chosen behavior that can—and should—be changed. What hurts me most is seeing the way this translates to how gay teenagers are often treated. Common sense alone can tell you that trying to suppress or change the sexual orientation you are born with is not only impossible, but also horribly painful to attempt. I know firsthand.

So I've made it my business to get to know as many ministers and congregants as I can. And I am struck that so many ministers are afraid of challenging their church leaders or congregants—even when they know in their hearts that such prejudice is wrong.

In 2007, our nonprofit organization, Faith in America, ran an ad campaign in local papers. The ads documented how some American churches had found endorsements for slavery and Jim Crow—and a basis to oppose interracial marriage and voting rights for women and blacks—in the Bible and religion. Our purpose was to underscore that those same churches are today using their teachings to oppress and denigrate gay people.

In response, the local organization of Southern Baptist ministers sponsored a revival in my town. I decided to attend. About twelve hundred people came to an event featuring a minister billed as a "former homosexual"; he acknowledged that being gay was how one was born and that gay people should be treated with respect and caused no physical harm—but he also preached that gay people can control their behavior by accepting Jesus Christ as their savior and having a personal relationship with God.

It devastated me to see people with their children there. Did they not realize what kind of message they were sending to kids who, after all, might themselves be gay? As I said above and will explain several times throughout this book, I know from personal experience that trying to change your sexual orientation gives rise to an inordinate amount of unnecessary suffering. That minister, and the parents who brought their children that evening, committed nothing less than child abuse. I realize that might seem like a very harsh thing to say. I believe most of these parents would not do this intentionally. I know they love their children very much. But the unintended consequence of their actions will be nothing less than horrific for their kids.

You will read about the debilitating effects teachings like that minister's have had on many people, particularly teenagers, in the coming pages. For every well-known gay person in this book, there are thousands of everyday people who have gone through similar, painful experiences. One of them is my friend Jeff Austin. Let me tell you a little about him.

Jeff grew up in rural Alexander County, North Carolina, where my furniture factory is located. His father was a "full-blooded Southern Baptist minister," as he likes to say, so religion played a big part in his life—a role that did not always jibe with who he knew he was. "There were so many times

I thought about going down to my dad's red barn, taking the rope that was there, and hanging myself from a beam," Jeff remembers. "That way no one would ever have to know."

But Jeff soldiered through instead. Being the son of a preacher in the South carries a lot of expectations, and for years he tried to live up

Mitchell Gold with Jeff Austin (left)

to them. He married and had children. When his marriage failed, he remarried. "If anyone should receive an Academy Award, it's a gay guy trying to live a straight life," says Jeff.

Oscar-worthy performance or not, Jeff was unhappy. "I thought I was supposed to be miserable: grow up to become a miserable man, a miserable husband, and live a miserable life." But about two years ago, he decided he couldn't continue acting—or being miserable—anymore. He didn't know how his children would react, but he decided to tell them the truth. He picked moving day.

His son, now in his twenties, was helping him carry a dresser off the U-Haul he had rented for the move to his new apartment.

"We got halfway through the door and I set my end down," Jeff recalls, "and I said, 'Chris, I need to talk to you for a minute.'"

"He said, 'Now?'"

"I said, 'Yeah, now. I need to tell you something.'"

"And he said, 'Dad. I know. You're gay. Pick up your end of the dresser, and let's go.'"

Jeff was dumbfounded.

"I want you to be happy," Jeff told me Chris continued, "and if this is you, then I love you no matter what. Now pick up your end of the dresser and let's go."

So they did.

His daughter was similarly warm and accepting, as was his brother. He was divorced amicably, and even his mother eventually came around. "It wasn't easy for her at first," Jeff admits, "but over the last year, she's told me, 'As long as you're happy, then I'm your mom and I'm gonna love you no matter what.' I've even brought my boyfriends over to meet her on the holidays."

Jeff confides, "For many, many, many, years, I really thought that I was gonna lose my family." Yet even Jeff and his sister—with whose Barbie dolls he used to play as a kid—are on good terms. Of all his family members, she was perhaps the most conflicted. Deeply religious and a Christian Coalition member, "it took her time to move beyond the 'love the sinner, hate the sin' thing," as Jeff says. But her love for her brother won out.

Achieving that kind of happy ending—without the prior decades of misery—is the impetus behind this book.

It is time to admit that the ideology of "love the sinner, hate the sin," like the ideology behind "separate but equal," is just another way of excusing discrimination and a way of teaching that ultimately leads to hatred, bigotry, and violence. The notion that someone can change his or her sexual orientation has been discredited by health professionals time and time again. Telling people they can pray away their sexual orientation must be recognized for what it is: harmful advice wreathed in saccharine loving-kindness.

Many people, including Governor George Wallace, once saw biblical verses in Genesis as a valid basis for enslaving African-Americans. Most people find that repugnant today—as did Wallace by the end of his life. He actually apologized to people of color some years ago. The Southern Baptist Convention officially apologized about ten years ago to black people as well. Many say that in time, biblical justifications for the oppression of gay people will seem just as offensive as biblical justifications for slavery seem now. But why must we wait?

I founded Faith in America because I did not want to see one more teenager go through what I did: The terror and fear I felt when I first realized I had intimate feelings for boys and not girls, the isolating belief that I was the only one who felt that way, the depression that haunted me from twelve until well into my twenties, causing constant suicidal ideation.

As a boy I saw how hatred cloaked in religion was used to oppress an entire race of people; I also witnessed their struggle, based in a different set of churches, to overcome that oppression and achieve equality.

As a closeted young gay man, I experienced the effects of prejudice and ignorance.

And now I see how bigotry disguised as religious truth has affected people like my friend Jeff and the men and women who share their stories in the pages that follow.

Making sure their stories get told so that the millions of others who come after them do not have to repeat their experiences was inspiration for this book. Please join me in ending the harm now, the roots of which grow in the soil of fear and lack of knowledge.

—Mitchell Gold, September 2008

STATS I WISH I DIDN'T HAVE TO SHARE

It is both devastating and enlightening to see so many of the same words running through the stories in this book: *depression, fear, isolation, loneliness, hopelessness, thoughts of suicide.*

When I read that list, however, one word is conspicuously missing: *anger.* Isn't it hard to imagine that being called "faggot" every day, having obscene drawings written on you in permanent marker, or being laughed at for the way you talk wouldn't make your blood boil? Of course it does. But what many gay kids do instead is turn their anger inward and take it out on themselves, emotionally and sometimes physically, because they believe they are at fault. This is one definition of depression.

The connections between gay kids and depression go further. Psychologists also find depression can come when significant people in your life don't accept or understand you—and if you're already having trouble accepting yourself, the pain can be doubled. Depression also stems from the idea that you've failed to live up to who you and your family feel you should be, a common theme for all teens, and especially gay teens. And what makes this even more significant is that depression is a major factor in suicide.

When I attended a volunteer training session for The Trevor Project Crisis & Suicide Prevention Helpline, they provided a fact sheet that made the risks clear:

- Suicide is the third leading cause of death among fifteen- to twenty-four-year-olds, and for every kid who takes his or her own life, there are twenty more who try.[1]
- Gay teens are four times more likely to attempt suicide than their heterosexual peers.[2]
- Gay youth in grades seven to twelve are twice as likely to make a plan to commit suicide and four times more likely to make a suicide attempt that requires medical attention.[3]

And this from a report by the American Academy of Pediatrics[4]:

- 45 percent of gay men and 20 percent of lesbians surveyed had been victims of verbal and physical assaults in secondary school specifically because of their sexual orientation.
- Gay youth are at higher risk of dropping out of school, being kicked out of their homes, and turning to life on the streets for survival. Some engage in substance use and are more likely than heterosexual peers to start using tobacco, alcohol, and illegal drugs at an earlier age.

The National Mental Health Association's website notes:

- Gay teens are at high risk because their distress is a direct result of the hatred and prejudice that surround them, not because of their inherently gay or lesbian identity orientation.
- 28 percent of gay students will drop out of school, more than three times the national average for heterosexual students.

Notes
1. Centers for Disease Control and Prevention and the World Health Organization
2. Massachusetts 2006 Youth Risk Behavior Survey
3. Seattle School System Study
4. American Academy of Pediatrics, Sexual Orientation and Adolescents (2004)

INTRODUCTION
All I Ask of You Is Your Compassion

All I ask of you is your compassion. Please read these very personal stories with an open heart and mind. They detail what it is like to live a lie—the cost of it and the impossibility of it, especially for young people. This is a book about human decency—about supporting and accepting your children and other people's children. It's also about the dangers of bullying. Maybe you remember what it was like to be bullied—or maybe you're going through it now with your own child. How painful it is to watch your sweet, smart, unique kid being harassed simply because he or she looks or acts differently. And how tempting to ask your kid to conform for the sake of safety and acceptance, even when you know it's impossible—and wrong.

If you're heterosexual, please put yourself in a gay teenager's place: Imagine being fourteen again—and scared to death. You know you're *different*, but you don't know why. It seems perfectly natural to you—but from all indications, others don't agree. You're afraid you'll lose everything—your parents' love, your friends' acceptance—if you say, "I'm gay." You're petrified of being thrown out of your house, kicked off the team, facing the bullying alone. But how long can you hide who you are? And is it even worth living if you can never tell those closest to you whom you love?

Recalling my own painful moments is what led to this book. My epiphany came during an interview for my nonprofit group, Faith in America, dedicated to stopping religion-based bigotry against the gay community. I was telling a reporter about it, and finally he said: "I don't get it. You're successful, well adjusted. No one's ever stopped you from visiting your partner in the hospital. Why are you doing this?" And in my frustration, I said: "*I'm doing this so not one more gay teen will have to go through what I did growing up.*" I started telling him what it was like—it had been years since I'd thought about it, and I'd never really talked about it—certainly not to the press. By the end of the interview, we both had tears in our eyes—and I was clear on the most important reason why we must stop the harm. Too many people just don't know it even exists.

If you think the Internet or *Will & Grace* have made things better for gay kids, you're maybe partly right for kids in urban areas. But not for kids in many, many other areas around the country. The families of these kids aren't watching that kind of TV and often have limited access to the Internet. In their towns, social life revolves around their church; if you're not accepted there, you're out of luck. And just as I was writing this, one of the young contributors to this book called from South Carolina with concerns that publishing his story might impact his job. So, yes, the problems continue today.

After years of trying to understand all this, personally and professionally, I have found one thing at the root of the problems: religion-based prejudice. You will see examples of this in many stories in the book. It leads to social intolerance. It is what many politicians use when they try to justify their resistance to marriage equality: Despite this country's great tradition of separation of church and state, they cite their religious convictions.

You see, I believe this is a problem we can solve—now. War in Iraq, that's complicated; the economy, tough. What this issue requires, first and foremost, is to stop treating people—children—badly. Protect them by law. Stop misusing religion and denigrating them from the pulpit. Help them feel safe and welcome in school. Don't threaten them with expulsion from the only home they know after they trust you enough to be honest about who they are.

So where can we begin? Here's a simple step: Believe the science. Let your children, family, friends, and coworkers know you accept the determination of the American Psychiatric Association, made all the way back in 1973, that homosexuality is not a mental disorder. Believe the American Medical Association and the American Pediatrics Association and other major organizations. Once and for all: Being gay isn't a choice. It's a human characteristic, like having blue eyes or brown. And if gay is what you are, it is perfectly okay.

What else? Don't allow bullying and name-calling to go on. It is not acceptable under any circumstances in a civil society, and we all know it.

Consider whom you vote for and the clergy you follow: Are they fair minded? Do they work for the safety, equality, and happiness of all? Are they deserving of your heartfelt support?

And think about this: Would you want your child to live tortured by a secret for thirty years? In the preface to this book, read about my friend Jeff Austin, who shared his truth with his Southern Baptist family only at age forty-four. When he first told me he had come out to them, I asked if they fully accepted him, and he described their attitude as more "love the sinner, hate the sin." "That's not good enough," I told him. "You haven't done anything wrong. They need to accept and love you for who you are." He went back and talked to them—and they did. He tells me it was one of the happiest days of his life. But why must we wait thirty years?

Exposing a Silent Epidemic

Through the words of people who have experienced it, this book exposes a tragic mental health crisis that is affecting hundreds of thousands of gay teenagers today. Right now, those kids are terrified because they are gay. And that terror leads to a depression that I can tell you is debilitating. I was once one of these kids. And the danger goes deeper because depression is a major factor in suicide.

I call this crisis a *silent epidemic* because even today many gay teens and adults are afraid to admit who they are and thus cannot share their depression, isolation, and pain. And even if they finally do, it can be hard for them to feel safe telling their "secret" and hard for the people they tell to know how to help them.

I call this book an *exposé* because in their stories the contributors have often revealed certain groups of people as sources of their pain, whether wittingly or unwittingly. I want those people to know they have the power to stop the harm. In some cases, those responsible may truly not be aware of the effects of their words and actions—or their silence. I created this book to help ensure they understand. "The Untold Story" (Part 7 of the book) details the issues and suggests ways to ameliorate the pain caused by:

- Religion gone awry
- Parents who will not allow their children to be who they are
- Educators who do not take responsibility for the safety of gay kids
- Politicians who do not stand up for equality for all
- The media's indifference to the crisis

I hope all of them can prove me wrong. Few things in life would make me happier.

How This Book Can Help You Understand

The stories are grouped into sections based on what the writers chose to focus on—their sexual orientation in the face of their religion, family, school, or workplace. Most of the stories, of course, also touch on discrimination experienced in other areas at the same time. I begin each story with an introduction about the author and the contribution the story makes to our understanding of the issues.

In addition to stories by well-known members of the gay community, the sections include accounts by young people that clearly show how the discrimination and pain continue today. Many of these younger writers have lived their lives openly from a much earlier age.

To give you a sense of how high the stakes are for gay teens, each of the major sections begins with a question to consider as you read:

- *Could you live with being called an abomination?* What must it be like for a gay teen of faith to hear that on too many Sundays and not be able to talk with anyone about it?

- *Would you be willing to test their love?* Imagine the risk a sixteen-year-old with no job and nowhere else to live faces. Consider the isolation of being without a family's love or a community's support at a time when such guidance is crucial.
- *How good would you be at pretending?* Think about having to watch every word and gesture to avoid being discovered and tormented. And try controlling your natural, involuntary physical reactions to another person, especially as a teenager. Could you stop your heart from racing when you realize you're in love?
- *Would you risk your career to be yourself?* Unless you're independently wealthy, you know what that's like. And if you're doing something you love, have trained extensively for, and are good at, should you have to give it up because other people are uncomfortable with whom you love?

How can we reasonably and rationally expect people—teenagers at that—to do this?

Additional sections of the book include the following:

- Accounts by two moms who have lost their children. They pose questions and share experiences that I know will inspire you to help stop future loss of life.
- An in-depth look at what many people of faith consider to be the core of the debate: sin.
- An exposé of who and what is contributing to the silent epidemic of depression, isolation, and fear, and what can be done about it.
- A resource section that lists organizations to call *and* organizations not to call because of the harm they can do to your child through a dangerous practice called reparative therapy.

Moving Forward

One thing I've learned from this project is how many important stories there are to tell. Transgender youth and gay homeless teens are two groups in particular I plan to focus on in the future. There are also many more lesbian and bisexual stories to tell. To do this, I have created a website for the book: www.CrisisBook.org.

The site will allow readers to share their own experiences and respond to stories in the book. Some of the most moving responses I've heard so far have been from parents who said they only wish they'd known what their child was going through and been able to prevent it. The website will foster a continuing dialogue about what we can all do to stop the harm.

Proceeds from the sale of the book will benefit several nonprofits working with gay teenagers and their families, including The Trevor Project, the Point Foundation, the Gay, Lesbian and Straight Education Network (GLSEN), and Parents and Friends of Lesbians and Gays (PFLAG). For anyone interested in helping kids, buying this book is one way to do so. And for gay people and those who care about them, giving this book to someone you love is a good way to start your own dialogue.

In the end, I hope this book inspires us to do for our gay children what I believe we must do for all our children: Let them know we love them unconditionally and that they can talk to us about anything. In these stories you will see how hard it is for kids to tell their parents they are gay. Research shows they come out first to friends, then siblings, then parents. I hope parents will be more accepting so they're not the last to know and can have input into their children's lives and be there to comfort them when they need it. Please don't let one aspect of who they are stop you from having a loving relationship with them for a lifetime.

EDITOR'S NOTE: In some cases, the names of the people in these stories have been changed to protect their privacy.

A NOTE ON LANGUAGE

This book is intended for a wide range of people: from the local ministers where I live in a small town in North Carolina to soccer moms in Minnesota to school board presidents in California to those gay teenagers out there in constant crisis mode because they can't figure out why they're attracted to the same sex—and maybe, just maybe, about to take a bottle of sleeping pills because of it. It is also intended for the media and for politicians. We want to have a conversation with everyone.

Thus, for the purposes of this book, I've chosen to use—and asked many of our contributors to use—the word *gay* as shorthand for *gay, lesbian, bisexual,* and *transgender* because it is direct, can apply to men and women, and is most familiar to the audience I hope to reach—namely, everyone. I know such a choice has long been the subject of debate in the gay community; however, I do not want to risk distracting readers from the crucial focus of the book with jargon that might be unfamiliar to them.

On occasion in this book, you will see the acronyms LGBT (lesbian, gay, bisexual, transgender) or GLBT (gay, lesbian, bisexual, transgender) used to emphasize the diversity of the gay community. In those cases, on first usage we've spelled out the acronym and included the letters in parentheses after it, then used only the acronym in following mentions.

Some contributors have also used *homosexual* because this is the term more commonly used in the evangelical religious community. I know some people also take issue with this term, but particularly in this case, I don't. I especially want those in the religious community to read these stories, immediately grasp the pain, and feel compelled to do something about it.

Unfortunately, sometimes people get distracted with wanting everyone to use certain words, especially their chosen ones. Obviously, language is incredibly powerful and important to consider deeply. But please don't let it distract you. Let's let nothing distract us from the importance of clearly and simply communicating the message.

PART 1
Religious Discrimination
Could You Live with Being
Called an Abomination?

COULD YOU LIVE WITH BEING CALLED AN ABOMINATION?

BY DAN KARSLAKE
Writer, Director, and Producer of *For the Bible Tells Me So*

Last week I bought the gun.
Yesterday I wrote the note.
Last night I happened to see your show on PBS.
And just knowing that someday, somewhere,
I might be able to go back into a church with my head held high,
I dropped the gun in the river.
My mom never has to know.

That's the e-mail I received from a gay kid in Iowa in 1998, the morning after a segment I produced about Rev. Irene Monroe aired nationally on PBS's gay news magazine *In the Life*. The piece was a simple profile of Reverend Monroe, a well-known "street theologian" at Harvard Divinity School who is also openly lesbian. Because Americans had never seen a person of deep faith who is also fully accepting of her sexual orientation on national television before, I knew the story would be controversial. But I never dreamed that it would save a life.

In subsequent e-mails with that boy from Iowa, I learned that he had felt completely overwhelmed because not only could he lose his biological family by coming out but also his church family, and indeed, God. Until he saw the story, he felt suicide was his only option. Yet there on television was a woman of deep faith who was also openly gay. I remember him asking, "Do you mean that I can be *gay* and still believe in God?"

My answer was, "Absolutely."

"Doesn't God hate me?"

"Absolutely not."

That gay kid in Iowa is the reason I recently made a film called *For the Bible Tells Me So*, and he's the reason why this book is so important. For hundreds of years, the Bible has been used to sanction discrimination, repression, and injustice around the world. It has been used to justify slavery, empower segregation, and excuse the subjugation of women—and the tradition continues. Today, a handful of religious passages are commonly exploited to justify condemnation of and violence against gay, lesbian, bisexual, and transgender people. (You can read more on this in Part 6 of the book, "The Sin Question.")

But what most conservative Christians don't know—or conveniently forget to tell you—is that the Bible says absolutely nothing about homosexuality as we know and understand it today. In fact, the word *homosexual* didn't even appear in any Bible in any language until 1946! And whether you think Jesus was the Son of God, just another prophet, or even simply a myth, the story of Christ is all about embracing outcasts, not creating them. A church that makes an entire group of people outcasts and yet calls itself "Christian" simply doesn't make sense.

"The Bible says absolutely nothing about homosexuality as we know and understand it today."

As you'll read in the incredibly personal and compelling stories that follow, words of judgment and condemnation from the pulpit have pushed many gay people toward suicide. Gay folks are three to seven times more likely to attempt suicide, and most of those who survive say they tried to take their own lives because of what they'd heard about themselves from their church, synagogue, or mosque.

What's even more sobering is that this condemnation doesn't only occur in the sanctuaries of religious institutions. Indeed, religion-based bigotry is echoed by many folks who rarely step into a church. The Bible is widely used to excuse discrimination at home, at school, and in the workplace by people without strong religious convictions to excuse their fear of gay people.

> **"The Bible is widely used to excuse discrimination at home, at school, and in the workplace by people without strong religious convictions to excuse their fear of gay people."**

The stories in this section tell what it's like to grow up in a religious environment and live a lie until one feels ready to undertake the monumental act of coming out under such conditions. My dear friend, the brilliant producer and manager Herb Hamsher, once noted that coming out is similar to the "hero's journey" described in Joseph Campbell's book *The Power of Myth*. Campbell says that in mythology, the "hero" must risk everything to fight for what he or she believes in and to be who he or she really is. That describes the coming-out process for many gay people. To be fully who God intended us to be, we must risk losing our families, our jobs, and sometimes our very existence.

In this section are several such heroes who struggled to be authentic in the face of fierce religious condemnation—the Reverend Irene Monroe, whose TV appearance helped saved that young gay kid from Iowa, among them. And though they may have initially regarded their sexual orientation as their own "dirty little secret," each came to know that their gayness was as much a part of them as their skin or eye color.

As Oprah Winfrey has said, in life, it all boils down to being authentic. I suspect that, like me, you will emerge from reading these stories newly inspired to live authentically, no matter what your personal story. We must all fully honor who God made us to be. Not doing so is the real sacrilege.

For more information on the award-winning documentary For the Bible Tells Me So, *please visit www.forthebibletellsmeso.org.*

*Above: Rev. Irene Monroe's childhood photo from the
cover of the 95th Annual Report of the Brooklyn Bureau
of Social Service and Children's Aid Society*

REV. IRENE MONROE
Minister and Public Theologian

From the humblest of beginnings, Rev. Irene Monroe has never given up. Abandoned at six months old in a trash can in Fort Greene Park, in Brooklyn, Irene went on to graduate from Wellesley College and Union Theological Seminary at Columbia University. She served as a pastor at an African-American church before going to Harvard Divinity School as a Ford Fellow for her doctorate. Irene is a syndicated religion columnist for online and print media; you can read her writings on her website, irenemonroe.com. She also appeared in the film *For the Bible Tells Me So*, speaking so eloquently about how misinterpretations of the Bible hurt gay people.

Her radiant smile, thoughtful message, and caring soul make her a role model for all of us. By the way she lives her life, you know Irene is a person of faith living in America and that she truly does have faith in America to do what's right.

"I ain't raising no goddamn bulldagger up in my house. Before I do that I'll send your ass right back to that damn agency where I got you."

Whenever my behavior revealed the slightest hint of masculinity, my foster mother always used those words to threaten me with expulsion from her house. My infraction one Saturday morning was getting caught playing an aggressive game of handball in the August heat with our neighbor's boys. Earlier that day, I had gone to Miss Pearl's Beauty Shop to have my black hair pressed, fried, dyed, and relaxed, and now I had sweated it out playing ball. Instead of hanging flat and listless on my shoulders, it had happily returned to its nappy roots, giving me, before it was fashionable, an Afro. Incensed by my behavior and the waste of her money, my foster mother made me stay home from church the following day. It was culturally unacceptable in those days for African-American women to publicly display their nappy hair, especially in the House of the Lord. And besides, many church members were already gossiping about my behavior. Their gossip shamed me because it shamed my foster mother.

My residency in my foster mother's house was always tenuous. It hinged precariously on my being a number of things for her, one of which was a dainty little girl. I desperately tried to be that little girl. However, sometimes I failed her. And in those times, before I learned to censor my undainty ways, the wild and happy and athletic butch girl in me would break loose. And I realized, in those wondrously fleeting moments, that not only did I enjoy competitive rough-and-tumble sports with boys, but also the sexual exploration that came with the sensuous joy of a touchy-feely game of "doctor" with girls.

At age six, my behavior was easily explained as precocious and cute; I was a tomboy who would outgrow this preadolescent phase once I learned cultural norms. However, by age sixteen I showed no signs of changing. Instead of precocious and cute, I was seen as a developmentally arrested teenager. The slang word for my "illness" was *bulldagger*, a colloquialism once commonly used in the African-American community to denote a masculine lesbian. This pejorative term had both tremendous sting and stigma, and my foster mother used it not only to spew her venom about my behavior but also to evoke fear in the hopes that it would straighten me out. It didn't.

I like women!

The realization of my attraction to them was affirmed weekly as I delighted in looking at the voluptuous mocha-colored to honey-brown complexioned centerfolds in *Jet* magazine. Oh how I dreamed of being sexy like those women so that they would lust and long for me the way men lusted and longed for them. And with my nightly fantasies of *Jet* centerfolds eyeing me, finally, I thought, I would make things up to my foster mother: Since I hadn't been able to be her dainty little girl, I would become her ultra-fem teenager.

I probably shouldn't have told my foster mother the reason why I wanted to become ultra-fem—so other women would like me. She yelled at me for my twisted thoughts, warning me that I would be homeless if I didn't take her demands that I become a normal girl seriously. My minister said I would go to hell if I didn't rebuke the homosexual demon in me and be spiritually treated by him.

> **"My minister said I would go to hell if I didn't rebuke the homosexual demon in me and be spiritually treated by him."**

As a ward of New York State, I had a third authority figure in my life: a social worker assigned to me by the Bureau of Child Welfare. And of the three—my mother, my minister, and my social worker—it was my social worker who showed the greatest optimism for my becoming a healthy heterosexual.

According to her, my sexual confusion was a textbook case. Having lived with my birth mother for six months before she abandoned me in a trash can in Fort Greene Park in Brooklyn, my behavior was merely an expression of my continuing search for her. In her usual distant and clinical tone, my social worker explained that the "tactile deficit" experienced by a child deprived of a parent's touch during infancy is often expressed sexually with someone of the same gender as the missing parent. I interrupted her to point out that I was missing both parents. Annoyed, she snapped back that it was the gender of the parent I missed most or who had hurt me most. Both my foster mother and my minister accepted her explanation.

So they sent me to weekly psychotherapy sessions, but I showed no progress. The child psychiatrist and my social worker seemed to realize I was incurably gay, incapable of modeling societal gender norms, and the frustration showed in their faces. At that point, my social worker gave me some advice: pretend to be straight.

Here was her reasoning: In those days, before there were group homes and interracial adoption, African-American and

> **"The child psychiatrist and my social worker seemed to realize I was incurably gay, incapable of modeling societal gender norms, and the frustration showed in their faces."**

Latino foster kids were the hardest to place (and still are). With many more children in need than foster homes available, my being a troubled African-American homosexual teenager assured me neither long-term housing nor permanent placement.

Her stories of the many foster children thrown out of foster homes for lesser infractions than being homosexual scared me enough to act straight. Moreover, she believed in behavior modification to change dysfunctional behavior patterns and remediate damaged thinking so one can better inter-act with the world. With her advice, I began accessorizing myself with the outward accoutrements of heterosexual culture. Being captain of the girls track and volleyball teams kept the question of my sexual orientation on the front burner for my foster mother, minister, and social worker, so I became a cheerleader. My biggest and best cover-up was my six-foot-three high school basketball-playing boyfriend. And while the cover-up worked beautifully Monday through Friday at school, I never felt comfortable with the lie I had created when I was in church on Sunday.

* * *

The centrality of the black church in African-American communities shapes the attitudes and mores of both its "churched" and "unchurched" residents. I joined my church at age five, was baptized at six, and served on the junior usher board from ages six until sixteen, becoming president of the junior board by fifteen.

I still remember the first day my minister called me into his study to share Jesus's special love for children. He read the Bible passage in Mark 10:13–16: "People were bringing little children to Jesus to have him touch them, but the disciples rebuked them. When Jesus saw this, he was indignant. He said to them, 'Let the little children come to me, and do not hinder them, for the kingdom of God belongs to such as these. I tell you the truth, anyone who will not receive the kingdom of God like a little child will never enter it.' And he took the children in his arms, put his hands on them and blessed them."

He told me no other place in the world so welcomes all children—espe-cially orphans—as the church. And since my church, a pillar of the commu-nity, was so welcoming, it was a nod for the larger community to welcome me, too. Growing up in the church was a refuge from the hostile and violent worlds of my environment and foster home, feeding and clothing me both physically and spiritually. To me, aside from Martin Luther King, Jr., my minister was one of the best representations of doing God's work in the world and an exemplary disciple of Jesus because he, like Jesus, loved me. Therefore I took his advice and admonitions about unjust acts and ungodly behavior seriously.

Over the years, I frequently met with him in his office—to sign an embarrassing report card, explain receiving detention for cutting class, discuss why I wanted to join the Dance Theater of Harlem instead of going to college, debate scripture or world events, and get advice on how to be a good Christian.

I will always remember my last visit to his office, when I was sixteen. It was my desire to be a good Christian that led me to make the appointment. When we met, I told him that my boyfriend wanted to have sex but the feeling wasn't mutual. I also confessed that if there were anyone I'd want to be with in that way, it would be my girlfriend.

As always, he listened attentively. Then he came around the desk with his Bible in hand and told me to open my Bible. He read Leviticus 18:22: "Do not lie with a man as one lies with a woman; it is an abomination." Next he told me to read aloud Romans 1:26–27 in which Paul writes, "Because of this, God gave them over to shameful lusts. Even their women exchanged natural sexual relations for unnatural ones. In the same way the men also abandoned natural relations with women and were inflamed with lust for one another. Men committed shameful acts with other men, and received in themselves the due penalty for their error."

When I finished reading, he slammed his Bible shut, knocked mine out of my hands, and said not only was I causing God's wrath, but also his own. Like my social worker, he too believed in behavior modification: He explained that if I pretended to like natural sexual relations with men I would eventually come to love it. However, he said, the best person to teach me was not my boyfriend, but him—and he was going to teach me now, once and for all.

The scuffle that ensued caught the attention of two male deacons, who ran frantically down the hall and knocked on the door. When my minister swung the door open, the deacons could see furniture overturned and the contents of his desk on the floor. Noticing that my minister and I were both straightening our clothes, the deacons asked what was the matter. My minister said, "I was fighting this harlot off me. After all these years of being a father figure to her I couldn't imagine anything like this."

News spread through the church and the community, with most people, even my foster mother, questioning the veracity of the story because there had been rumors of his predilection for young girls. Nevertheless, because I brought shame to the minister, in less than a week, with a black garbage bag of my worldly possessions in tow, I was an emergency placement in another foster home. When I told my new foster family what had happened, they threw me out of their house for fear that my homosexuality would lead me to prey on their other female foster kids or cause them to "catch it" from me.

With no place to go—no help from the foster care agency and the loss of both my community and my church—I would have attempted to take my life were it not for the help of my high school guidance counselor and teachers.

* * *

When I left for college in the 1970s, I was the beneficiary of three civil rights movements—black, women's, and gay. I assumed my choice of school—renowned liberal Massachusetts women's college, Wellesley—would be the most open and affirming. It wasn't. Although Wellesley had many white openly lesbian students, the African-American ones were closeted. Controlled by the homophobic ethos of black nationalism, as well as the social isolation and cultural intolerance of the campus milieu, many of us African-American lesbian sisters performed our requisite black heterosexual roles in order to be part of the black community. I played my role so well that by my senior year, I was elected president of the black student governing body.

After college, I decided to attend seminary. I wanted to go to an African-American seminary because I felt there was no better place to learn about the black church. But by this time I had come out, and the two African-American seminaries to which I applied had rejected me because of my sexual orientation. Instead I attended Union Theological Seminary in New York and then Harvard Divinity School, where as a doctoral student my focus became gay rights.

* * *

In recent years, the black church has yet again rejected me. Because I am openly lesbian, I have not found a home church in my faith tradition from which to do AIDS ministry—and black heterosexual women are the new face of HIV/AIDS, so there is much work to be done.

So I have become a public theologian. I have found a home and my ministry on the streets, with Boston's gay, lesbian, bisexual, and transgender community. The foundation for my life's work is in what Jesus said in Matthew 25:45: "In truth I tell you, in so far as you failed to do it for the least of these, however insignificant, you failed to do it for me."

My work is a public theology in tandem with a struggling community. While it is easy to see how economic disadvantage because of racial bias leads people of color to the streets, it is less determinable as to how many gay people are forced into homelessness. Abandoned by family and friends because of their sexual orientation, many have only the streets.

> "Abandoned by family and friends because of their sexual orientation, many have only the streets."

Part of my outreach ministries is reporting on religion in the news for gay and mainstream publications. In this era of dominance by the Christian Right, I try to inform the public of the role religion plays in discrimination against gay people. And because homophobia, like other prejudices, is a hatred of the "other," and usually acted upon in the name of religion, my writing allows me to highlight how intolerance and fundamentalism not only hurt the gay community but also perpetuate other forms of oppression such as racism, sexism, classism, and anti-Semitism. And in the process, prejudice and intolerance in the name of religion also shatter the goals of American democracy: life, liberty, and the pursuit of happiness for every citizen.

*Rev. Mel White in college, above, and today,
opposite, with his spouse, Gary Nixon (on left)*

REV. DR. MEL WHITE
Author, Filmmaker, and Former Ghostwriter for Jerry Falwell, Billy Graham, and Pat Robertson

Rev. Mel White grew up in a loving Evangelical Christian family deeply involved with the church; as Mel puts it, any time the church was open, his family was there—and Mel loved it. His Evangelical ties go deep: He has been a Christian filmmaker, pastor, seminary professor, and ghostwriter for Evangelical heavyweights, including Billy Graham, Pat Robertson, and Jerry Falwell. At the time he was hired by various publishers to write "autobiographies" of these religious leaders, Mel still believed his homosexual desires were a sickness and a sin.

In 1995, after reconciling his homosexual orientation with his Christian faith, Mel and his spouse, Gary Nixon, founded Soulforce, devoted to achieving religious and political freedom for the gay community guided by the principles of relentless nonviolent resistance as lived by Mohandas Gandhi and Martin Luther King, Jr. Mel has authored twenty-four books, including his best-selling autobiography, *Stranger at the Gate: To Be Gay and Christian in America*, and most recently, *Religion Gone Bad: The Hidden Dangers of the Christian Right*.

I first discovered the agony of gay adolescence at the 1953 Boy Scout Jamboree in Irvine Ranch, California, where I experienced my first "crush" on my tent-mate, Daryl, another thirteen-year-old. While all the other boys were whispering about their girlfriends, I was hopelessly infatuated with a boy. Those unexpected and unwanted feelings started me down a long and painful road toward self-understanding and acceptance.

From that moment until I was roughly forty years old, I felt guilty, lost, and afraid. I was unwilling to tell my parents, my pastor, a counselor, a teacher—anyone. I'd heard just enough about same-sex attraction to believe (quite wrongly) that it was a sickness and a sin. It was clear to me then that something terrible had gone wrong in my life.

I came home from the jamboree feeling totally alone. I was infatuated with Daryl, but I could tell no one. I thought about him constantly but never once had the courage to share my feelings with him. That kind of loneliness—when you don't see any options, when you can't talk to anyone, when you fall in love and have no way to express it—feels absolutely overwhelming.

During my junior and senior years of high school, this same-sex attraction continued. I was constantly afraid of being revealed as a "pervert" or a "sicko." So I overcompensated. I served as student body president, played in the band, ran the mile, and had an almost-perfect grade point average. And I did it all to make sure God and my parents would find me worthy because I felt so unworthy to myself.

> **"I did it all to make sure God and my parents would find me worthy because I felt so unworthy to myself."**

All those years I told no one about my feelings. In fact, I tried desperately to overcome them. I went to the altar as an Evangelical and prayed that God would take away my same-sex desires. Looking back now, I'm convinced that God was probably saying to me, "Your homosexual orientation is my gift to you. Quit trying to give it back. Accept my gift. Celebrate it. Live it with integrity." Instead, almost every day of my childhood and adolescence I prayed, fasted, memorized "thou shalt not" verses from the Bible, and continued to hope with all my heart that somehow I would overcome my need for same-sex intimacy.

I'm sixty-eight years old, and now I can say without a shadow of a doubt, "I'm gay. I'm a Christian. And God loves me without reservation." But for all those lonely, unhappy decades, I was a victim of misinformation that came into my life through ignorance and prejudice that began in the church.

One of the first horror stories I ever heard about "what happens to those sick and sinful gay people" concerned the city manager of Santa Cruz, California, where my father was mayor. The manager was an attractive young guy. I liked him. Then one terrible day my dad told me that on a business trip to New York City my friend had been killed in a homosexual bondage scene. I had no idea what he even meant, but it wasn't hard to guess. The looks of horror and the quiet whispers that followed this bad news convinced me that if I continued on my path, I would end up dead and disgraced as well.

Today there are gay-straight alliances in schools, gay-friendly counselors and community centers, and books, magazines, and TV shows about healthy gay lives. There are more than 350 Metropolitan Community Churches and other open and affirming mainstream congregations in almost every city. But when I was young, there was no gay community, no gay church, no positive gay role models. I didn't even dream that one day I would accept my homosexuality as a gift from God. I was certain that what I felt was sinful and that being homosexual was the worst sin of them all.

The struggle went on forever. There were many times when I reached the point where death seemed the only way out. I remember completing a film assignment in Paris. The crew had left for home and I was alone in the City of Lights wandering the streets, attracted to other gay men who seemed attracted to me, terrified that I would "give way to my sinfulness" and ruin my life and the lives of those I loved.

While walking on a bridge across the Seine, I decided that rather than "give in to my temptation," I would kill myself in some kind of "accident" so that no one would ever know. I was tired of the struggle. So I wrote a long suicide note to my family and then stared into the dark waters below—but I just didn't have the courage to end my own life. Thank God I didn't during those long, lonely years. I would have missed so much.

Even today, when we have all the evidence we need to know that homosexuality is not a sickness or a sin, there are still gay people who are victims of religion-based oppression who have struggled all their lives to accept their

CRISIS

"I decided that rather than 'give in to my temptation,' I would kill myself in some kind of 'accident' so that no one would ever know."

sexual orientation. They get tired of the struggle and honestly believe death is the only way out. Many gay teenagers take their own lives before they discover how good life can be if and when we accept our sexual orientation and refuse to believe the antigay teachings of our churches. I believe that the Protestant and Catholic leaders who condemn homosexuality are sincere, but they are sincerely wrong, and their antigay teachings have tragic consequences in the lives of my sisters and brothers. They are responsible for the deaths of many of my sisters and brothers, and they were almost responsible for my own death as well.

Fortunately for me, I met Lyla Lee Loehr in the seventh grade. We were neighbors and gradually became best friends. In high school we dated, but I was a strange boyfriend to be sure. Even Lyla's parents couldn't understand why we would sit outside in the car talking for hours and never end the evening with a kiss. No one, however, suspected the reason. And even without understanding, Lyla loved me still. She even enrolled at Warner Pacific College, a small Christian school in Oregon, because she refused to give up on me.

Although I loved Lyla as my best friend and favorite conversationalist, it did not stop my attraction to other young men. I didn't want to give in to those attractions, so I clung to the hope that the "love of a good woman" would save me. We married in 1962, shortly after graduating from college.

From the beginning I told Lyla about my feelings for men, and we decided to work to overcome those feelings together. During the first years of our marriage, I got involved with "reparative" therapy. I was willing to do anything to make our marriage work. My wife and I were two of the first donors to the ex-gay movement. We gave $1,000 to help start Exodus, a group for "formerly gay" Christians "cured" of their homosexuality who met in a church near Disneyland. I remember passing out "ex-gay" tracts in New York City with this headline: "Your homosexuality can be cured." I asked my pastor, "How do I know who should get these tracts?" And he answered, "Don't worry. God will lead you." You can imagine how conflicted I was handing tracts to gay men and at the same time feeling attracted to them.

In those days, my efforts to become a heterosexual were endless. I even went to a psychologist friend and asked him to treat me with electric shock. An Evangelical himself, my friend warned me that shock treatments might not be wise. "I don't believe that homosexuality is right," he explained, "but I don't think you should have electric shock treatments either." When I insisted, he said I would have to administer the shocks to myself. I agreed.

He had me bring in pictures of men I thought were handsome and pictures of beautiful women as well. Then he gave me the controls. One by one I turned over the pictures. With every handsome man, I shocked myself. With every beautiful woman, I switched off the electricity. It didn't work. In fact, while I was shocking myself, I was feeling attracted to the student assistant helping with the treatment.

I was very determined to "overcome." I can't blame my psychologist friend or any of the other Christian counselors who treated me. All the misguided and worthless aversion therapies I tried were my own decisions—and I tried them all, from biting my tongue when I was attracted to a man to working with a Catholic priest to exorcise my "demon of homosexuality."

> **"In those days, my efforts to become a heterosexual were endless. I even went to a psychologist friend and asked him to treat me with electric shock."**

After Lyla and I married, we settled in Portland where I worked on my master's degree and Lyla continued her graduate program in education. The next summer my youngest brother, Dennis, came to visit us. He was only fourteen, and my mother had been reluctant to let him come. She made me promise to take good care him. While I was directing my first film for my master's thesis, Dennis got bored and borrowed a neighbor's bike. Riding in our neighborhood, Denny strayed quite accidentally onto a bike trail that ended without warning. He fell more than fifty feet, and though he survived the fall, a few days later he died from a severe case of spinal meningitis that he contracted in the hospital. Needless to say, we were devastated by his death.

I share that story because when Denny died, I honestly believed it was my fault. I actually thought God was punishing me for my sick and sinful feelings toward other young men. Of course I knew it didn't work that way. I knew in my head that God was loving and forgiving, but I had trouble believing it in my heart. By then, although I had almost no homosexual experience, I believed that because of my homosexual thoughts other people had to suffer. I saw my brother's death as the ultimate sign that God had taken his hand of blessing off my life.

I'm not sure people who weren't raised in Evangelical circles can fully understand what it means to believe the lie that God would ever say, "Enough. I'm finished with you." I was a victim of sick and manipulative theology. For centuries the threat of hell and damnation kept believers in line. I lived in fear that God had given up on me. I hadn't discovered yet that in spite of anything we say, do, or think, God never gives up on us.

The Bible has been misused through the centuries to support bloody inquisitions, slavery, apartheid, segregation, even holocaust. Now it's being misused to support prejudice and discrimination against gay, lesbian, bisexual, and transgender people. Martin Luther King, Jr., once said that the church is "adjusted to the status quo, standing as a taillight behind other community agencies rather than a headlight leading men to higher levels of justice."

"By then, although I had almost no homosexual experience, I believed that because of my homosexual thoughts other people had to suffer."

But now the Church is changing. And it isn't changing through empirical data or psychological enlightenment. It is changing because more and more of its members know someone who is lesbian or gay, bisexual or transgender. They discover that there are gay couples who sit in the pews beside them. They've heard that these gay people are sick and sinful, but what they experience is very different from the antigay propaganda of the televangelists and their denominational leaders. These gay couples are in loving, committed, long-term relationships. They serve the church as pastors, youth leaders, musicians, deacons, and elders. They are loyal, tax-paying Americans. They have children of their own and are excellent parents. When gay people come out, when they share their lives with others, little by little the prejudice and intolerance are worn away and replaced by love and acceptance.

This issue will go on ruining lives, destroying families, dividing churches, and crippling the nation until our religious leaders have the courage to take a stand on our behalf. Until then, we must not confuse Jesus with the people who go by his name. His church is sick and needs healing. Fundamentalist Christian forces that use homosexuality as an issue to divide and conquer are still gaining strength. They are better financed and better organized than the forces of justice

> **"Although these are the best of times for sexual and gender minorities, these are also the worst of times for young gay Christians who are bombarded with antigay messages from their spiritual leaders."**

and truth. I never heard a sermon against homosexuality when I was young, yet for almost forty years, I was a victim of the lies. Although these are the best of times for sexual and gender minorities, these are also the worst of times for young gay Christians who are bombarded with antigay messages from their spiritual leaders.

Fundamentalist Christians do not use homosexuality just to raise money and mobilize volunteers. It is dangerous to doubt the motives of those who crusade against us. They are true believers. They are sincere in their antigay tirades, but they are also sincerely wrong. Back when I still believed they were right, I saw Falwell, Robertson, and other fundamentalist Christian leaders up close and personal. I know these men; I ghostwrote their autobiographies. They genuinely believe that if homosexuality is recognized as an acceptable minority in this country, "God will remove his hand of blessing from our nation." That's why they fight to deny us the rights and protections the Constitution promises all Americans. They fight to deny us marriage equality and the right to serve in the military. They even work to defeat hate crime legislation and equal rights to housing because they truly believe that once we're recognized as a legitimate minority, the country will go down in flames.

Because I'm a fairly well-known gay clergyman, I've officiated at funerals for gay people who have killed themselves or been killed by those who hate gays. One young gay man laid down on a plastic sheet in front of a mortuary and killed himself there so he "wouldn't make any more messes for his parents or his priest." Benny, a young man in San Antonio, Texas, hanged himself in his grandmother's garage on Gay Pride Sunday. He had been sitting in a park with other gay men the day before, talking about Sunday's celebration, when they were caught up in a police sting, arrested, and thrown in jail. The local chapter of Pat Robertson's (un)Christian Coalition took it upon itself to print Benny's name in the newspaper. At the request of his angry and grieving brother, I conducted Benny's memorial service on the steps of the newspaper whose reporting led to his death.

All the experiences I've had burying kids who have killed themselves, some after emasculating themselves as well, have left me angry with religious leaders and impatient for them to end their campaigns against gay people. However, I'm convinced that anger can be empowering if not misdirected. That's why I cofounded Soulforce based on Mohandas Gandhi's principles of nonviolent resistance.

First, volunteers of Soulforce attempt to talk with our enemies. If dialogue is refused, we stand in quiet vigil before their national conventions and even face arrest in nonviolent direct actions. Our Equality Riders campaign to end intolerance in Christian schools and the military academies. For churchgoing folk, Soulforce is experimenting with a program called "Faithful Dissenters." It encourages congregants to put a note in the offering basket saying, "I'm not giving financial support to this church until gay people are fully accepted here." Psychological enlightenment, empirical data, and neighborliness aside, as Dr. King knew, change can also come about by refusing to support one's own oppression.

Wherever I travel I invite people to join us in nonviolent dissent. On every occasion I repeat these simple words: "God created me gay and loves me exactly as I was created." It is my sincere prayer that one day the Christian churches, Catholic and Protestant alike, will respond with a resounding, "Amen!"

THE RIGHT REVEREND GENE ROBINSON
First Openly Gay Episcopal Bishop

The son of tobacco sharecroppers from Fayette County, Kentucky, Gene Robinson was seriously ill at birth, and his parents were told his death was imminent. For a long time, they believed he would soon die. Knowing this made it all the more touching when I watched the documentary *For the Bible Tells Me So* and saw their joyous faces during the ceremony in which he became the first openly gay Episcopal bishop. His mother talked about how she always knew God had some special plan for Gene and that this must be it.

Gene attended General Theological Seminary in New York City and was ordained in 1973. He then served in churches in Vermont, New Jersey, and New Hampshire before becoming the ninth bishop of the Diocese of New Hampshire. Gene has two daughters with his former wife, Boo, and two granddaughters. He was joined in civil union to his partner of twenty years, Mark Andrew, in 2008.

I entered my teenage years as the prim, proper, and prosperous 1950s gave way to the turbulent 1960s. The civil rights movement was in full swing. Members of the beloved and now-benign folk trio Peter, Paul & Mary were considered outright agitators. When Martin Luther King, Jr., came to Fayette County, where we lived, my father called him a commie.

The whole country was in chaos. But while the nation's fears may have been as clearly articulated as my father's, there was no name to put to what I was feeling and fearing. The closest I remember anyone alluding to someone being gay was saying they were "that way." The word *homosexual* was as unspeakable as the forbidden love it described. "Please God," I prayed, "not me."

I had reason to worry. A few years earlier, friends of mine had obtained a copy of *Playboy*, the magazine that, over the years, has separated not only the men from the boys but also so many gay boys from straight boys. As we looked at the forbidden pictures, it was clear they were doing something for my friends that they weren't doing for me. And at almost the same instant, I realized that revealing how I felt would be dangerous to my relationship with my friends, and possibly physically dangerous as well. That's when I began to pretend to be one person while fearing I might be another.

I had a friend with whom I would get together on Sunday afternoons. While purporting to play Monopoly in the basement, we were exploring our fast-changing bodies and discovering the mystery and excitement of human touch, affection, and arousal. For just a couple hours, I could set aside all questions and fears and simply enjoy my own body and his. But those wonderful moments were always followed by guilt, self-loathing, and fear. Yet I always went back for more.

> **"I realized that revealing how I felt would be dangerous to my relationship with my friends, and possibly physically dangerous as well."**

My church, the Disciples of Christ, which I had loved since birth, became an added burden. Without ever speaking the word *homosexuality*, its members made clear what God thought of people who were "that way." I didn't know exactly what sodomy was, but I knew that the penalty for it was condemnation and death. Being an "abomination" sounded totally beyond God's love.

Finding a book on sexuality in my mother's chest of drawers was no help. There were only one or two paragraphs devoted to homosexuality, in the chapter on perversions. There it was in plain print: I was a pervert!

Finally, there came a point when my nature seemed inescapable. Up until then, I had been able to avoid gym class; however, for high school sophomores, it was required. I worried about it all summer. Come fall, I would have to go to the boys' locker room, undress with other boys, play the seasonal sport, return to the locker room, and shower with my classmates.

> **"Self-hatred and fear would become a way of life."**

Showing up for gym class on the first day, my worst fears were compounded. Through a fluke of scheduling, I wound up in a class with the toughest boys in the school, known for drinking, swearing, and fighting. I was small, unathletic, and brainy. I would go on to be class valedictorian, but for now, I was in gym class with a bunch of Neanderthals, any one of whom could break me into little pieces. And my fear, of course, was that in the midst of all the undressing and showering, I would get an erection, and one or more of them would beat me to a bloody pulp. I still get an ache deep in my stomach when I remember the constant, unrelenting fear.

In the end, an unanticipated turn of events saved me. Gym class was on Mondays, Wednesdays, and Fridays, but on Tuesdays and Thursdays, we were subjected to health class, at which I excelled—unlike my classmates. I don't remember how, but I began to tutor my potential abusers. The mysteries of the endocrine system were Greek to my tough peers, but I got them through their health exams. And they got me through gym. We struck up a most surprising alliance, even friendship. I knew that as long as I didn't make any missteps and reveal my true nature, somehow I'd live through this. But I've blocked much of that period out. It's too painful to remember.

This was in 1962—years before New York's Stonewall Riots between gays and the police. Before San Francisco became known as a gay mecca. Before Billie Jean King, Martina Navratilova, Melissa Etheridge, and Ellen DeGeneres. Before openly gay congressmen Gerry

> **"Being an 'abomination' sounded totally beyond God's love."**

Studds and Barney Frank. Before *Will & Grace*. Before Lance Bass and the Indigo Girls were even born. When the word *gay* still meant "lively." I would spend many more years suppressing my feelings. Self-hatred and fear would become a way of life.

Eventually, in graduate school, I underwent reparative therapy. One of organized religion's cruelest ruses, it preys on gay men and women desperate for affirmation from the churches and families in which they were raised, pretending to enable them to abandon their homosexuality for the sexual orientation God intended for them. And indeed, I believed myself "cured" and ready for a heterosexual relationship. I married and had two wonderful children. But in the end, I could not deny or suppress who I was—who I am.

Coming out at thirty-nine, I was a late bloomer. But better late than never. In 1962, I could never in my wildest dreams have imagined a life in the open, partnered for twenty years to a wonderful man and happy beyond words. But that is my life now. I certainly could not have imagined all that and a life in the church. Nor could I have imagined the honor and privilege of being the first out gay man elected bishop—even though the storm that ensued from around the world included death threats and necessitated my wearing a bulletproof vest at my consecration ceremony. And the controversy continues to rage: I was the only duly elected and consecrated bishop not invited by the Archbishop of Canterbury to attend the once-a-decade worldwide gathering of bishops at the Lambeth Conference held in England in July 2008.

"I long to tell them that it will be all right, that they are not an abomination, that they are gloriously made precisely as God wants them to be."

The controversy also continues to rage in the lives of gay teens. Not a day goes by that I don't think of some teenager fearful and terrified that his secret will lead to his betrayal by those closest to him. Despite all the progress we've made, it still happens today. Young people who do not yet know that God loves them beyond their wildest imaginings are hating themselves, ashamed for who they are. I long to tell them that it will be all right, that they are not an abomination, that they are gloriously made precisely as God wants them to be.

BRUCE BASTIAN
Co-inventor of WordPerfect

The fifth of six children from a conservative Mormon family, Bruce attended Brigham Young University. After earning a master's in computer science, he and his faculty advisor, Alan Ashton, started a software company. In 1983, soon after the IBM PC debuted, they introduced the WordPerfect word-processing program. Bruce's business success has led to his appearance on the Forbes 400 list of wealthiest Americans. He was chairman of WordPerfect Corporation until the mid-1990s, when he began focusing on philanthropy. Today, the B.W. Bastian Foundation is a major donor to lesbian, gay, bisexual, and transgender groups, as well as to the arts, environmental causes, and homeless shelters.

Bruce says he learned the importance of equality from his father, who taught him to be free from prejudice and aid those less fortunate. His father gave food from their family-owned grocery to those in need and took meals to black musicians who couldn't enter all-white restaurants in town before the Civil Rights era. But Bruce still felt he had to keep his sexual orientation secret at all costs because his faith would not allow him to be who he is.

Being a teenager is never easy. So many things are changing in your body; so many ideas are bouncing around in your head. And there are new pressures from friends and other outside influences. Now add to that being from a Mormon family and having the strict Mormon social structure constantly "guiding you to happiness." Then imagine waking up every day to the secret knowledge you're attracted to others of the same sex.

I grew up in Twin Falls, Idaho. Most Americans know about the strong influence of the Church of Jesus Christ of Latter Day Saints in Utah but are unaware that Mormon pioneers also settled much of Idaho, Nevada, Arizona, and parts of California. My family's history is deeply rooted in the Mormon faith. My father grew up in Utah, the grandson of a prominent Mormon pioneer, and my mother's parents were British immigrants and converts to the Mormon faith.

Being Mormon is much more than church on Sunday: It is a way of life and, for many, an entire social network. The church expects that your friends, and certainly your spouse, be Mormon.

Although at times I wasn't the most faithful Mormon boy, I knew I had to obey the commandments. I didn't always go to church and felt guilty about not wanting to. At age twelve—and again at fourteen and sixteen—Mormon boys are expected to be "worthy" to receive the Mormon priesthood. A bishop asks you about your character, including direct questions about sexual purity. There are even questions about masturbation, which is thought to lead to homosexuality. There's a lot of pressure to "pass" these oral exams. It is a way for the church to keep boys from straying.

"I was certain nobody else in my school or town could possibly have the same feelings."

It was in junior high, in the 1960s, when I began figuring out my sexual fantasies were about boys instead of girls. That would have been scary for any boy, but for me, it was unbearable. I was certain nobody else in my school or town could possibly have the same feelings. It was never discussed. I had been told numerous times I shouldn't even "touch myself," let alone another man. So I tried very hard to bury those frightening feelings.

As freshmen in high school, young Mormons are strongly encouraged to go to seminary to study church doctrine, the Bible, the Book of Mormon, and Mormon history. I did as expected, attending until I graduated. Each year I became more certain I liked boys more than girls—at least sexually. I got teased about not having a girlfriend. Many of my "dates" were with my best friend and his girlfriend. I never got called names like fag, but I am sure people whispered behind my back. My family never bullied me about not having a girlfriend, although my grandmother often made rude little comments. But she was rude to everyone, so it didn't bother me much.

My real torment went on inside my head. In high school, we started hearing things in church that made it clear sex between two boys was an abomination. I got the message that if anyone learned the truth about my sexual attractions, I would lose my family and most, if not all, of my friends. I felt more and

> **"But I couldn't decide which would be the bigger sin: being homosexual or taking my own life."**

more like there was something wrong with me. I believed I was a disappointment to my God and would certainly be a disappointment to my church if anyone found out about the feelings I kept hidden deep inside. I became introverted because it was easier and, of course, safer. I was convinced that if anyone discovered my secret, my life would be over.

I never had any sexual experiences when I was a teenager—not with boys or girls, though I did feel pressure from boys to have sex with girls. I actually had the chance once, but couldn't go through with it. I guess that's when I really knew I was gay—imagine a teenage boy turning down that opportunity. And not because I felt it was wrong—because I didn't want to!

There were times when I thought seriously about suicide. But I couldn't decide which would be the bigger sin: being homosexual or taking my own life. I think if anyone had found out I was gay then, I would have considered suicide more seriously. But I was able to keep my ugly, dark secret hidden. I even started denying it to myself. I tried to believe I could change and be "normal" if I followed church teachings more closely.

And yet, my most difficult years were still to come. Most of my good friends from high school went to the University of Idaho, which at the time was very liberal and known as a party school. It even made a *Playboy* list of the biggest party schools in the country.

Instead, I attended Brigham Young University, the church-run school in Utah. The next three years were some of the darkest of my life. There was a period when I did not want to go on. I sat in my living room and drank almost an entire bottle of rum with Coke and ended up vomiting blood. If my roommate hadn't found me, I would have died. And I wanted to. I felt like I was cursed. I felt so alone, so "queer" in every way, so evil and bad.

I majored in music, playing clarinet and sax, and got a degree in music education and a master's in computer science. At first, music was my escape from reality; later, computer programming became my savior. Focusing on those things let me forget my troubles. But I was still living a lie, going through the motions of being what everyone expected of me. Since I was a child, I had been told the road to happiness was to follow all the teachings of the Mormon Church. So why was I so unhappy?

At twenty-one, in the middle of my college education, I decided to go on a two-year Mormon mission to Italy. Young men usually go on a mission at nineteen. I "repented" and went two years late. I hoped it would cure my evil sexual feelings. It did not. Still, following church leaders' advice, I got married to a wonderful woman, my best friend, even though I knew I wasn't being fair to either of us.

I kept trying, remaining a faithful member of the church and even serving in leadership positions for several more years. But I was still unhappy and unfulfilled emotionally. I could not understand why God would continue to allow me to have these evil feelings if I was doing everything He had told me to do. It was then that I started to seriously question the church and its teachings. By then I was in my thirties, married, with four beautiful children. And then I fell in love.

I could no longer be anything other than who I was. I left my family and also the church. It felt like I was giving up everything that had grounded me since birth. It caused great pain for my family. I am sure they were told by church members that being gay was a matter of choice and that I could have changed my inner feelings if I wanted to.

"Happiness only came when I started to believe in myself and follow my own feelings."

Most Mormons believe they can achieve happiness only by following the teachings of the church. It's what they are taught from childhood. For me, that was anything but true: Happiness only came when I started to believe in myself and follow my own feelings.

Coming out did not make everything better overnight, however. It was a long and sometimes scary journey. Yes, it freed me from a life of lies and let me be who I really am, but in the end, it takes more than the courage to be who you are to be free. You need to feel safe, secure, and accepted in and by society; you need to feel part of your religious community if that is your choice; and you need the right to marry and make a life for yourself with the person you love. Boys and girls must feel free to feel different without being wrenched with guilt.

> **"When the church is the center of your life and you're not accepted there, what do you do?"**

I was lucky. I had parents, brothers and sisters, and friends who loved me unconditionally, regardless of who I was inside. And even after I began living as the person I really am, they did not turn away from me.

Some fortunate young gay people today have so much freedom to be themselves. And yet, there are so many others who don't—in religious communities, in rural areas, maybe even in your own town's schools. When the church is the center of your life and you're not accepted there, what do you do? Without family and friends who love you unconditionally, where do you turn? How can you tell if that guy is "like you," or if that girl will be accepting? You can't. And so you always feel alone and at risk. You fear what others will think of you when they learn the truth. That fear stops you from reaching your potential. The fear is what damns you, not the truth of your sexual preference.

Even after all I've been through, I still believe good things are taught in churches. Jesus taught forgiveness, charity, and love. But control over whom someone loves was never part of Jesus's teachings. Religious institutions could do so much good. They could open the door to these kids simply by letting them know it's okay to be who they are—and reap the benefits of all the great things those lonely, frightened people may someday do for this world. They could help believers reach their full potential instead of trying to channel that potential. Jesus never taught controlling others, only self-control. His teachings are summed up beautifully in the Sermon on the Mount. It is a sermon of understanding, peace, and acceptance. I'm sure there were homosexuals in His audience, and I hope they took solace from His message.

> **"Religious institutions could do so much good."**

H. ALEXANDER ROBINSON

Executive Director and CEO,
National Black Justice Coalition

When Alexander Robinson told his mother he was gay, she felt he was asking her to make a choice between her son and her church. She chose her church.

Alexander, a long-time civil rights leader, is the executive director of the National Black Justice Coalition, a gay rights organization focused on social justice, equality, and ending racism and homophobia.

Alexander's personal experience has helped make him one of the most effective leaders we have in educating black church leaders about the harm caused by their homophobia. Unfortunately, spurred by antigay Christians, some black churches have taken a lead in speaking out against full and equal rights for their gay children. Alexander's work gives fair-minded black leaders a platform from which to speak out and let it be known that there are many blacks, such as NAACP Chairman Julian Bond, who believe gays are a natural part of society and deserve full and equal rights.

Life in my conservative Christian household outside Richmond, Virginia, was filled with going to school, going to church, and reading the Bible. At home I was sheltered from more or less everything else, although my family did travel extensively, and my parents strongly encouraged us to get a good education. Growing up, I was never very childlike—I always felt like a little adult. I got married at eighteen, and my first real sexual encounter was on my wedding night.

I've never not felt different. Other people saw it in me, too: I've been called "queer" and "sissy" all my life. And I was a sissy, but I was always clever. I built a kite in third grade—no one else could do that. On the first windy day in March, I took my kite to school. And then everybody liked me.

Around that time, however, I also experienced one of my saddest moments. I'd always been very close with my mother. Then one day, a woman from our church told my mom that she was turning me into a sissy and that she should stop being so close to me. From that moment on, my mother began pushing me away. It hurt even more because my father, a career military man, spent a lot of time away from home; so I had nowhere to turn. I didn't give up on her, though. I learned to cook. I learned to sew. I did a lot of things to keep close to her.

"I've never not felt different."

My parents' fears about me went further. In fifth grade, a music teacher gave all the students an aptitude test, and I did so well that he told my parents I should pursue music. But my mother and father were so worried that music would be a feminizing influence that they never let me take music lessons. Their fear only created more dissonance between what I was feeling inside and what was going on outside.

Growing up in the capital of the Confederacy added to that pervasive sense of fear—and difference. Even though segregation was officially illegal, in the mid-1960s water fountains still had signs over them reading "colored" and "white." I was one of the black kids who integrated my school. And we lived in a neighborhood where white people lived on one side of the street, and black people lived on the other. Most black people I grew up with felt tormented because they couldn't live on the other side of the street, but it didn't bother me. I never felt deprived of anything.

I actually heard about being gay before I heard about the birds and the bees. My father sat me down and told me about a deacon in a neighboring church who was "funny." When his preferences were discovered, the people in the church tied him up, cut off his penis, stuck it in his mouth, and stuffed him in the closet of the church, where he bled to death. I was probably ten or eleven at the time. It was clearly a cautionary tale.

In seventh grade English class, each of us had to choose a vocabulary word from the newspaper to study. I chose *homosexuality*—causing nervous laughter in

> **"Every other story I'd heard about gay men ended in lonely desperation or worse."**

the classroom. Intuitively I knew what it meant. But that was the first time I'd actually looked it up. I knew there were "funny" men and gay people—I had a gay cousin. He was extraordinarily flamboyant. But until that week I didn't make the connection to myself. I understood that I had same-sex attraction. But to me, gay people looked like my cousin. After that week I at least understood that I was like him in some way.

By the time I graduated high school I knew there were men who had occasional sexual encounters with other men; once again, my father, the worldly military man, had filled me in. He said they nonetheless got married and became part of the community. A lot of good things derived from being married, after all, and no thinking person would ever give them up. So I got married.

It wasn't until I went away to college that I realized there was such a thing as a gay community. Two doors away from where my wife and I lived, there were two men who lived together. It was the first time I had ever heard of such a thing. Every other story I'd heard about gay men ended in lonely desperation or worse. But those two men seemed quite happy.

People had whispered when I got married. But because I was smart and could sing and was a good orator, all important qualities in the church, and because my wife and I were an attractive couple—and because I never pushed back—there were never any messages that I needed to butch it up. I dressed, talked, and walked the way I always had, and I was accepted as heterosexual by my family and my church—just as I had been in school in the 1970s when I wore bright colors, midriff shirts, platform shoes, and a big afro. Because I was in a predominantly white environment, much of that was written off as "ethnic." I could be as flamboyant as I wanted: Even my long nails were seen as an ethnic affectation. It wasn't until many years later that I realized I had become so compartmentalized that it was impossible for me to know who I really was.

My marriage started going south—for many reasons, although my desire to explore my sexuality was part of it. Given my fragmented state, it doesn't really surprise me that at the time I didn't feel terribly troubled about my desire for men.

It wasn't 'till my wife and I had separated, however, that I had my first sexual encounters with men. I was twenty-one and going through a divorce before I fully realized there was an alternative to the life I had been leading. I had moved to San Francisco for graduate school and was finally able to be myself. But my parents did not yet know who I was.

After a few years in San Francisco, I moved back to Richmond, where I had an affair with a beautiful dark-skinned black man. The first time I saw him, he was wearing tight jeans, a white dress shirt unbuttoned to the navel, and a stainless-steel chain with a padlock around his waist instead of a belt.

He was a member of the church where my father was an elder.

"My biggest fear—of losing my mother—had been faced."

After a couple months, he felt guilty about our affair and went to the church to confess. What ensued would have been classic Hollywood—if movies at the time had portrayed black families and their gay sons. When my parents found out, my mother began wailing and fell to the ground. My father said, "Look what you've done to your mother. She's going to have a heart attack and die." It would almost have been funny if it hadn't been so grim.

For years I had feared that moment. Now denial was no longer possible. And it was then I realized that this was also the moment my parents had feared—that on some level they'd known all my life.

My mom kept asking, "How could you do this to me?"

Finally, I said, "This is not about you."

At last, the bubble I had always lived in had burst. And although my parents saw me as a sinner, I felt almost righteous. My biggest fear—of losing my mother—had been faced. From that moment on, I was out to everybody.

From that day until they passed away, I never had a real relationship with my parents because they didn't want to accept me as an openly gay man. Ironically, it was they who had given me a sense of self-confidence and self-worth. They had taught me as a young black child that other people's prejudices were other people's issues. I went on to apply that lesson to all areas of my life.

I found my father to be a little more accepting than my mother. He was both a man's man and a ladies' man. And although not much into sports, he did enjoy most things stereotypically male. But he was also a gentle man, and he seemed to have an intuitive understanding—and tacit acceptance—of homosexuality. For him it was part of the human experience—sinful, but not more so than anything else. I have often wondered whether he himself had feelings for men. When I came out, he expressed that he felt more than anything that I was being selfish because I had had a good life with my wife and child.

> "Would my life have been different if I had known about the possibility of being gay when I was much younger?"

Of course, both my parents felt pressured by the church's way of dealing with any kind of dissension—excommunication. And that's essentially what happened to me. Family and friends were not even supposed to associate with me.

Would my life have been different if I had known about the possibility of being gay when I was much younger? My marriage lasted for three pretty good years—I'm not so sure I regret it. What I regret, however, is feeling like I didn't have a choice.

Young people today must grow up with choices. They need a chance to explore their feelings—to understand what those feelings might suggest and where they might lead. They need to do this so that they can make good decisions for themselves and for the people their lives touch.

All my years of lying have taken their toll. There's the outside world and people's perceptions of who I am, and then there's who I know I am. Even

"All my years of lying have taken their toll."

today I don't always let the world see that—it's so instinctive that I don't necessarily have control over it, although I've done enough work that I know when I'm shutting people out. To stand up and come out and talk openly about being gay—first to my parents, and then to others—was a big deal. For me, it was not just about sexual orientation—it was totally new to reveal anything about what was going on in my head. Living that way is very lonely. But that's what the closet does.

ARI GOLD
Singer/Songwriter/Producer

Born and raised in an Orthodox Jewish family, Ari Gold was discovered while singing at his brother's bar mitzvah at the tender age of five. He soon began a professional career, crooning more than four hundred jingles, providing voices for the *Cabbage Patch Kids*, and singing backup for Diana Ross. Today he is an award-winning recording artist, and his politicized pop/R&B music videos have been featured on VH-1, HBO, and Logo. Ari donates songs to CDs benefiting gay and progressive causes and helps raise money and awareness for organizations such as the Ali Forney Center, Soulforce, and the Human Rights Campaign.

Growing up, Ari's world revolved around his Orthodox community. He couldn't imagine ever telling his "secret" to anyone. But as a teenager, he couldn't keep it bottled up anymore, and so he shared it, and himself, with a thirty-five-year-old stranger—taking the kind of risk that keeps parents and other caring adults up at night. What Ari had really wanted more than anything, however, was to be able to tell the truth to those he knew and loved. We can give that to our children—and in return, get the chance to try and guide them in life's situations.

I was sixteen and felt straighter than I had in years. Dara, my girlfriend, was a "slut"—an "older woman" (she was a senior, I was a junior) with a bad reputation. I even found myself looking at photos of women in a *Penthouse* I found in my dad's closet. True, the photos I liked best had men in them, but I did enjoy looking at girls by themselves. It was my own personal aversion therapy. So what if I hid *International Male* catalogs in my *Wonder Woman* comics? So what if I had a shrine to Madonna in my bedroom? There was hope for me yet.

Our high school in Manhattan was a yeshiva, a strict Orthodox Jewish parochial school. It was a sin to have sex with a woman before marriage. It was a sin to have sex with a man—ever. (It was also a sin to eat pig or shellfish or mix milk with meat.) You were not allowed even to touch someone of the opposite sex.

"It was a sin to have sex with a man—ever. (It was also a sin to eat pig or shellfish or mix milk with meat.)"

I still tried to pressure Dara into having sex with me—nothing made me feel like more of a man than pressuring a girl to have sex. I wanted so badly to shed the *faygele*, sissy-boy image that had followed me around since elementary school. And Dara did turn me on. There was something about her outcast status, dyed jet-black hair, and long black trench coat. It all somehow made me feel closer to my own sexuality, which I had been doing a pretty good job of keeping a secret for as long as I could remember. Dara was the perfect antidote to my lead role in the high school musical, my obsession with designer labels, and my performance of "Vogue" at Arts Night.

There was also Dara's superhot ex-boyfriend Joseph—the guy she had actually slept with. I didn't know if I wanted to *be* Joseph or be *with* Joseph, but making him jealous of me was the next best thing to either. Just imagining Joseph and Dara together made me want Dara even more.

But Dara broke my heart and wouldn't have sex with me. So, like Tom Cruise's rebound with Katie after Penelope, I quickly found a new girlfriend— my best friend, Gabrielle. She was the prettiest girl in my grade—and an *actress!* She even had her own 8 × 10 glossies. We were a yeshiva supercouple. We looked great together. With Gabrielle, I could be as faggy as I wanted, with my heterosexuality still intact. For a while, I was safe.

* * *

The short time traveling home to the Bronx from school on the 5 train was the only time I had to myself—and to fantasize about guys. And when the 5 wasn't working and I had to switch to the 2, I could steal some time at the magazine store. I'd check out the latest *Rolling Stone* and *Interview* and then get to the men's exercise magazines with photos of muscle guys in Speedos. I occasionally even got the nerve to peek at some real porn.

One day, as I was leaving the store, a man was walking in. I held the door for him, and we locked eyes. I don't know why, but I said, "Hi," before I walked out. As I headed home, I turned around, and there he was, behind me. My heart was racing, but I wasn't scared: I was desperate to connect with another man. I stopped to tie my shoe. It was a precocious move, especially for a yeshiva boy. He introduced himself as Greg.

My parents knew exactly when I left school and were expecting me at home. But I wasn't thinking about that when I walked into Greg's apartment. We talked for a while. When I told him I thought I was gay, it was the first time I had ever uttered the words out loud. I told him my family would never accept me and that I would be kicked out of school if anyone found out. And then I seduced him. I didn't particularly enjoy it, and he felt guilty. He said he was worried that he had molested me: He was thirty-five; I was sixteen. But I felt like I had been in control of everything. Of course, I never thought about how dangerous that was—what could have happened to me—alone with a stranger in his apartment. I saw it as my only chance to express my burning desire.

> "I had been hiding the truth of who I was for so long that when she guessed that I was gay, the dam broke and the tears wouldn't stop."

"Where have you been?" my parents asked as soon as I came home. "Your brother is out on the streets looking for you!" I don't remember what lie I told them. I don't think they really cared, as long as I was home safe.

Soon afterward, I let me friend Leah guess my secret. I had been hiding the truth of who I was for so long that when she guessed that I was gay, the dam broke and the tears wouldn't stop. All I had heard about homosexuality in school was that it was a sin punishable by death, and all I heard at home was my brothers calling gay men "fudge-packers" and my parents talking about gay people like they were lonely lepers. I told her I felt hopeless and thought I was destined to be unhappy for the rest of my life, keeping this deep, dark secret from everyone.

Leah didn't say much to console me—but she didn't hang up or say she would never speak to me again, either. Finally, someone in my life knew—not just some stranger I had met in a magazine store.

I didn't tell Leah about Greg, though. I didn't know what happened to boys like me if they actually did what I did with a man.

* * *

I convinced myself that Gabrielle and Dara were the only two girls I would ever be attracted to, and that I had better end up with one of them. So I told Gabrielle I was bisexual. She seemed okay with that. She didn't judge me, and she didn't tell anyone. She even stuck up for me when other boys called me "faggot." It turned out Gabrielle had a secret, too.

Gabrielle's parents were separated and she lived with her mom, an ex-actress. I spent a lot of time at Gabrielle's apartment—there was much more privacy there than at my house. One day, Gabrielle burst into tears and told me that when she had visited her dad, she discovered he and his long-term "friend" John slept in the same bedroom with the door locked. No one in her family had bothered letting her in on her father's secret. She had banged on the door demanding an explanation. I, of course, didn't need one. And I also understood Gabrielle's pain in a way no one else could. We now both shared the knowledge that the world we lived in was not the one we had been taught about in yeshiva. Our relationship felt *bashert*—meant to be. It was us against the world now. And to solidify that bond, we had sex: innocence lost.

* * *

Much to my mother's dismay, after I graduated high school, I decided to pursue my music career at NYU, not study Torah in Israel like most of my class. And much to Gabrielle's mother's dismay, she decided to study Torah and not become an actress.

I was out of yeshiva for the first time since nursery school and free from the constraints of Orthodox Judaism. I was eighteen, living on my own, and around all kinds of different people at school who thought it was okay, even cool, to be gay. Soon I ate my first cheeseburger and went to my first gay bar.

When high school friends Noah and Amy visited me, I came out to them in a marathon session that turned into a five-hour conversation about the meaning of life, art, and love. When Dara visited, I came out to her—and then we had sex. Maybe I wanted to know if I could be heterosexual for the one girl I thought I wanted but never truly had. Or maybe we were just horny college kids. It didn't stick—for either of us: Dara came out as a lesbian a few months later.

I did have to be careful about who I came out to, as word spreads like wildfire in the Orthodox community, and I still hadn't told my family. I wanted full control over that. So I wrote an eighteen-page letter and made copies for each family member. I held an unprecedented family meeting—it was the first time we had ever sat down as a family to really talk about anything, as opposed to just *kibitzing* about *nurishkeit*—yapping about nothing. I addressed issues of Judaism and homosexuality—and included additional reading materials in the back! Somewhere on page three was where I wrote the words *I am gay.*

I almost broke down when I read those words aloud, especially once my brother Elon started crying. But I needed them to see I was okay. Finally, I read the last line: "I may be a sissy, a faggot, a fudge-packer, a queer, a *faygele*, but I am still Ari, the same Ari who loves you all very deeply." We all cried together. The first thing my father said was, "The only reason we are crying is because of the pain we caused you." I could not have asked for a better response—even if it was probably not the only reason my family was crying. My mother said it was great news because now that this secret was out of my body, I wouldn't get sick anymore, as I had through much of my childhood and adolescence. I didn't know then that my journey was only beginning, and that it would take my family much longer to let go of their dreams for their son. But at the time, their acceptance was all I needed to feel free to live as a gay man and let go of the secret I had been holding inside for so long.

However, my newfound freedom left little room for my girlfriend, Gabrielle. And so I became the focus of her anger toward her father for being gay and abandoning her mother, and toward her family for keeping that secret from her and leaving her to put the pieces together. Our bond could not withstand all that.

> **"Their acceptance was all I needed to feel free to live as a gay man and let go of the secret I had been holding inside for so long."**

I don't speak to Leah, the first person in my community I shared my secret with, anymore either—she allowed her homophobic husband to disrespect our relationship—and our friendship could not withstand that.

But Dara is still in my life. She and her partner of ten years share a brownstone in Brooklyn with their twins. I was even the best man at her traditional Jewish—lesbian—wedding, where I sang my song "Bashert (Meant to Be)" to honor their love.

Rodney Powell as a medical student in 1961,
above, and today, opposite, with his partner of
thirty years, Bob Eddinger (on right)

RODNEY POWELL
Civil Rights Leader and Medical Doctor

As a medical student in Nashville from 1957 to 1961, Rodney Powell was a student protest leader in the African-American civil rights movement, where he had the honor and privilege to learn and apply the philosophy and strategies of nonviolent resistance under the guidance of Dr. Martin Luther King, Jr. Today, Rodney continues his activism, serving on the board of directors of Faith in America and Soulforce, organizations dedicated to achieving equality for gay Americans.

Rodney grew up in an era before civil rights, and his story illustrates the strength it takes to rise above dual prejudices. It also shows how much harder it is for a young person to face prejudice alone, without a supportive community.

I met Rodney through Jimmy Creech, a former Methodist minister and straight ally. One concern among some in the black community is that the gay rights movement is appropriating the rhetoric of the black civil rights movement. Jimmy suggested I talk with Rodney. Because he lives in Hawaii, with his partner of thirty-one years, Dr. Bob Eddinger, we first met via computer. Later, we spoke by phone. Finally, we had dinner in Los Angeles. In any medium, his words are compelling — breathtaking even. As measured as he is, there's no mistaking the fire in his belly.

As a teenager, I was painfully aware that American society had consigned me to the edges of the social order. I was always aware that I was marginalized by race, and that during childhood my identity as a "Negro," and a "colored person," was burdened with lowered expectations, limitations, and liabilities. Nevertheless, growing up a Negro and colored person was relatively easy compared to growing up with my secret.

In 1945 I was only ten years old, but I already knew I harbored a disturbing secret. At ten, I couldn't give it a name or even begin to articulate it, yet I knew I was somehow different from other boys my age, different in a way that could put me in danger and isolate me from my family, friends, teachers, and especially the ministers of my church. I instinctively knew that this secret, and the fear I felt, must be faced alone and suffered in silence. Of course, I had no concept of heterosexual or homosexual orientation at ten. I barely knew what sex was. But I did know I had feelings that, if discovered, would be condemned, considered a serious offense against nature and God, and marginalize me far worse than the worst aspects of racism and segregation. It was a numbing, terrifying fear. And I was only ten years old!

> **"I instinctively knew that this secret, and the fear I felt, must be faced alone and suffered in silence."**

By comparison, at that same age, I already understood that the discrimination and other injustices I experienced growing up in Philadelphia were based on both social class and race, and that I wasn't alone. I knew that within the Negro community, there was resistance and struggle against this prejudice, and that there were also people of goodwill in the white community who opposed the evils of Jim Crow practices. This knowledge, and the constant mantra that black children heard from their elders when I was a child—get an education and be a credit to your race—inspired me to strive toward the center from the edges to which American society consigned Negroes.

> **"It was a numbing, terrifying fear. And I was only ten years old!"**

There was, however, no resistance or struggle or community that cared about or buffered the oppression and injustices heaped on children with a similar secret. There was no language that I knew to describe my sense of alienation. I knew for sure that my secret meant disgrace, if not rejection from family, friends, and community. Fortunately, at age ten, I didn't fully understand that my secret—the sense that I was different from other boys—was punishable by death according to the Bible, Leviticus 20:13. However, I did understand that it was something that put me beyond the pale, beyond the margins, with no hope of moving toward the center.

Language is an important tool with which minority people are marginalized, whether by race, sex, ethnicity, social class, nationality, or sexual orientation. Yet "faggot," "fag," and "queer" were far more demeaning and threatening taunts to me than "nigger." During my youth, a Negro child called "nigger" could always retreat to the safety of the Negro community and the comfort of family, friends, teachers, and clergy. During my lifetime, the word *nigger* has been stigmatized to such a point that any white person who utters it is now quickly vilified as a racist. Between 1945 and 1965, the labels Negro and colored gave way to newly felt pride and more positive self-identification labels—first Afro-American, then black, and finally African-American.

> **"Fortunately, at age ten, I didn't fully understand that my secret—the sense that I was different from other boys—was punishable by death according to the Bible, Leviticus 20:13."**

However, during that same period, if you had the gnawing, shameful insight and were able to admit to yourself that, indeed, you were "homosexual," then came the sickening awareness that the labels faggot, sissy, and queer summarily described the way white and black society viewed and valued who you were. And, for lack of affirmation to the contrary, it might have become the way you viewed and devalued yourself. There were no words to describe in a positive way who I was or what I was feeling. It wasn't until 1965, after my protests as a student in the civil rights movement in the South, when as a black American I had new language and positive ways to affirm my racial identity, that I found positive language to acknowledge my sexual orientation and affirm unconditionally who I was. By then I was thirty years old, married, the father of two children with a third on the way. I found that courage in a three-letter word: gay.

Gay . . . what an absurd little word to have such power. Author and culture critic Richard Rodriguez made the following observation about the term:

**"I found that courage in a
three-letter word: gay."**

"Before it became a public word, a defi-
ant political term, gay was a code word, a
nonsense word spoken in private, in shadows, nothing innocent or carefree about
it, but a word coded with irony . . . and
double meaning . . . a way of saying it without having to say it: 'I am homosexual . . . a fag, a queer.'"

I was liberated, and my life transformation began with the admission and
affirmation "I am gay!" I was finally empowered by a three-letter word, gay,
and three simple words, I am gay, to begin my second passage from the edges
toward the center.

That second passage was fully informed by my first and most critical
passage toward the center, which was based on race and occurred during the
decade 1945 to 1955, from ages ten to twenty. By the time I graduated high
school in 1953, I understood the significance and limitations of Abraham
Lincoln's 1863 Emancipation Proclamation, and I understood the manner in
which racism and segregation had been institutionalized into the very fabric
of American society. My high school education had taught me to understand
and firmly believe in the foundation of American democracy, the principles
and lofty ideals that underscore our Constitution and Bill of Rights. During that ten-year period after World War II, there were monumental executive, legislative, and judicial gains for African-Americans. Most notable were
President Harry Truman's executive order in 1948 ending segregation in the
military and his December 1951 order creating a committee to enforce non-
discrimination clauses in federal contracts.

As president of my high school Student Government Association in
1952, I led a delegation to protest Senator Joseph McCarthy's witch hunts
against our teachers suspected of being communists or communist sympa-
thizers. Little did I understand the kind of power and political polarity I was
opposing, but it certainly gave testament to the fact that, at age seventeen,
I had discovered it would require active opposition to survive racism, segregation, and homophobia in order to move toward society's center. I also

understood that overcoming the limitations of racism necessitated unswerving determination to excel academically. Yet my secret still filled me with fear that all this wouldn't be enough—that exposure would condemn and doom me to live my life in the shadows, at the edges of society.

"Yet my secret still filled me with fear that all this wouldn't be enough—that exposure would condemn and doom me to live my life in the shadows, at the edges of society."

As a young black American, and eventually as an adult gay American, one seminal event and fundamental force propelled me to expect justice and claim equality and first-class citizenship. It was without doubt the May 17, 1954, decision by the U.S. Supreme Court in *Brown v. Board of Education* to end segregation in public schools. All my future experiences as a civil rights leader, and eventually my liberation as a gay American citizen, are based on my faith in the unswerving truth in Brown: that separate is not equal and that the constitutional provision that all men are created equal and have an inalienable right to life, liberty, and the pursuit of happiness applies to everyone, including all racial groups and ethnicities—and all sexual orientations.

Despite these advances, my second passage toward society's center, from the destructive edges of religion-based homophobia, was still painful and tortuous, as I began the process of openly acknowledging those three simple words—I am gay!—and coming out of the closet to family, friends, and colleagues. It took ten years to prevail over my fear of condemnation and rejection and fully give myself the right to an authentic life as a gay person. By then I was forty years old.

"It took ten years to prevail over my fear of condemnation and rejection and fully give myself the right to an authentic life as a gay person."

A year and half later my life was fulfilled when I met my partner of thirty-one years, Dr. Bob Eddinger, who is an incredibly supportive and loving parent to our three children and our grandchildren. Bob has enriched all our lives and enhanced our family bonds.

I have been extremely fortunate because I found encouragement, resiliency, and sufficient educational success to resist and overcome being marginalized by race and sidelined by sexual orientation. Others have not been as fortunate, and the stories of the recurrent tragedies of today's teenagers victimized by religion-based bigotry are told in the pages of this book.

For me, the most poignant question the book asks is, What more could I have contributed without this struggle? The answer is difficult to quantify. Bigotry leads to incredibly lamentable opportunity loss. So much time and energy—emotional, psychological, and cognitive—have been expended in coping with the vicissitudes of religion-based bigotry toward race and sexual orientation. My medical career over the past forty-plus years has been in the public sector, where the influence of race and sexual orientation as a factor in career success

"I suffered more fear and numbing anxiety from my 'secret' as a teenager than I did from racism and segregation in Philadelphia in 1950."

has diminished over time. Nevertheless, earlier in my career I decided not to accept certain academic appointments as well as certain domestic and international public health assignments in which I thought I would be vulnerable if my sexual orientation were known.

Let me be clear: I suffered more fear and numbing anxiety from my "secret" as a teenager than I did from racism and segregation in Philadelphia in 1950. I can only imagine how my life would have been transformed and enhanced without the cloud of religion-based bigotry punishing me because I was born black and homosexual. The perverse interpretations of Christian doctrine used to justify slavery, racism, and segregation, as well as the condemnation and rejection of homosexual American citizens, were destructive and draining during a critical maturational period of my character and my education. Perhaps I emerged stronger, but I think I would have emerged more creative, productive, and prepared to make more substantive contributions to society if those survival and coping efforts could have been directed toward more positive endeavors.

Above: Jody Huckaby on his father's lap in a 1967 family portrait

JODY HUCKABY

Executive Director of Parents, Families & Friends of Lesbians and Gays

Just as people of many races helped achieve civil rights in the 1960s, Jody Huckaby knows achieving gay rights will be a joint effort with the heterosexual community. The organization he leads, PFLAG, has been building this connection since its founding in 1972 by a mom who saw her gay son on the nightly news being beaten at a gay-rights rally while police stood by.

Jody also has extensive personal experience with family acceptance despite religious convictions on a large scale: Raised in a family of deep Catholic faith, he and three of his seven siblings came out to their parents as adults. None of them knew the others were gay growing up.

"**M**eet the Huckabys."

That's the way my family story was introduced on March 10, 2006, to tens of millions of people across the globe when Oprah Winfrey welcomed me and some of my siblings to a special episode of her show featuring "extraordinary siblings." Before an audience filled with sets of sisters and brothers, I sat on Oprah's sofa and told her that not only was I gay but that I also have three gay siblings among my seven brothers and sisters.

In many other ways, however, my family was just like countless others across the country. Dad owned his own small electronics repair shop, John's TV Service, located not more than two hundred yards behind our house in the small town of Eunice, Louisiana. When she wasn't busy cooking meals, doing laundry, and cleaning the house, Mom served as part-time receptionist and bookkeeper for "the shop," as it was known. The Huckaby household was always busy and never without some special project or activity.

Our small three-bedroom house with one bathroom was cozy, almost always spotless, and somehow rarely felt crowded. When their sixth child was born, my parents purchased a small mobile home and nestled it between the house and Dad's shop to give us extra room. We also had plenty of yard space and, it being the Deep South, my sisters and brothers and I spent time outside year-round.

My parents' income was meager, but they sacrificed so we could receive a Catholic education. The statues of the saints, the pictures of Jesus and Mary, and the rosaries throughout our small house, as well as the porcelain altar of the Last Supper that occupied much of one wall, were constant reminders that the Catholic faith was at the core of everything we did as a family.

I was about ten years old the first time I felt a same-sex attraction. I was watching *Love American Style* on TV with two of my brothers. John Davidson was the guest star. I don't remember the setup for the sketch, but when Davidson took off his shirt, I was drawn to him and wanted to kiss the TV screen. But something stopped me: I knew the way I felt made me different from other boys.

There was one older boy at school who particularly reinforced that idea for me. I wasn't an athlete, and I had only a few friends. He and his posse of pals called me "sissy" whenever they saw me alone in the school courtyard. I had never heard the word before, and I was too embarrassed to ask a friend what it meant, so I asked my mom. She told me, "Jody, a sissy is someone who loves the Virgin Mary." I remember thinking that it must be a good thing because the nuns who ran our school were Marianites of Holy Cross, devoted to the Blessed Virgin. It was barely a week before I learned from a friend what sissy really meant. And then I felt bad because I realized that my mom had lied to make me feel better.

I was first attracted to another boy in high school. Jeremy was taller and had started shaving much earlier than any of us. A linebacker on the football team, even as a freshman he was performing so well that everyone believed he would be a big star. At the time, I had a girlfriend to whom I felt no great physical attraction. The first time I saw Jeremy naked in the locker room after gym class, I knew I never would.

Not long after that I heard from a friend that a man in our town was gay and even had parties at which "other men like him" got together. He said it in such a way that it made me think the whole thing was scandalous. That's when I knew that I could not tell anyone about my attraction to Jeremy.

In my last two years of high school, I became increasingly interested in my faith. The nuns at school even encouraged me to consider the priesthood. I joined a Catholic group for high school students, and for a while my connection with those charismatic young Christians helped me focus less on my ever-growing attraction to guys.

* * *

I worked hard in high school, and it paid off: I got a free ticket to a public university. The summer after high school, I moved into a dorm for honor students at the University of Louisiana. The other guys in the dorm were party types, something I had had little exposure to. One night I went out with a group of them to a series of fraternity parties, and somewhere beyond the fourth drink, I lost track of exactly what was happening. Around 2:00 a.m., I found myself in a room down the hall from my own, attempting to push someone off me. I don't remember how I got there.

He was a large, muscular guy whose strength far exceeded mine. I saw his face as he lay on top of me. With his hands, he pressed my arms against the bed. Then he raped me. The alcohol did nothing to numb the physical pain. Finally, I broke free and ran down the hall to my room.

I felt terribly ashamed. I didn't come out of my room the next day. I was terrified by what had happened, and not sure if I could ever face the guy who had done it to me. In the back of my mind, I had a sinking feeling that maybe in my drunken state I had somehow done something to cause it. Later that week, I ran into my attacker. He smirked at me. Terrified, I acted as if nothing had happened.

Somehow I still put one foot in front of the other and got on with freshman year. It wasn't until nearly five months later, during the spring semester, that I told a priest what had happened. I cried uncontrollably as he consoled me and helped me relive that night, giving me a safe place to feel all the hate and fear that I had suppressed.

That priest invited me to participate in Catholic campus activities, and I joined in immediately. I met people and created a circle of friends. Many of them encouraged me to consider the priesthood, just as the nuns in high school had. I prayed, consulted other priests, and spoke with the diocese's vocations director. Ultimately, I felt a call. I left the university and entered Holy Trinity Seminary in Irving, Texas.

At seminary I found a spiritual director—a Jesuit priest and psychologist—who helped me deal with the reality that I was gay and navigate long-buried family issues such as my father's alcoholism. By then, my older brother Jason had already come out to my parents—but I had not. My parents' politics were extremely conservative, like those of many in our extended family. Their negative reaction to my brother's news sent a strong message: Being gay would never be accepted in our family.

A few years later, another older brother, Jonathan, came out to them. He had a fiancée at the time—and even I had been clueless about his struggle. Our parents told him he was pursuing a "choice" and a "lifestyle" that they didn't agree with or understand, and as when Jason came out to them, they didn't want to talk about it.

Meanwhile, I completed my undergraduate degree and began my six years of study to become a priest. Midway through, in 1986, I told my parents that I was gay. Also about this time, some of my siblings and I confronted my father about his alcoholism. It was a turning point for my family, albeit a terribly tumultuous period.

As was the case with my older brothers, coming out to my parents had its consequences. My mom wrote me a letter in which she said that being gay was far worse than Dad's addiction to alcohol, and that like him, I needed to change my ways. I cried when I read her letter. But I was on track to become a priest and was making a commitment to being celibate. I knew being a priest would make my parents proud, and I convinced myself that for now my parents' reaction didn't really matter.

A few weeks later, I found some brochures created by Parents, Families & Friends of Lesbians and Gays (PFLAG) in a library. I sent them to Mom with a note inside that simply said, "I love you." As was typical in my family, we didn't discuss the PFLAG materials or my being gay any further, and I was content not to rock the boat any more than I had already.

* * *

I was two years into graduate school in Chicago when I decided I could no longer reconcile my life as a gay man with the Catholic Church's punitive teachings about homosexuality. I left school and moved to Houston to live with my brother while I got on my feet with my first job as a counselor. I went through my own gay "adolescence," exploring who I was as a gay man at twenty-four.

A year later, yet another sibling came out to my parents. By then, my parents had done so much reading, research—and soul-searching—that they were ready to support and love all their children, straight and gay.

It was, in the end, my parents' deep faith that brought them around to embracing their gay children. My mother recently told me that after constant prayer and reflection she realized that her church's demonization of gays and her strong belief that Jesus was about embracing, not rejecting, those who were different simply did not go hand-in-hand. While she, like many mothers faced with a child coming out, asked herself whether she had done something to make her children gay, she ultimately came to understand that her love for me and my siblings was her first priority.

Today my parents and straight siblings are completely affirming of my gay siblings and me. They are much more open with neighbors, friends, and extended family, too. And my parents are proud of the fact that I now lead PFLAG as its national executive director. In many ways, PFLAG is the conduit through which families like mine can have honest conversations about a parent's initial feeling of guilt or shame. It is also the means, in many cases, for transforming those feelings into unconditional love and support. I believe my parents' pride in my work at PFLAG is their way of showing support for others who are grappling with the same issues they faced as their own children traveled that same road.

As Oprah would say, our appearance on her show was a real "full-circle moment" for the Huckabys. For my parents and some of my straight siblings, that circle has included moving from rejection to tolerance, from tolerance to acceptance, from acceptance to affirmation, and from affirmation to celebration. We now love and support each other. And, importantly, most of us are still people of strong faith: We rejoice in all that we are as part of God's unique creation.

When Oprah asked my older sister Jann about having four gay siblings, Jann shared her own struggle from rejection to celebration. She was raising young children at the time and had such conflicting opinions, she explained: "I loved my siblings dearly, yet I didn't want them to have an influence. Then I prayed about it, and I realized that I didn't need to judge. I needed to love."

MATT COMER
Editor
Age: 22

Matt Comer's words are a harsh reminder to those in big-city bubbles with constant Internet access—and even gay TV—of the struggle that young gays and lesbians still face in so many parts of the country. Even his family has had to bear the pain of this bigotry. Parents of some friends of Matt's younger brother have refused to let their children come to the house when Matt is there, for instance.

Although Matt is still shunned by his Southern Baptist church community in Winston-Salem, North Carolina, he has nonetheless refused to give up his spiritual life or the religion he was raised in simply because he is gay.

Today, at twenty-two, Matt is the editor of *Q-Notes*, a gay news publication in the Carolinas.

"**P**ut all the queers on a ship, cut a hole in the side, and send it out to sea," my pastor said with a half-smile and eerily happy eyes. For years, that statement and others like it were part and parcel of my childhood religious teachings at my small, conservative Baptist church right outside Winston-Salem, North Carolina. With the stereotypical rabidity of a Southern country preacher, my pastor condemned gay and lesbian people from the pulpit almost every Sunday. So conservative that the Southern Baptist Convention seems almost liberal by comparison, my church was a place full of hatred and bigotry. Though the people there were family to me, their sheer disdain and disgust toward gays was a fact of life.

How does an eleven- or twelve-year-old "preacher boy" with a promising future in the church—one who had already gained the respect of being called brother—come out as the very thing so hated and condemned by the people he loves and cherishes as family? With such a heavy burden added to the almost unbearable weight every adolescent feels naturally, I had only one option: Faith in Christ and His everlasting love was my only solace.

People ask, "How can you continue to have such great faith?" The answer is simple: When everyone around you seems as though they'd be the first to cast you out, a person has only Christ to turn to. But to be fair, even the presence of God wasn't always enough. Many times the unthinkable became plausible—a way out of the life I'd come to despise.

"Many times the unthinkable became plausible—a way out of the life I'd come to despise."

Those thoughts of suicide didn't last long, though. I believed suicide would have sent me straight to the depths of hell, landing me in the same spot as being gay. So, I turned to begging and pleading. I tried compromising with what I had been taught God wanted.

Alone in my bedroom, I'd lie on the bed, crying and praying, "Well, God, what if I'm bi and I eventually get married? If I try my very best to not think about guys the way I do, will you still condemn me?" It wasn't just the act of being with a guy that scared me. I thought just thinking about guys was enough to send me to hell.

The summer before eighth grade, I began doing odd jobs for my uncle. He owned a business downtown just close enough to walk to from my school, so I was able to continue working there when classes started again in the fall.

It was through this opportunity that I eventually found the strength and courage to find the answers I so desperately needed. My family didn't own a computer, so my only option was the public library—which was one block from my uncle's company. In addition to the religious bigotry at church, my library visits might be the only other childhood experience I have in common with gays who were teenagers long before I was born. However, unlike the scant and often negative information they found there, the texts I read at the library were positive and uplifting. In the corner of the second-floor nonfiction section, I'd gorge myself on stories of gays living proudly in such far-off places as New York and San Francisco. One of the first books I had the courage to check out was *One Teenager in Ten*. Teenagers just like me? I was in heaven. I finally began to understand that I wasn't alone. I wasn't sick. I wasn't worthy of death. And I wasn't headed to hell.

And yet, I wasn't totally convinced. I'd go home and, like hundreds of times before, read Leviticus. My death was on my own hands—my sin was my own fault, it said. No matter how many books I read to the contrary, I couldn't help but still think I was a sinner. I stayed at my church.

Over the next few months, I continued to read both my Bible and the books I checked out of the library. I'd compare the two and then pray. I'd cry and then plead with God. I'd fall asleep and do it all again the next day.

I don't know exactly when it happened, but I eventually became more comfortable with myself. The pain I felt when hearing my pastor's sermons subsided. In its place, I felt anger. How could he say those awful things? I wondered.

The rubber band I wore on my wrist—to snap whenever I thought about my male middle school crush—had to come off. And my church and preacher had only themselves to blame for what came next. They had raised a future fire-and-brimstone preacher, full of conviction and a hardheaded spirit, and those were all the life lessons I needed once I found the courage to speak out. Right after turning fourteen, at the end of my final year in middle school, the doors of the closet swung wide open. The Bible-toting, scripture-quoting preacher boy of only a few months prior turned into the most flamboyant, outspoken queer teen Winston-Salem had ever seen.

When I found out about a gay youth support group in town, I told myself I was going no matter what. Against my mother's wishes, I made my way to a place where, for the first time, I was surrounded by people who loved me just as I was, without reservation. I felt whole. I felt safe. It was ecstasy.

But that didn't stop the condemnation I continued to feel from my church. Although I eventually quit going to the weekly church services I'd attended every Sunday for my whole life, I still had to deal with the religious bigotry the church had instilled in others around me. My mother said I was crazy and sick and told me I was going to hell. It wasn't until I ran away from home that she started resolving the outright hatred of that part of me she couldn't understand.

> "The Bible-toting, scripture-quoting preacher boy of only a few months prior turned into the most flamboyant, outspoken queer teen Winston-Salem had ever seen."

The summer before my first year in high school, while flipping through the channels on TV, I saw the Millennium March on Washington broadcast live on C-SPAN. Two teenagers just barely older than me were speaking about a school club called a gay-straight alliance. My mind went crazy with plans of how to start one as soon as I began school. And luck was on my side: I wasn't the only teen in my school system attempting to "start trouble."

And trouble it was. The school board battled the Gay-Straight Alliances (GSA) like they were waging war. As the students at the other school in my district finally won their right to start their group, I put my plans in action. I approached my principal and started R. J. Reynolds High School's first-ever gay club. My mother condemned my involvement in the group, and for a time things were very tense at home.

Sometime that year, though, my mom began to change. In fact, she changed a lot. At the time, I didn't understand that my mother had to very quickly travel the journey her son had taken years to walk. I know now that she couldn't change overnight—it took time. Today she is my strength and my most avid supporter, and I know she loves me no matter what. I can only forgive her for the things she once did and said.

> "The school board battled the Gay-Straight Alliances (GSA) like they were waging war."

That old country church, however, hasn't changed. Three years after graduating from high school and seven years after coming out and leaving the church, I made my way back. I sat through the service, hoping and praying I wouldn't hear those familiar strains of hate and condemnation; my hopes were dashed.

I spoke to the pastor about his bigotry after the congregants left. He said he had never preached what I know I remember—his words are eternally imprinted on my memory. Yet he then immediately went on to compare me to a contagious disease, saying children had to be protected from those who would "influence them." By saying these awful things yet again, he again made me feel the way he did when I was a kid.

> **"I know that I've had an effect on my family and friends, my high school and college, and so many others."**

I have God to thank for making it through those times. In the very moments I thought about ending it all, or the times I thought about forsaking God and saying, "Enough already," He somehow had a way of pulling me back.

But all that I was taught as a child wasn't in vain. My life has proven that when there is nothing else, God will be there. Ever since becoming that huge flame of pride at the end of my eighth-grade year, I've sought only to create a world in which gay people can experience the full love of God. It saddens me to know that all my work has fallen on deaf ears at my old Baptist church. At the same time, I know that I've had an effect on my family and friends, my high school and college, and so many others across the Carolinas.

Maybe one day, the picture-perfect, happy-go-lucky gays we see on MTV and on Logo, the gay-and-lesbian TV channel, will have a chance to exist everywhere. Perhaps rural America and the South will one day wise up. But until then, we all have more work to do.

JARED HORSFORD
Student, Texas Tech University
Age: 26

If your child is gay and you want that child to "change" his or her sexual orientation because of your religious beliefs, please read this chapter carefully, with an open heart and mind—it could save your child's life.

Unfortunately, the story is not an isolated one. I beg you to understand the harm, both spiritual and physical, done to people who feel forced to try and change the sexual orientation they are born with. Jared Horsford grew up in an environment that told him he was sinful and an abomination and that he had to change his ways. He tortured himself emotionally and physically trying to change. My hope in asking him to recount the painful details is that his honesty will touch you—and from that another type of change will come. Recently I met a mother of two gay children who told me she had come to understand that it was not her children who needed to change, but rather the leaders of her Southern Baptist church. Please give your gay children that kind of unconditional love. Please know how important it is for them to receive it.

"**F**AG" ran across my chest in letters eight inches high, their dimensions blurring and elongating as the blood dripped down. I stared in the mirror, bitter irony rolling through my mind about how illegible it was, bloody and backwards, in the bathroom mirror. I wouldn't make the same mistake a few months later when I carved "I HATE YOU"—backwards this time—across the same skin, both relieved and disappointed that my previous message left me unscarred. I liked that I could create tangible, visible reminders of what a failure I was. My arms bore lines, some faint and pale, others pink and puffy rubber-like keloids, each a reminder of the futility of my efforts to "change" myself.

In January 2005, I decided to make a final try at changing. I left college at Texas Tech University, in Lubbock, to attend an ex-gay ministry in Dallas. I would soon turn twenty-three. I couldn't live like this anymore. Long gone were the childhood days on the cotton farm where I grew up—back when I thought being gay was just a phase because I was an artistic, intelligent, and misunderstood high school student trapped in a small town.

No one in my high school or the conservative Southern Baptist church I grew up in knew I was gay. To my knowledge, no one even suspected it. At six feet ten inches tall, I was the school basketball star—as well as the valedictorian and student government president. I was the church youth group leader and the "golden child" of my hometown. I was the guy that moms wanted their daughters to date and the friend to whom those same daughters would lament, "Why can't my boyfriend be as sweet as you?" I was a walking teen movie cliché . . . except for that one small secret. I wouldn't admit it for a few years, but I knew.

I chose to attend Texas Tech because they offered me a full-ride academic scholarship and a chance to walk onto their basketball team. I would be close to my family, and in a good Christian town as well. College was my chance to reinvent myself. I could start dating girls who didn't view me as a big brother. I could succeed in my pursuit of a lucrative career in landscape architecture. I could finally shake the notion that I was gay. After all, I hadn't really had a

"I told one minister when I was on a weekend spiritual retreat in high school, and he suggested I quit basketball so that I wouldn't be tempted by the locker room antics."

girlfriend in high school because I was too busy, and the girls were all friends. College would fix everything.

Besides, no one knew I had homosexual thoughts. I told one minister when I was on a weekend spiritual retreat in high school, and he suggested I quit basketball so that I wouldn't be tempted by the locker room antics. That response gave me an excuse to write him off. I decided Jesus would just fix me, or I would grow out of it.

To my dismay, the attractions persisted at college. I went to Bible study classes during the day and watched gay porn on the Internet

> **"I don't know how the idea came into my head to start cutting myself. I remember reading about some cutters on the ex-gay support website."**

on nights when my roommate was out of the dorm. The summer after my freshman year, I disclosed to one of my church leaders that I "struggled with homosexuality." But I was not gay. It was a test, nothing more. I would fight and prevail!

I found an ex-gay ministry with an online support group and joined eagerly. But over the next few years, I continued to struggle. Feeling exhausted by my attempts to hide my secret and keep up my reputation as a "good Christian," I began to spiral into depression. I was lonely and hurting. The church leaders I talked to—at this point, I had spoken to a couple more, along with a few of my closest church friends—encouraged me to keep fighting it. They said Jesus would heal my sin and that He would fix me if only I stayed faithful.

So I fought. I got counseling; I fasted; I prayed; I dated a girl from church; I worked at a Christian summer camp.

I don't know how the idea came into my head to start cutting myself. I remember reading about some cutters on the ex-gay support website. Then on Easter Sunday in 2003, I went online late at night and, for the first time, met another gay man from Lubbock. I had still never done anything with a man, and I told myself, "It's now or never." We hooked up, messed around, and I went home and cut myself for the first time. I could hide scars, no problem. I had plenty of experience hiding, so this would be easy. As my depression escalated, I found myself meeting anonymous guys regularly. It was always clandestine, and far too often, it was risky. I was naive, yes, but more than that, I hated myself so much that I really didn't ever think about self-preservation. In a two-month period I had experimented with more than thirty guys, yet no one in my circle of friends knew.

Fast-forward a few months. That type of behavior left me tired, more depressed, and struggling with school. I enrolled in a hardcore Christian residential ex-gay program, but got scared and didn't go.

The cycle continued for another year and a half until I quit school and moved to Dallas to join the ex-gay ministry that ran the online site I'd been with for a few years. By then, all my church friends knew of my struggle. Some wrote me off as a fraud. Some tried to support me. Most ended up drifting away due to my self-imposed isolation and depression and their ignorance about what to do for me. I felt the move to Dallas truly was my last option.

> **"I began to think that the only way I could resolve my crisis was either to write off God or be straight. Since my faith was so important to me, I chose the latter."**

In Dallas, I worked at the home furnishings store Pier 1 Imports, went to church, and attended ex-gay meetings. And I went online to find sex, to clubs to meet guys, and to my bathroom mirror to cut myself. Looking back on that period of my life is difficult because I see myself as ridiculous. I don't feel pain about it now because I didn't feel anything then. At ex-gay meetings, the leaders would say our goal was "holiness, not heterosexuality," but now I know they really didn't separate the two.

I began to think that the only way I could resolve my crisis was either to write off God or be straight. Since my faith was so important to me, I chose the latter.

I would go to the ex-gay meetings for a while, start feeling defeated because I wasn't getting "healed," and go home and cut myself. Then I would stop going to the meetings, be isolated in my depression—but I would stop cutting myself. I told the ministry leaders this. They said the reason I didn't cut myself when I skipped meetings was because then my spirit wasn't fighting my flesh; my faith was no longer standing strong against my desires. They said even though cutting wasn't good, it was a positive sign that I was fighting my desires.

I look back and have to laugh, albeit bitterly, at how long I bought that line. I was hurting myself. I had carved words into my chest to remind me how much I hated myself—and they said that was better than not fighting. They seemed to think that being an ex-gay cutter was better than being a healthy, happy homosexual. Of course, at that point in my life, I'd never met a healthy, happy homosexual. Or if I had,

> **"They said even though cutting wasn't good, it was a positive sign that I was fighting my desires."**

I'd let the ministry's brainwashing affect my perception of the person.

Luckily, a few things happened all of a sudden that changed everything.

I was one of three gay men in a very open-minded workplace. I was in the closet, but it was a glass closet. One day, I found out that one of the other gay guys had outed me to everyone. Obviously, I was irate at first and very hurt. But then something odd happened. People still liked me. My coworkers didn't write me off or shun me. They didn't suggest I fight it or get counseling. They affirmed me. And then they just let me be. They didn't bring it up all the time. And I suddenly realized that they thought it was normal to be gay. I wasn't an aberration in their eyes.

Slowly, I stopped going to ex-gay meetings. I stopped cutting myself. I stopped hating myself. I started learning to like myself, and even love myself.

It's funny how quickly things turned around once I got away from the ex-gay ministry. I joined a local gay volleyball league and met plenty of happy, healthy gay

> **"It's funny how quickly things turned around once I got away from the ex-gay ministry."**

men and women. I made friends, and we did normal things friends do. They were not, as the ex-gay ministry tried to tell me, a bunch of sex-crazed people who just used social gatherings as an excuse to find their next sex partners. After all those years, believe it or not, what I finally realized is that gays are people, too—not animals or abominations. We love, we laugh, we hurt, we cry, we pray, we live.

After about a year in Dallas, I decided to move back to Lubbock to finish my degree in landscape architecture at Texas Tech so that I could pursue the career I'd dreamed of since I first started college. It was a rough transition.

A study had just named Lubbock the second-most conservative city in the nation, and here I was back as an out gay man. But things went okay. Things are okay. I have gay friends, many of whom I knew before I moved and had been taught were unhealthy and troubled. Now they're some of the truest friends I've ever known. I also now attend a gay-affirming congregation, and, although small, it is right for me.

None of the words I wrote on my chest left a scar. In spite of all my attempts to dissect and divide myself to remove my sexuality, something kept me knit together. I like to believe that it is God's way of reminding me that no matter how much I hated myself and how much hate the ex-gay ministry taught me I deserved, God always loved me.

JARROD PARKER

Emergency, Fire, and Aeromedical Services, Greenville, South Carolina
Age: 22

I wish Jarrod Parker had less painful memories. He doesn't deserve the ones he has. He grew up in a place where religion-based bigotry continues to be used to hurt gay people, and his story illustrates how it affects areas of life beyond the church, including Boy Scout camp, school, and a town itself. Yet, through it all, Jarrod has stayed committed to his faith, even when his religious community rejected him. He has suffered isolation, fought depression, and spent two years in reparative therapy, which as a teenager he paid for with his own money, attending in secret so his parents wouldn't find out he is gay.

In the end, it was the ultimate tragedy that gave him the courage to accept himself. His stepbrother Sean Kennedy, a twenty-year-old gay man, was murdered in their hometown of Greenville, South Carolina, because he was gay.

Jarrod told me if he could help one person by reliving the painful events detailed here, it would be worth it. He dedicates his story to his stepbrother Sean.

In the summer of 2000, when I was fourteen years old, I worked in the first aid lodge of a Boy Scout camp in northern Greenville County, South Carolina. While on staff for what was to be an eight-week session, I had many good experiences and learned a lot about myself.

At the end of the sixth week, I got a one-night break from camp. I returned the following day and began preparing the next week's activities. After the evening program, I made my way to my cabin by the light of a full moon. None of the other staffers I shared the cabin with were there yet. I changed into my pajamas and crawled into my sleeping bag. Before I fell asleep, I thought about how much fun I'd had over the past several weeks. I woke briefly during the night to the sound of people talking and loud music playing, but it didn't bother me—I was used to it. I just took a sip of water from the bottle beside my bed, rolled over, and went back to sleep.

The next thing I knew, a fellow staffer was shaking me and telling me I had overslept. It was 8:30. I went to take a shower so that I'd be ready to teach my campers first aid at 9:00. But I never made it.

When I looked in the bathroom mirror, I saw that someone, or maybe a group of people, had written all over my body. The first thing I saw was "FAGGOT" across my forehead and a picture of a penis at the corner of my mouth. I took off my pajama shirt and saw "cock sucker, faggot" on my chest. There was an arrow pointing to my penis with the words "dick lover" beside it. I turned and saw more of the same on my back, plus an arrow pointing to my butt and the words, "insert dick here fuckable hole."

I was scared out of my mind. All I could think to do was call my grandparents to take me home. My grandmother left work immediately and picked up my grandfather at his office on the way. When they got there, my grandfather told the camp leaders they had three short hours to find out who had done this, or the sheriff's office would come and find out. Then he walked me to my cabin to get my things. I was so glad to be with them but still scared because I had no memory of what had happened.

To this day I don't know why I didn't wake up during that awful event, which was truly a hate crime. I can't remember anything from the time I took the sip of water till the next morning. Did someone put something in my water bottle or in my dinner? I don't know.

When we got home, my grandfather called the sheriff's office to file a report. The sheriff's deputy arrived and said he needed to take pictures of all the markings on my body. Then he wrote down the case number on a card and left.

That was all that was ever done for me. The sheriff's office just said that I had been "intimidated."

* * *

Growing up, I never knew openly gay people existed. I saw TV shows with gay characters, but I never considered that those actors might actually be gay in real life; I just thought it was a TV thing. I didn't meet other gay kids online; I never had the chance to explore the Internet that way. There was no one I felt comfortable talking to. I was raised very conservatively; you just didn't tell people how you felt or what you thought.

I felt isolated in my own body. Alone in my bed at night, I would think and cry, think and cry, recalling all the hatred I experienced over the years. I thought about things the church said about homosexuality and the hatred taught there. I would get so depressed that I would want to run away to another world.

My lowest points were when I was alone—and they still are. I'm someone who enjoys being around people. But when people realize I'm gay, most of them choose to have nothing to do with me.

That was always my biggest fear about coming out: that my own family would hate me and throw me out into the streets. Because of the way my so-called school friends treated me and because my church taught me I would go to hell for being gay, it really seemed possible.

Here in the Bible Belt, you'll find a church on just about every corner. And almost all of those churches, and the families who attend them, will not accept a gay person. Some young gay teens run away from home because they can't take the hatred anymore. If the kids are under sixteen years

> **"I thought about things the church said about homosexuality and the hatred taught there."**

"Law-enforcement officers do not have the training and resources needed to understand what gay kids go through."

old and their parents call the police, the police tell them they have to go home or go to jail. Law-enforcement officers do not have the training and resources needed to understand what gay kids go through. Some kids actually commit crimes to get a record so that they'll be sent to juvenile hall instead of home—and these are otherwise good kids! Still others take matters into their own hands: They take their lives to get away from all the hatred.

* * *

In 2004, at the age of eighteen, I was very involved in the large community church my family attended. I was a youth-ministry volunteer and worked closely with the youth pastor as well as middle school and high school students.

Hearing what the church was teaching these students about homosexuality made me feel condemned. I'd leave youth group meetings feeling bad about myself and soon entered a deep depression. The only way I can describe it is as a "mind over heart struggle": My heart loved God and liked men, while my mind told me I was a horrible, nasty, worthless person who did not deserve anything unless I changed my sinful ways.

I struggled for about a year; the depression would get better and then bad again. I finally confided in a pastoral leader I considered a friend. He told me he already knew I was gay. I said I did not want to be that person.

He said if I wanted to inherit the kingdom of God (heaven) when I died that I needed to remove all homosexual contacts from my life. I believed I had to do this to be able to see my family members who had already passed from this earth to heaven. He recommended a counselor who specialized in "people who want to come out of the homosexual lifestyle," and I agreed to go. He told me he had to discuss this with certain people, including the church pastor, and that I had to step down from all my roles in the church and focus on my issues. I felt so isolated and especially missed working with the students.

The counselor was a leader of one of the well-known "ex-gay pray yourself straight" ministries. He began by telling me the reason I was gay was because

I had an overpowering mother and no strong father figure. That should have been my first red flag. My father did work on the road, but he was still a big part of my life; and my mother had not been very involved until I was in high school. But since the only people I had shared my struggle with were the leader of this ex-gay ministry and my pastor friend, I had no one to discuss my concerns with.

The counselor said I'd need to attend a weekly group meeting and a monthly one-on-one session for about a year and a half to be "cured." I went to the group meeting twice but felt very uncomfortable because it consisted of participants talking only about whom they had hooked up with over the past week, and the counselor asking each of us why we weren't dating a woman yet. At my one-on-one session, I told the counselor I wouldn't go to future group meetings and explained why. He didn't say a word. Over two years, I paid the ministry fifty dollars a month, sometimes a hundred dollars a month, in hopes of becoming "normal."

> "He began by telling me the reason I was gay was because I had an overpowering mother and no strong father figure. That should have been my first red flag."

I soon found myself even more depressed because I wasn't changing—and even more isolated. My church treated me like I had a disease. People who had been friends stopped speaking to me. I once sat in the second row at church, but I began to feel I had to sit in the very back.

I never told my parents I was going to therapy because I wasn't sure how they'd react. I was too afraid of losing the only thing I had left. I know now that keeping it from them made my life much harder.

* * *

There are two important spiritual dates in my life. The first was the day I became a Christian, at age seven. The second was the day I came out—July 19, 2007, two months and three days after my stepbrother Sean Kennedy was murdered in our hometown of Greenville because he was openly gay.

Even in Sean's hospital room on the night of the murder, when a friend of his mentioned in front of my family that he had thought I was also gay, I denied it. When I did come out to my parents, I found that they, as well as Sean and my other four siblings, already knew but had felt it was not their place to say anything until I was ready. I remember sitting on the floor of my parents' home office and crying. It felt like a part of me had died and that I had become a new man.

I realized that I was not meant to change. Jesus says in Jeremiah 1:5, "Before I formed you in the womb I knew you, before you were born I set you apart; I appointed you as a prophet to the nations." I believe He is saying He created me as a gay man—even before I was born. I feel that as a young Christian boy I had a relationship with Jesus Christ, but since I came out, my relationship with Him has become stronger.

My stepmother told me Sean wished many times that he could talk to me about being gay but saw that I was too scared, even after witnessing how our family accepted him. Because someone's hatred took his life, I had to come out without him, but in my heart he was with me the entire time. His murder opened the door for me to live.

I used to get mad seeing him so alive and having fun and not caring what people thought while I was still hiding. Now I wish there was a way to let him know what a role model he has been. Since I won't have a chance to tell him in this life, I'll honor him by being who I am. That is all he ever wanted from people.

AN EVANGELICAL CHRISTIAN APOLOGIZES

BY BRENT CHILDERS
Executive Director, Faith in America

"I'd rather be shot dead than know my daughter married a black man," said an older man in our Sunday school class in North Carolina during a 2006 discussion on race.

Ugly words? Horrible. And imagine being on the receiving end of the attitude behind those words. Yet the man saw no need to apologize—not even for saying it in church.

Although interracial marriage has become more and more accepted, for many white evangelical Christians there is still some apprehension below the surface—and sometimes out in the open, as the man in our Sunday school class demonstrated. It wasn't long ago that we were taught that the Bible condemned mixed marriages.

For gays and lesbians, that same kind of religion-based bigotry—hostile and discriminatory attitudes reinforced with scriptural passages—doesn't conceal itself at all. It's blasted across airwaves and typed into print every day.

"They are immoral," says a top U.S. general; "Worse than terrorists," says an Oklahoma lawmaker; "Undeserving of rights," says a presidential candidate; "Faggots," according to at least one Religious Right commentator; "An abomination," say countless pastors who claim their interpretation of scripture represents the message of Christ.

And again, no one sees a need to apologize—not even for saying it in church. For evangelical Christians, black and white, considering that we may have missed the mark with our attitude toward gays and lesbians hasn't been an option. We've been taught that they are an abomination for a very long time.

So wouldn't it be heresy for a Christian—evangelical or otherwise—to believe homosexuality isn't sinful? Wouldn't it place the believer in direct opposition to God? From my own experience, I have found the opposite to be true. Once I walked away from the church's teachings of rejection and condemnation, my relationship with God transcended to a higher spiritual plateau. I realized an unparalleled sense of spiritual clarity when I opened my heart and mind to a genuine expression of love, compassion, and acceptance of gays.

"I'd rather be shot dead than know my son is queer." That's the place from which I started my spiritual journey. It makes pretty clear how genuine my love for gays and lesbians was when I was espousing the church's message: "Love the sinner, not the sin."

Back then, because I was raised a conservative evangelical Christian, I know what my reaction would have been if my son had told me he was gay. I would have prayed to God that He make it not so. I wouldn't have been alone in my reaction. Over the last three years, I've talked to many Christian parents of gay and lesbian children who prayed that prayer to no avail. God didn't make their children heterosexual or change their "lifestyle."

But I've also met parents who found that God instead changed their lifestyle—from a spiritual life that included rejection to one that embraces acceptance. And like me, once they walked away from religion-based bigotry and the condemnation it breeds, they experienced a spiritual awakening.

Religious Right organizations have long preyed on the fears of Christian parents with their hateful messages. What Christian parent would want their child snatched away from them by evil homosexuals who only want innocent, disease-free young men and women to satisfy their carnal lusts? How could parents of a gay child continue belonging to their church family, knowing that on any given Sunday the pastor might characterize their child as an abomination?

Yet thousands of wonderful, loving parents have been forced to choose between either rejecting their church's interpretation of certain Bible passages, and thus alienating themselves from their church communities, or rejecting the children they love. Sadly, many have chosen to reject their own children. And while it may sound heartless, I believe it is never easy for these parents to do. For many years, I lived in fear that any of my four children would be gay and that I'd have to disown them. I can't imagine something so painful.

I remember a deacon in a church I used to attend who went through this. I knew the deacon's son growing up; he was a wonderful, sweet, and tender child. When he told his dad he was gay, his dad forced him to leave home. The church pastor instructed his dad to do it, insisting it was the right decision. Before my spiritual awakening, I would very likely have done the same thing.

So it was divinely ironic to be in another church one Sunday morning in late 2006 asking my fifteen-year-old son what he thought about being gay.

"I don't think it's right," he said. "I was taught it's wrong."

In the quiet confines of our pew, I couldn't escape my feelings of disappointment. I knew I had played a role in passing on that attitude, as part of those "traditional values" so often stressed today.

My response to him conveyed my sorrow, and I think he sensed my apologetic tone. "I used to believe that, too," I said, "but I was wrong."

The journey that led me to that conclusion began at a Sunday lunch with my parents two years earlier. I was taking a hostile and hateful attitude toward gays when my mother asked me if I thought my attitude was very Christ-like. I didn't realize it then, but her question began to open a door in my heart and mind.

Soon after, in a talk with my fiancée about whether gays and lesbians could be Christians, I proclaimed they absolutely could not. She said I was definitely wrong, as she knew a number of gays and lesbians who professed their love for Christ.

I would come to know many myself.

I began to learn more about sexual orientation and about how my attitudes and opinions were based on a particular interpretation of scripture. And soon that door—long sealed shut by the James Dobsons and Jerry Falwells of the world—opened.

A highlight of my spiritual journey occurred during a Town Hall meeting in Ames, Iowa, in 2006. A gay Jewish professor from a nearby university stood up and said he hoped there were some Southern Baptists in the audience because he wanted them to apologize for the harm they had caused him and others.

After the meeting, I approached him, told him I was a Southern Baptist, and apologized for my ugly words, and, more importantly, the attitude behind those words. I asked for his forgiveness, which he gave.

To all the young gay teens being harmed by society's attitude of rejection and condemnation—which I once helped promote—I ask the same. I also ask forgiveness from their parents.

As for those gay teens and adults who ended their lives or were killed because of hatred toward them, I believe I still have to answer for promoting a social climate that makes it easy for them to be hated or even killed. Hopefully, our generation will be the last to have to answer for it. There have been moments with my son that give me hope.

Since our conversation in church, my son began dating a classmate. During this time, he saw how painful it was for his girlfriend when someone at school started a malicious gossip campaign about her parents, a lesbian couple. He said many of the boys spoke badly about gays and lesbians and used their religious teachings to justify it.

Earlier this year, I spoke with the grandfather of one of my children's friends, a pastor who is where I was before starting my spiritual journey. I told him I worked for an organization that helps people better understand the harm religion-based bigotry causes gays and lesbians. He soon voiced the all-too-familiar "I love the gay person but not their sin." Then I explained to him how so many gays and lesbians feel completely rejected by the church, and he said he loved them but could never allow "one" to attend his church.

Later that day, I shared those comments with my son. He was dismayed. He said that a convicted sex offender attended the grandfather's church. I could see him making the connection in his mind: The church accepted a convicted sex offender but not a gay person.

"Can you believe it?" he said.

Behind his words was an attitude void of rejection and condemnation—one for which he'll never need to apologize or answer.

PART 2
Family and
Community Rejection
Would You Be Willing to Risk Their Love?

WOULD YOU BE WILLING
TO RISK THEIR LOVE?

BY CHARLES ROBBINS
Executive Director,
The Trevor Project

A call came in from a sixteen-year-old gay boy from just outside Boston. He told our counselor that he had taken ten Klonopins, an antianxiety medication, spent the night passed out at a friend's house, and thought he had been raped. A frequent abuser of drugs and alcohol, he revealed that he had been overdosing on Klonopin regularly just to see if it would kill him. The counselor was urging him go to the hospital for medical care when he abruptly hung up. We called emergency services, and he was found and hospitalized.

Kids who can't take it anymore—and can't tell anyone—call us every day.

When journalists ask about my work at The Trevor Project, the questions I hear most often are, "Don't you think it's easier for teens to be gay today than, say, ten years ago?" and "Isn't it a different world from when you were growing up?"

My answer is always, "It's not that simple."

For me, growing up in the 1970s in Colorado, just being a teenager from a dysfunctional family with divorced parents was hard enough. Being gay? That was something unfathomable, and I didn't want to think about it. As a matter of fact, the kids in the neighborhood knew I was gay before I did. I recall being called antigay epithets as early as middle school because I was perceived as effeminate. Even my two older brothers teased me about it—all the time.

I felt different from other boys since puberty, but didn't quite grasp why until I had my first same-sex experience when I was sixteen. It felt wonderful—but elation quickly turned to shame. I felt alone with my thoughts. In the 1970s, the world around me told me my attraction to boys was abhorrent. My internalized homophobia was so strong that in high school I turned to drugs and alcohol to suppress the pain.

I finally came out at twenty-five. Once I did, I felt relieved and exalted, but unfortunately, I still could not stop the drug and alcohol abuse. After a near-fatal overdose at twenty-nine, I committed myself to a drug treatment program, where I faced my demons and got the help I needed.

> **"My internalized homophobia was so strong that in high school I turned to drugs and alcohol to suppress the pain."**

Despite a decade lost to substance abuse due to lack of self-esteem—or perhaps because of it—I've been able to devote myself to making sure that others find help where I found none when I was a kid. For more than seventeen years I've worked in the gay community as a "professional homosexual." I founded Project Angel Heart, a meal program for people with HIV/AIDS, before joining the Gay & Lesbian Alliance Against Defamation (GLAAD) and later the National Gay and Lesbian Task Force.

Now I'm proud to channel these experiences into my work as executive director of The Trevor Project. A decade old, Trevor operates the only nationwide, round-the-clock crisis and suicide prevention helpline for gay and questioning youth.

As I review the call reports from our helpline, it is heartbreaking to see the exact same issues I faced as a teenager cropping up today. Although they all have very different stories, the majority of our callers describe a sense of loneliness and isolation. Sure, there is greater social acceptance of gay men and lesbians today, but the private pain of fear, loneliness, and rejection still abound, eating away at the hearts, souls, and self-confidence of young people at a most vulnerable point in their lives.

"As I review the call reports from our help line, it is heartbreaking to see the exact same issues I faced as a teenager cropping up today."

* * *

Calls to Trevor spike during the holidays, traditionally a difficult time for many people, including gay youth. I remember a call over Thanksgiving weekend from an eighteen-year-old in Gallup, New Mexico. He was home from college on break and feeling depressed and terribly lonely. He said he wasn't close with his mother, who refused to acknowledge that he was gay. He was feeling conflicted about his future as a gay man. He told the counselor that earlier in the evening he had had a knife to his wrist, but he hadn't really wanted to kill himself and had called the helpline instead. Talking with our counselor helped the young man feel less alone.

A twenty-four-year-old transgender woman from Santa Rosa, California—I'll call her Kate—told one of our counselors that she was going to kill herself by jumping off the top of a tall parking structure. She had recently been

"The private pain of fear, loneliness, and rejection still abound, eating away at the hearts, souls, and self-confidence of young people at a most vulnerable point in their lives."

forced out of her job and was having major problems at home because religion was standing in the way of her family's acceptance. Kate said that before she began to present herself as female, she hated pretending to be someone she wasn't. But as the woman she felt she was born to be, she was faced with scrutiny and discrimination she hadn't anticipated. As Kate stood on the top floor of that parking structure, she told our counselor about her abusive, alcoholic father and a family history of sexual abuse and rape.

For Kate, suicide seemed to be the only alternative in a world she felt rejected people like her. In fact, she talked about trying to jump about a month before, but two friends—or as she told the counselor, "my *only* friends"—were there to stop her. This time, her friends were not around. Thankfully, Kate called The Trevor Project. As our counselor coaxed her to talk about herself, another counselor alerted the police, who were dispatched to her location (which she had unwittingly disclosed). The counselor kept Kate talking on the phone until the police found her. At that point, the call ended.

> **"For Kate, suicide seemed to be the only alternative in a world she felt rejected people like her."**

A month later, Kate called again. She wanted to thank the counselor for "tricking" her into revealing where she was, because it saved her life. Kate let us know that when the police had showed up, she decided to surrender to them. A two-week stay in a mental health facility followed. She is now on medication and in the care of a therapist and social worker. Through counseling, she's learning more about gender identity and is starting to feel more hopeful. She met two other transgender individuals in her area, and they formed a social support group. For the first time in her short life, Kate is finding the acceptance all young gay people so desperately need. She couldn't thank our counselor enough for helping her—and saving her life. She said she used to feel like there was no tomorrow to look forward to, but that although tomorrow might be difficult, she now wanted to live.

* * *

Most people I talk with are stunned to learn the truth about teenage suicide in America. According to the Centers for Disease Control and Prevention, suicide is the third leading cause of death for young people ages fifteen to twenty-four. Suicide is now the second leading cause of death among college students. Unfortunately, the odds of substance use for lesbian, gay, bisexual, and transgender youth are, on average, 190 percent higher than for heterosexual youth, according to a study by University of Pittsburgh researchers published in the *Journal of Addiction*. And most alarmingly, Youth Risk Behavior

Surveys in Massachusetts and Washington, DC, affirm that gay youth are up to four times more likely to attempt suicide than their heterosexual peers.

My partner of nearly a decade, Damon Romine, is the entertainment media director of GLAAD. His upbringing in Kansas during the 1970s mirrors that of many others of our generation: Without any gay media images or positive reinforcement, he remained stuck in the closet until early adulthood. Because of his work at GLAAD, he's the first to tell you that celebrities like Ellen DeGeneres, Rosie O'Donnell, and Elton John; films like *Brokeback Mountain*; TV shows like *Will & Grace* and *Brothers & Sisters*; and images on MTV have increasingly made it easier for young gay people to be open and authentic at an earlier age, and to find acceptance from those around them.

Anecdotally, we know this to be true. But looking at the calls we receive at Trevor makes it clear that problems surrounding coming out are not disappearing. From 2006 to 2007, we saw a dramatic 28 percent increase in call volume. Young people continue to need someone to talk to, and they continue to consider suicide because they are gay or questioning their sexuality. In 2007 alone, our counselors spoke with nearly twelve thousand youth.

"Young people continue to need someone to talk to, and they continue to consider suicide because they are gay or questioning their sexuality."

The vision, compassion, and social action of the founders of The Trevor Project have given hope to thousands of gay and questioning youth. I can only imagine how my teen years would have been different had a helpline like Trevor existed. I'm so glad it exists today to meet the continuing, overwhelming need of our nation's youth. Still, I look forward to the day when a helpline isn't needed—and being out of a job.

The stories in this section make clear how vital family and community are in the lives of gay teens and how crucial being included and accepted by those they love and respect is to them . . . even if they can't always express how they feel. May these stories inspire you to find ways to be there for them.

For more information on The Trevor Project, please visit www.thetrevor project.org, call its helpline at 866-488-7386 (866-4-U-TREVOR), and see the resource section at the back of this book.

RICHARD CHAMBERLAIN
Actor

Richard Chamberlain will always have a special place in my heart: He was my first crush. As a boy I watched him play the handsome physician on the 1960s TV series *Dr. Kildare*; I never took my eyes off him to look at any of the nurses. Even then, I knew I was smitten. And yet, even then, I could sense others would feel it was "wrong," and that frightened me.

Born in 1934 in Beverly Hills, Richard lived both a thrilling public life and a painful private one. In addition to playing Dr. Kildare, the beloved stage and screen actor starred in two popular 1980s' miniseries, *Shogun* and *The Thorn Birds*. He was also the original Jason Bourne of *The Bourne Identity*, playing the character in the original 1988 TV movie that Matt Damon later made famous on the big screen. He was more recently seen on *Desperate Housewives* as the gay stepfather of character Lynette Scavo, and as Councilman Banks in *I Now Pronounce You Chuck and Larry*.

But in one area of his life, acting did not serve him well. In 2003, at age sixty-nine, he published his memoir, *Shattered Love*. In it, he came out publicly for the first time—sharing with the world the private agony and costs of an inauthentic life.

Here he recalls all the acting he did as a young person to hide who he was—and what a struggle it was to undo all the consequent damage later in life.

Growing up in the forties, certain things were quite clear. The clearest of all was that girls were inferior and utterly other, and for us guys, any deviation from the sacred masculine was unthinkable, loathsome. To be thought a sissy was social death. The key to life, to happiness itself, was a firmly fixed male gender identity. Polarity was sacrosanct. Androgyny was verboten.

By the time I was ten or eleven, it became obvious to me that my gender ID was disastrously off the mark. I was attracted to boys. To me and, as far as I knew, to just about everybody else on earth, this meant that I was despicable and unworthy of existence.

But I did exist, and instinctively knew that to survive, I must pretend to be someone else, someone other than deformed me. Which brings us to the fifteen-year-old Richard I was inventing.

Ah, high school and its raging cauldron of adolescent angst. Luckily, I was good looking, agile, reasonably intelligent, and a budding actor. Acting became my life. I acted Richard the Straight and pretty much got away with it. I had girlfriends whom I genuinely liked and enjoyed. Kissing was fun and, in the fifties, not much more was expected. (And who knows, perhaps I might magically transform into a genuine male.) Nearly all my friends were straight.

My deep fear of being unmasked and revealed as an emotional leper was somewhat glossed over by friendship, scholastic requirements, sports success (I was a four-year letterman in track), and some unexpected distinctions. I was chosen as chief justice of our student court, received an art award trophy and a summer scholarship to Art Center School in Los Angeles, and was accepted by Pomona College in Claremont, California, despite my mediocre grades. And to my total surprise, I was chosen most reserved, most sophisticated, and best physique by our senior high school yearbook.

"I acted Richard the Straight and pretty much got away with it."

So Invented Richard was doing pretty well. Except for the fact that his sexuality, a very big deal at fifteen, had been banished to a dark, dank cellar lockup where it languished, fearful, vexed, and angry, through four years of college and two years in the army.

In 1959, I was living in a tiny apartment in LA pursuing my longed-for career, deeply involved in acting, singing, and dancing lessons, and occasionally even working in television. Sounds good—sounds just right. But I found myself becoming inexplicably fatigued and withdrawn and vaguely fearful. My real self, the self I had been taught by my family and culture to hate, was beginning to agitate for recognition, for light and air and life. Living a lie day after day can be exhausting, even dangerous. But I was psychologically ignorant and had no idea why I was sliding into depression.

My singing teacher, noticing my thinly disguised unhappiness, suggested I see a psychologist she knew. I made an appointment. Our first session was, in retrospect, hilarious. She asked me how I was. "Fine," I said. And how was

> **"My real self, the self I had been taught by my family and culture to hate, was beginning to agitate for recognition, for light and air and life."**

my work? "Fine," I said. And my family, how were we getting along? "Oh, just perfectly," I said. And my romantic life? "Great, just fine," I replied. After a pause, she asked why a person so fine and great and perfect was consulting a psychologist. Well, there I was, caught right in the middle of my Great Lie: that I was the absolutely perfect person my absolutely perfect family had always wanted me to be. Despite being totally busted, or rather because of it, I realized the way I was living my life had to change. I stayed, and our serious work began.

It has taken me many years—decades in fact—of psychological and spiritual exploration to begin to understand the power and tenacity of our social conditioning. The imprint upon a child's mind and heart of family and cultural fears, prejudices, and hatreds can be deep and almost indelible.

Despite my loving relationship with my partner of thirty years, the last vestiges of self-loathing remained into my sixties—and then vanished in a moment of grace. Suddenly, I at last realized that I had been sabotaging myself with a totally absurd, completely fallacious belief that being gay made me despicable. Suddenly, it was clear that being straight or gay tells us next to nothing about people—not whether they are good or bad, smart or slow, kind or cruel, loving or hateful. Being gay is simply

> **"The imprint upon a child's mind and heart of family and cultural fears, prejudices, and hatreds can be deep and almost indelible."**

"Being gay is simply a benign fact. Barely interesting. How I wish I had known this early on."

a benign fact. Barely interesting. How I wish I had known this early on.

So parents and teachers and preachers beware. Your unexamined fears and prejudices are powerfully contagious and can infect and deform the young, whereas mindfulness and loving-kindness will free their spirits to fly toward great things.

EDITOR'S NOTE: Years after my TV love affair with Dr. Kildare—and still in the closet—I was working at Bloomingdale's as an assistant buyer in the comforter and blanket department. My sassy colleague from towels came over, beaming: "There's Richard Chamberlain with his partner." Partner? I must have looked dumbfounded. She said, "Oh, everyone knows he's gay." What she meant, however, was that lots of people knew, but it wasn't publicly known. I stood there in shock, watching what looked like two normal guys shopping for a comforter. And in that moment, I realized it could be okay—that maybe I could live my life somewhat openly and honestly. Some in my New York City world could know, but back home, my parents and old friends need not know. Although this is not the message we want to send to our gay teens—that they can only be who they are in certain areas of their lives—it was, for me at least, a first step toward living authentically, and for that, I thank Richard.

Above: Mitchell Gold (on right) at age thirteen
with his brother, Richard. Opposite: Mitchell
(on right) with his partner, Tim Scofield

MITCHELL GOLD

Cofounder and Chair-Man,
Mitchell Gold + Bob Williams

NOTE: In 1989, with an investment of $60,000, Mitchell Gold and Bob Williams started a furniture company in rural Taylorsville, North Carolina. Today, their company has more than 750 employees and $100 million in sales. From the beginning, the heart of their company has been "comfort." To Mitchell, this means so much more than the sit of a sofa or the feeling you get when you enter a welcoming home. It encompasses all areas of life. It's what led him and Bob to create company benefits that make life easier for their employees, including an education-based on-site daycare center for children of employees and members of the community. And the company's success has allowed Mitchell to extend his efforts toward comfort for all through regional and national philanthropic efforts. Among them is Faith in America, a nonprofit organization he founded in 2005 to help stop religion-based bigotry against the gay community. When asked why he works so hard for this cause, and why he created the book you are now reading, he says, "It's because I don't want one more gay teenager to have to go through what I did." Here is his story.

rowing up, I loved going to the Glendale Tavern. There was something welcoming about the restaurant, set in a middle-class neighborhood in my hometown of Trenton, New Jersey. Its houselike exterior blended with its surroundings. Inside, it felt equally calm and pleasing. (Yes, I thought about home décor even then!)

I remember eating there with my parents and brother one Sunday night in the mid-1960s. Just the four of us. Everyone was in a good mood. My parents worked very hard, so sometimes they were tired and edgy. But not that night. The conversation was lively and cheerful. Everyone was smiling. I was fourteen, and my brother was eighteen. He was home from college. I was always excited to see him. He was the greatest brother on earth.

And then, like always, the black cloud hit me. That's what I called it: the black cloud. I remembered that I had this enormous problem that I couldn't solve, no matter how hard I tried. The other guys my age were talking about dating girls and kissing girls and feeling them up. Not me. By then, I had been with a few girls—and with a few guys. There was little question which felt more natural.

So there we were at dinner, all smiles and conversation, when the black cloud descended. In an instant, I remembered there was no way I could ever be 100 percent happy because I had this affliction. Like so many other times, I had to multitask—keep the smile and conversation going while dealing with the emotions overtaking me. I couldn't wait to get home. I would make some excuse and go lie down. At least then I could be by myself and try to sort out my feelings.

Nights were horrible. The cloud always set in then. I'd be alone in my bed, trying to sleep, and all I could think about was my problem. Or some guy I had a crush on. Especially troubling was the realization that I didn't just want a sexual connection with other guys, but that I had a desire to be intimate with some—to cuddle and share feelings I might not share with others. And I was realizing I didn't want to marry a woman, but would rather spend my life with a man.

In the 1960s, this was obviously taboo. The only "homos" I knew about were the few effeminate ones I saw on TV and the two guys who lived in town. One was a dress designer, and the other, a beautician. They were oddities. Many of my parents' friends were friendly with them—but made fun of them behind their backs. One of my biggest fears, as strange as it sounds now, was that if I continued to desire guys, I would become increasingly more effeminate until I was just like them. And then people would laugh behind my back, and my only job opportunities would be designing dresses or being a beautician. That really scared me.

In those days, being a homosexual was actually considered a mental illness. Fortunately, in 1973, the American Psychiatric Association removed homosexuality from its list of mental disorders. However, even afterward, being gay still wasn't something people discussed much.

> "It's one thing to be depressed, but to feel you have to hide your depression is torturous."

When gays were shown on TV shows or news reports, they were depicted as lonely, depressed, sick, fearful individuals. In one now-infamous 1967 broadcast, Mike Wallace of CBS interviewed a "homosexual" so afraid of being identified that he spoke from behind a potted plant. Not much to aspire to.

I can't remember when I first fully realized I was gay, but I do remember throughout my teen years being incredibly depressed. For me, being a gay teenager meant being two people all the time. I had to live as "normally" as possible—be cool, take girls out on dates, go to dances. But my "other person" lived in constant fear and confusion, which led to my depression. It's one thing to be depressed, but to feel you have to hide your depression is torturous. I remember thinking, *Why did God create me this way?*

I thought about suicide often. I made a pact with myself: If I could not change and want to be with a woman by the time I was twenty-one, I would commit suicide.

I debated over how to do it. An overdose of sleeping pills seemed somewhat painless. But when I told our family physician,

> "I made a pact with myself: If I could not change and want to be with a woman by the time I was twenty-one, I would commit suicide."

Dr. Kurt Zeltmacher, I was having trouble sleeping, he wouldn't give me the pills. He said I was too young.

I was getting desperate. One evening, Kurt and his wife, Muriel, came over to play bridge with my parents. In those days, people didn't always lock their cars. So I went outside to his car and—bingo—it was open, and his medical bag was on the front seat. I carefully held the little button as I opened the door so the automatic overhead light would not go on. I searched the bag, naively thinking he'd be carrying some kind of pills I could use. There weren't any. But I did find his prescription pad, so I took a few sheets, thinking I could write myself a scrip, but I couldn't figure out how to write it.

I considered other tactics—driving a car off a cliff, running in front of a train, jumping off a building—but I knew I didn't have the guts. And then it sank in: Even if I could muster the courage, my parents and brother would be devastated. Surely, if any of them took their life, I'd forever feel guilty and be hard pressed to deal with such enormous loss.

With no one to talk to, I cried myself to sleep more times than I can count. It was like living through a nervous breakdown—my own little world of pain. I barely got through school with a C average. I hated going because each day was a challenge to keep my secret, so I often played hooky. I got caught once and was suspended. For a Jewish boy in the suburbs, that was unheard of. My father and mother were crazed by my behavior, yelling at me and smacking me occasionally, asking why I would do such a thing. I just looked at them blankly and said I didn't know. Once again, I was lying.

Yet I'm one of the lucky ones. Several years later, I was about to go back to college in Rhode Island after winter break. I was a complete mess, and it must have showed in my face. My father asked me what was wrong, and I broke down. I still couldn't tell him the truth, but I did manage to say that I had troubles and needed to see a psychiatrist. He was startled, but his unconditional love took over. He told me to find one and send him the bill. This was no small gesture on his part. Business was not great, and I knew it was a difficult financial time for the family.

> **"It was like living through a nervous breakdown—my own little world of pain."**

The psychiatrist I was lucky enough to find through my school may well have saved my life. At the very least, he helped set me on the path to affirming who I am. He told me my homosexuality was not something to be cured. I began to accept myself, even if I wasn't ready to come out to those close to me yet, and I began to have hope for the future. I transferred to a new college, and in a sense, started over. It was truly as if I had been born again and become the person I was meant to be. The experience was that powerful.

The number one reason I work toward equal rights for gay, lesbian, bisexual, and transgender people is because I do not want kids to go through what I did. Today I live and work in an area of North Carolina that falls squarely within the Bible Belt. Too many families here torture their children spiritually and emotionally if they happen to have been born attracted to others of the same sex because they believe "their" Bible compels and obligates them to do so.

It would be one thing if religious leaders had never before misinterpreted and misused the Bible to dehumanize, degrade, and marginalize minority groups. But they have. And they are doing it again. When they influence congregants to vote for candidates who would legislate discrimination, they continue to cause indelible pain.

> **"The psychiatrist I was lucky enough to find through my school may well have saved my life. He told me my homosexuality was not something to be cured."**

I often wonder what my life would have been like if, when I was a teenager, there had been laws condemning hate crimes, protecting me in the workplace and housing, and providing for marriage equality. I would have grown up feeling whole and equal—not marginalized and less than others.

Thankfully, there are more and more religious leaders of all sects who have the courage to speak out against such bigotry. I have heard Christian clergy tell their religious communities that if Jesus Christ were here today, he would say shame on those who use the Bible to inflict pain on the gay community. They are joining forces with Jewish and Muslim leaders who are fighting fundamentalist teachings about gay people in their own communities.

I believe the world's great religious traditions emphasize loving

> **"I often wonder what my life would have been like if, when I was a teenager, there had been laws condemning hate crimes, protecting me in the workplace and housing, and providing for marriage equality."**

thy neighbor as well as loving God. There is no room in such great traditions for the kind of small-mindedness that would incite violence against anyone or deny anyone his or her civil rights. And I have been heartened to learn that many people agree. They are coming together through Faith in America, as well as through other grassroots organizations to emancipate gay people from bigotry disguised as religious truth and to create a world in which no child has to grow up fearful just because he or she is who they are.

JORGE VALENCIA

Executive Director and CEO, Point Foundation, and Former Executive Director and President, The Trevor Project

Jorge Valencia remembers counselors at The Trevor Project, a crisis and suicide pre-vention helpline, getting calls from kids whose parents told them, "I would rather have a dead son than a gay son."

The son of immigrant Mexican Mormons, raised with a strong Latino and reli-gious upbringing, Jorge had to face down his own struggles with his sexuality, as well as his parents' understanding of it, before he felt he could take a public role in his vital work at The Trevor Project. Today, Jorge works for the Point Foundation, which provides scholarships to students marginalized because of sexual orientation, gender identity, or gender expression. It has been a source of hope and a chance at a future for a number of students of merit whose families rejected them when they disclosed their sexuality. In its seventh year, the foundation currently supports eighty-four lesbian, gay, bisexual, and transgender scholars at colleges and univer-sities across the country. Several of them share their stories in this book.

In school, I was the guy with the thick glasses and braces. I was quiet. I wasn't into sports. Nobody would sit with me at lunch. The other kids called me names—"sissy," "queer," "girl"—painful epithets for a young boy growing up in Texas's Rio Grande Valley in the 1970s. I would get stomach cramps every morning because I knew what I would have to face that day. But I never told my parents. It's one of those things you don't want to share with them. You don't want them to be embarrassed that you're their child.

My sister was my complete opposite—eleven months older than me and beautiful, popular, and smart. Had it not been for her, I don't know what my future would've held. There was not a day that she did not invite me to have lunch with her and her friends. And by virtue of her popularity, I was somewhat left alone. But to this day, I remember the name-calling very clearly.

In my sophomore year of high school, things changed for me. I grew taller; the braces came off; I got contacts—and so I was treated completely differently. I was voted "Mr. Sharyland High School" and received other popularity awards that young people somehow deem so important. Yet, inside, I was still the same Jorge.

"You don't want them to be embarrassed that you're their child."

My high school had only a few hundred students. My university, Brigham Young, in Utah, the most prestigious Mormon university in the country, had more than thirty thousand. All I wanted to do was fit in—I never wanted to go back to how I'd felt as a kid. So I ran for student body vice president and won. I dated popular girls, including a cheerleader or two. I was even recognized as "Most Photogenic Model in Utah" and got some modeling contracts from it.

"All I wanted to do was fit in—I never wanted to go back to how I'd felt as a kid."

But despite everything, I still knew something was not right, and I couldn't stop thinking about it. While my male friends spoke about the excitement they felt when dating, deep down I knew I didn't feel what I should be feeling when I was with a woman. I hadn't yet internalized that I was gay, but I knew I was hiding a lie—and what else could it be?

After my freshman year of college, I made a major attempt to fight my feelings. I took off two years to go on a mission, as good Mormons do. I went to Brazil, and there I lived by the rules: We got up at a certain time, went to sleep at a certain time, knocked on doors to introduce people to the church at a certain time. During the entire mission, I got up late, after 6 a.m., only once because I was sick—and I felt guilty about it. I truly was a good Mormon boy.

When the mission ended, I returned to college, but no matter what I tried, nothing made me happy. By my junior year, it was becoming frustratingly clear that all the success and popularity weren't going to provide what I needed. I was sure I was destined to feel this emptiness forever.

One day, my roommate was out of town and I was alone in our apartment. I felt I had to talk to someone, to tell someone the truth. I tried to reach my family but no one was home. The one person I reached was really busy. So instead, I went into the bathroom, grabbed the sleeping pills, and took all of them. Two days later, I woke up. There hadn't been enough to end my sorrow. I like to think the Lord was on my side.

* * *

It wasn't until I graduated college and moved to Washington, DC, that I knew I needed to explore the part of me that the mission and college life hadn't changed. I went with a friend to a gay club. The identification was immediate and overwhelming—I understood why I had felt so different for so long.

After that, I struggled with a double life, hanging out with my church friends, trying to slip away early to hang out with my gay friends, and hoping the two worlds would never collide. I assumed that if I told my family, they wouldn't want anything to do with me. For the first time in years, I didn't go home for the holidays. I wanted to find out what life might be like without them.

I'm first generation American; both my parents are from Mexico. My father moved to the States when he was sixteen. When he and my mom married, they literally had nothing. But they are hard workers, and their hard work paid off. My father owned several businesses, and we did well. My first car was my father's old Mercedes. How many people with immigrant Mexican parents can say that? They had four children, two boys and two girls—a small Mormon family and a small Latino family.

I came out to them in my sister's kitchen. I said, "I have not been living my life the way you expected. I have been involved with a man for a year. There's nothing you can possibly say that I haven't thought of a million times myself as to why I'm sitting here telling you this now." Then I said, "All right, have a good night; I'll talk to you soon," and walked out of the house. As I drove away, I thought, *They'll never speak with me again.*

But they did: They offered to pay for a therapist—a church therapist, of course. I drove all the way to the appointment and then sat out front for an hour and a half while the session was supposed to be going on. Finally, I thought, *Why am I here? There's nothing wrong with me*, and drove away.

But my parents were relentless. There wasn't a single conversation we had that did not go back to religion—and the eternal ramifications of those who did not live the way God intended. This continued for a long time. It didn't help that I still felt conflicted myself. When I moved from Washington, DC, to Los Angeles, I tried going back to church. But I couldn't live that lie again.

* * *

I never imagined myself working for a gay organization. But when I attended a benefit for The Trevor Project helpline and heard the statistics on gay and questioning teen suicide, I was so saddened and horrified, that I wanted to do something. I became Trevor's first executive director. My family already knew I was gay, but I wasn't ready for the whole world to find out; the founders agreed to be the front people and let me work in the background. There was just enough money to keep Trevor's helpline open; I ran things from my dining room. But that work changed me: The issue of suicide prevention touched me personally, and I felt a powerful call to speak out about Trevor's importance. I soon found that I could no longer remain behind the scenes.

And yet, although I was a spokesperson for Trevor, I still never told anyone about my own suicide attempt. It would seem natural for someone talking about suicide prevention every day to do that. But until last year, when I was at the Point Foundation, I couldn't get past the stigma. I didn't want to be perceived as weak, and I didn't want my loved ones to be perceived as uncaring. That's one reason why many gay people don't tell, and why it can be hard to get full statistics. People don't want to discuss it because they don't want it to be the focus of everything they've ever done.

* * *

I was in a relationship with my boyfriend for about three years when I asked my parents if I could bring him home for the holidays. My family considered him my "roommate," but they had to have known. My parents asked me if he didn't have anywhere else to go. I was shocked by their response. I said, "I cannot believe I'm hearing this from my parents, who talk about religion, and God, and what Christ would do." We still made the trip, but stayed in a hotel.

Later my parents called, crying, saying how terrible they would feel if we didn't stay with them. The last night we were in town, we relented. We stayed in separate bedrooms to make them feel a little more comfortable.

Even so, they both pulled me aside the next day. My mom told me I was being selfish because I was denying her grandchildren. I said, "Who says I can't still have children?" My dad said, "Can't you be in a relationship with a woman that's just platonic?" And I said, "Dad, to whose benefit is that? Mine? Yours? Certainly not hers."

> **"I felt it wasn't my issue anymore: Whether they chose to be proud of their son was something they had to deal with."**

They finally had to come to terms with the fact that I'm gay when *People en Español* did a feature on me—a full-page photo and three pages of text. They started getting phone calls from family and friends in Mexico and the United States. I felt it wasn't my issue anymore: Whether they chose to be proud of their son was something they had to deal with.

Things have gone well, although there has been an occasional hiccup. Just a year ago, my dad said, "Hey, I've heard of a group that can make people straight through religion!" And I said, "Yes, Dad. And some of their own leaders are still going to gay clubs."

Although they've never attended a charitable event for a group I've worked for, they do ask me about my work all the time. I talked out the challenging decision to move from The Trevor Project to the Point Foundation with my dad.

Dad has always understood the importance of my work at Trevor. Being Mormon, he believes that suicide is unthinkable—why would you take your life when you've got God on your side? When my dad found out the suicide rate of the kids I work with, he was shocked.

But maybe he shouldn't be. Society casts away gay people. Some religious leaders actually tell parents it's the right thing to do—to reject their own kids. What those parents may not know is that even gay teens with supportive parents are prone to suicidal thoughts. When parents are ambivalent, the situation worsens. And when parents are openly hostile, their children's suicide rate jumps up seven times or more.

"Some religious leaders actually tell parents it's the right thing to do—to reject their own kids."

If parents knew that their actions, as well as those of their religious leaders, could drive their children to suicide, I'd like to think they'd watch what they say and tell their religious leaders, "What you are saying is harming my child." What good parent wants to risk his or her child getting hurt?

Nate, at age fourteen, with his mom, Nancy Golden

NATE BERKUS
Designer

As a featured designer on *The Oprah Winfrey Show*, Nate Berkus earns kudos from audiences for his smart and stylish decorating ideas, presented in a charming and friendly manner. I can tell you that Nate is as warm and genuine in person as he appears on TV. Watching him so at ease on camera, it's hard to imagine the teenage boy who lived in fear of anyone finding out he was gay.

Nate grew up between Minnetonka, Minnesota, where his mom lived, and Orange County, California, with his dad. The oldest of four brothers and one sister from his parents' second marriages, he attended boarding school in Massachusetts, an internship in Paris, and college in Chicago. In 1995, at age twenty-three, he opened his own firm in Chicago, Nate Berkus Associates. He is the author of *Home Rules: Transform the Place You Live into a Place You'll Love.*

I knew I was gay when I was really young, maybe even at two. I truly was conscious of a physical attraction to men, yet an emotional attraction to women, and it made me sense that I was different early on. My deep-rooted fear was that because I was different I'd lose the love of the people close to me—that my family and friends would be disgusted by who I am. That fear stayed with me for years.

Today, I don't define myself solely by my sexual orientation, just as I don't define myself by my race or my religion or even by having almost died in the tsunami in Sri Lanka. I live a very open life, even on television. I can hold hands with my boyfriend walking down the street. I can talk about being gay anytime, anywhere.

That wasn't always the case. From ages thirteen to seventeen, growing up in the suburbs of Minneapolis in the 1980s, I was in crisis mode. I couldn't think about anything other than being gay and how to deal with it. And since I felt I couldn't tell anyone, I had no help in figuring it out. It stopped the growth in almost every area of my life. Now, looking back and knowing the man I've become at thirty-six, I wonder, "How could I have been so obsessed with that one issue?"

"From ages thirteen to seventeen ... I was in crisis mode."

Because of that issue there were many things I didn't allow myself to do. I could have started in fashion or gone to design school, but I didn't because it seemed "too gay." And now here I am on TV as one of America's best-known designers. It's what I do not only proudly and publicly but also gratefully. I knew in high school what my interests were, but I wouldn't admit it to my friends because it seemed so stereotypical.

Yet even though I spent tremendous energy concealing that part of myself, other kids still sensed it. Kids are smart; they know when you're trying to hide something, and they pick up on your attempts to compensate for it. Not only sexual identity—it could be trouble at home, trouble with food, whatever.

There were times when I thought I was safe—and then got caught off guard by the bully on the other side of the classroom yelling something like "Hey faggot, why don't you play any sports? Skiing isn't a real sport." In adolescence it often feels like there are electric prods on either side of you, and just when you start feeling good about yourself, you get a "zzzzz," reminding you to get back in the center lane. For gay teens, those prods are doubly painful, frightening reminders of all you stand to lose if you let down your guard.

This is one of the greatest tragedies of not being able to come out: You must lie all the time—to yourself and others. Even after you come out, it can take years to get back to being honest. For so long I led a day-to-day existence of covers-ups and masked feelings—of trying to talk myself out of my feelings. It prevented me from getting to know myself and kept me from being proud of who I am.

Often when people finally come out, they say, "I'm telling you because I care about our relationship and want you to know me. I'm tired of lying." When you lie to someone you love, it robs you and them. Yet when you're gay and closeted, you must lie out of necessity.

> **"For so long I led a day-to-day existence of covers-ups and masked feelings—of trying to talk myself out of my feelings."**

It reminds me of stories about European Jews in World War II. They had relationships in hiding during the war, when they were pretending to be Catholic, and years later, they admitted to being Jewish. Two years ago, I met an eighty-year-old woman in Paris who admitted to me she was Jewish—and that was the first time she ever spoke the words out loud. It was a mind-blowing experience.

Even though I knew my parents loved me, and even though my mother was a decorator with gay friends who often visited our house, I was still afraid.

In fact, it was my mother who broached the subject of my sexuality with me, when I was a freshman in college. She began by asking about my friends:

"Is Vanessa gay?"

"Yeah," I said.

"Is Scott gay?"

"Yeah."

"Do you have anything you want to tell me?"

I couldn't get the whole truth out so I said, "I think I'm bi."

"I have two things to tell you," she said. "You're too old to get sick because you've been raised in an era when people have information and aren't afraid to talk about it. So it would be a crime if you didn't practice safe sex and allowed yourself to get sick. And two, there's nothing more lonely than a gay person growing old alone." Then she got up and said, "I have to pick up your sister at dance class, we'll talk more about this later. Bye, fag."

That was truly how I came out to my mother. And yet, as positive as her initial reaction was, and despite her acceptance of gays in general, she still mourned. Why? I don't believe any parent wants a child to have to deal with anything more challenging than the quintessential cookie-cutter life, whether the issue is sexuality, or a career at which they have a slim chance to succeed. So parents go through an adjustment when children stake claim to how they want their lives to go. When coming out is the issue, they need time to deal with their fears of their child being hurt or sick or alone.

That's something I hope gay teenagers will remember: No matter how liberal your childhood or your parents' lifestyle, whether you're raised in the city or suburbs, almost all parents need time to adjust. And the person coming out needs to respect that.

With my father, although we'd always been close, we almost ended up with no relationship because he was so uncomfortable. I remember him saying, "You're so good-looking; you could have any girl you want. You're choosing such a hard life. This doesn't make sense. I don't *know* any gay people. I work in sports. I can't see why you're doing this."

At the time I was living in Chicago, and he was in California with my stepmother; so we only saw each other occasionally. My stepmother is religious, and based on her Christian faith, she told him I had made a choice, but that they didn't have to agree with it. Her attitude was, "We love him, but we're worried about him." I wasn't there to address it with my dad and didn't care about winning him over then.

It wasn't until several years later that we had our first real conversation about it. My father had hit a crisis in his own life and had come to Chicago to have dinner with me and discuss it.

I wasn't on *Oprah* yet, but I had a successful design firm, a lake house in Michigan, and a penthouse in Chicago. And I had started my own firm when I was twenty-three years old. I felt I was doing pretty well in life.

We talked a long time, and just before he had to go back to the airport, he said, "There's one more thing. This life you've chosen can be really lonely. Your stepmother and I worry because we don't talk to you often and don't know what goes on day to day. We're always afraid that someday we're going to get a call."

"What do you mean?" I asked—and then said incredulously, "A call that I killed myself?"

Now I *know* my dad. He's an intelligent guy. And this is what he was carrying around, afraid to say anything to me and afraid of what might happen to me.

I said, "Change your flight. We have to finish this talk."

We went to the airport bar, and here's what I told him: "Dad, I'm the last of your four boys you'll ever get that call about. What makes me sad is you know me so little that you think it's a possibility.

"I'd love for us to be back laughing and joking like we used to when we were so bonded. But we can't unless we agree on one thing: People don't choose to be gay. I know you. You're a businessperson. You don't respect people who make decisions you don't understand. If I *could* choose, I don't know what I'd do because I love my life. But I never chose it. It chose me. So, while I'm aware there are two schools of thought on this, you and I cannot have a real relationship unless I know you believe that."

> "If I *could* choose, I don't know what I'd do because I love my life. But I never chose it. It chose me."

And he said, "I've never thought about it much. I've just been listening to your stepmother. You're my son. If you say you feel you were born that way, then you were born that way."

Had we not had that conversation, our relationship might have been lost. There are countless parents and children in that position. I think it was brave of my dad to bring it up.

I remember when my mom called her parents—my grandparents—to tell them I was gay. She was terrified—and they're not scary people. My grandmother's reaction: "Thank God he loved you enough to share it with you. Some parents never have any idea who their own child is. Now you'll be able to be a part of this."

A shocker to my mom and me at the time, but I think that as people get older and have the grace to look back on life, they realize that those conflicts you're able to avoid are your greatest triumphs. You never have to try and get back wasted years that way.

* * *

After I lost my partner, Fernando, in the tsunami of 2004, Oprah Winfrey aired a segment about us. Having my personal story recounted on television was a huge awakening for me, one that gave me hope for the future. I saw my loss understood as a loss—not a gay loss. I saw my relationship presented as a relationship—not a gay relationship. The story wasn't told for political reasons, but to help bring aid to those who desperately needed help. I shared it straightforwardly, without apology or second thoughts. I believe people could feel that energy and honesty. The acceptance I received was unbelievable. Thousands of people wrote to me. Many sent their prayers. It kept me going at such a difficult time.

That's why this book is so important to me—like my *Oprah* segment, it is important for what people can learn from it. People who had thought horrible things about gays until they watched my story wrote me in sympathy. Parents who knew their children were gay sent letters asking for my advice on how to approach them. And I heard from kids who saw the beauty of our relationship and decided to come out because they wanted the chance to have that.

We must remember, however, that even today coming out is still such a risk for many young teens. It shouldn't be, but it is. For one thing, they're not financially independent. And when you're risking the very roof over your head, and the very school you're attending, you start to wonder if it would be worth it, or if it would be better to stay quiet until you're eighteen and can get a job—because a fourteen-year-old can't even get a legal job with which they can support themselves.

They shouldn't have to wait, and they shouldn't have to lie. With kids coming out younger and younger, more than ever they need our acceptance, our support, and our love.

James McGreevey and his sisters

JAMES MCGREEVEY

Seminary Student and
Former Governor of New Jersey

Jim McGreevey was the governor of New Jersey from January 2002 to November 2004. Born in Jersey City, he earned degrees from Columbia, Georgetown, and Harvard before serving three terms as mayor of Woodbridge, New Jersey. He currently attends the General Theological Seminary in New York City and lives with his partner, Mark O'Donnell, in New Jersey.

This book illustrates how society—be it parents, community, peers, or religious upbringing—often forces gay people to live a significant part of their lives as a lie. Many must also choose between being open about who they are and their careers. This chapter illustrates how early in life the painful decision to hide or live openly must often be made. Coming out can free gay people from our greatest fears and help us find, in Jim's words, "what unites us to all humanity." Jim hopes to be able to use his hard-earned wisdom to focus on becoming a minister and helping people in a more authentic way.

My memories of growing up are idyllic scenes from a Norman Rockwell calendar—loving parents, family dinners, baseball games, VFW picnics, and bike rides through a maze of suburban New Jersey streets with little more than change in my pocket for an ice-cold soda at a corner convenience store. I loved that life. And from a very young age, I was afraid I could lose it if anyone discovered my dark, ugly secret.

As early as first grade in St. Joseph's Grammar School, in 1963, I knew I was different. If you had asked me how, I couldn't have explained it. I looked like all the other boys in our uniform of gray flannel pants, starched white shirt, and plaid clip-on tie. I don't know if the other boys and girls on the playground noticed, but I already sensed a difference in the way I interacted with others. The vast majority of kids liked members of the opposite sex, while I felt something for other boys. I didn't know why I felt that way, but it scared me.

Back then, nobody told me I was gay or what that meant. This stands in sharp contrast to the way I learned about the rest of my identity—my ethnicity, family history, religion. My parents, teachers, and pastors gave me an appreciation for the members of my tribe who had come before me: wonderful tales of my Irish and English grandparents traveling to America by steamship; the willing sacrifices of my family during World War II; the charisma of the first Irish Catholic president, John F. Kennedy; and the dedication of Catholic clergy in their adopted homeland. No one, of course, knew anything about gay heroes and struggles, and even if they had, they wouldn't have mentioned it. Unlike race or gender, being gay isn't necessarily obvious—and in those days it was definitely not something you talked about. So I tried to learn all I could about it from my peers, my church, and my local library—without ever directly asking anyone. And everything I learned told me that it was taboo.

"It made me feel that I needed to hide this secret at all costs."

It made me feel that I needed to hide this secret at all costs. So while trying to understand my own sexuality, I also worked hard to learn the behaviors of heterosexuals. In that area, I had help: Like invisible electric lines that restrain dogs, my peers punished me every time I crossed a hetero-normative barrier. I had to look and act heterosexual, but it wasn't easy. The behavior didn't come naturally.

I remember an early scouting trip during which I helped another scout put on his backpack. I stood behind him and raised the pack, performing what the Servant Sisters of my Catholic grammar school would call an act of compassion. But in the eyes of the other boys, I did it wrong. I stood too close: I had crossed a boundary line. That night, lying in my tent, I heard the older boys swapping stories around the campfire. And then I heard, "That McGreevey is a fag, a homo, a cocksucker." In that instant, they articulated my greatest fear. How had they discerned my secret? My tent-mate told me to ignore them, but I knew they'd found my deepest vulnerability. I cried myself to sleep, asking God why I wasn't like every other kid in America.

By the next morning, I had a plan. I strutted up to the head scout and challenged him to give me more work, more duties, more tasks. I'd show him, the other scouts, and the entire Boy Scouts of America that I could be the toughest, most determined scout in their ranks. If I showed him and all he represented that I could do everything scouting wanted of me and more, maybe I could will away the stigma of being a "homo." Or at least I could distract from it by out-hustling and outperforming my peers. And that's just what I did, at scouts—and later, in other arenas. Yet while I publicly observed the boundaries, I also secretly continued to explore who my heart, mind, and soul told me I was.

In eighth grade, I had my first gay encounter, with a skinny athletic blond kid a year behind me in school. Walking home, he told me about his older brother's *Playboy* collection and invited me to look at it. I didn't need urging; the tension in my chest and excitement in my bones were palpable because I intuited this boy wanted the same things I did. Paging through *Playboy* provided the cover for our passion. Afterward I ran home, the excitement replaced by humiliating shame. For the first time, I had crossed the great chasm of lesser venal sins to a mortal sin of the worst kind. The Bible called it an abomination. The Holy Roman Catholic Church condemned it as unnatural and perverted. My actions had put my soul within the grasp of eternal damnation. If I were to die in a freak accident, my soul would burn for all eternity in the fires of hell . . .

I jumped into the shower and turned up the hot water, letting the scalding liquid "cleanse" my skin of the impurities of the past hour and wash away my perverse desires. Then I collapsed on my bed and fell asleep, temporarily sexually gratified and not quite convinced that I had mitigated my iniquity by punishing my body.

If my physical nature had won a battle, I was determined to use my intellect to win the war. The answers I found were not comforting. At the library, I discovered that although ancient societies had embraced homosexual love, and certain nineteenth-century English authors had written beautifully of it, in twentieth-century America it enjoyed no such acceptance. It was an aberration and a particular threat to children. Psychiatry condemned it as an illness; medical authorities thought it might one day be eliminated. My beloved Catholic Church was in the vanguard, providing "moral leadership" against its corrupting influence. The military saw it as a treacherous and divisive substratum that harmed its unity. In politics, sports, and business, it went largely unmentioned, except for the occasional joke.

> **"My actions had put my soul within the grasp of eternal damnation."**

I did not want to be something so reviled. So I made the agonizing—adolescent—decision to deny my sexual orientation by changing it. I would force myself, through my own form of aversion therapy, to reprogram my mind. I'd no longer be stimulated by the near-perfect male bodies modeling briefs or swimsuits in catalogs. I'd be like almost every other kid in town—and, for that matter, in the state and the country.

I began studying the pin-up beauties in *Playboy* and *Hustler* and reading the sexual antics described in their pages. As the months wore on, these and other efforts felt increasingly futile, of course. After I started high school at an all-boys Catholic prep school, it got worse. I saw my friends at weekend parties flirting, making out, and being sexually playful with the neighborhood teenage girls. I could spend every day trying to be sexually responsive to girls; I knew in my heart it would never work. Changing my wiring wasn't like changing a CD; my sexual longings were encrypted in my soul.

> **"Changing my wiring wasn't like changing a CD; my sexual longings were encrypted in my soul."**

That self-realization led to an intense loneliness and isolation worse than being ridiculed had felt in my youth. I'd leave those parties and walk the streets by myself. Never actually listening to God, but to the "inspired" wisdom of the church in which I was immersed at home and at school instead, I determined that living a gay life would be sinful and result in alienation from God. In the midst of deep depression, I struggled with every possible "solution"—even suicide. Thankfully, God's grace and the love of my family sustained me.

* * *

As the years passed, I moved on to college and law school and into politics, which became my attempt to satiate myself by doing good. But I was still a fractured person. I relegated my secret to dark places where, ironically, my actions were sinful and unhealthy. Because I thought I could never express the love in my heart—the way young men and women who happened to be attracted to the opposite sex did—I began to seek anonymous interludes with strangers. The sadness of my closet was that love, friendship, and joy didn't matter. All that counted was keeping my secret and experiencing sexual excitement in those hidden places. By day, I lived a "wholesome" all-American life

> **"I relegated my secret to dark places where, ironically, my actions were sinful and unhealthy."**

that included marriage, children, and career goals I felt I could only achieve as a heterosexual, while by night, as the late gay writer Oscar Wilde put it, I was "feasting with panthers."

Even in the closet, there are shades of gray. You hide from certain people, but—out of necessity—you signal others about the truth. Still others you make complicit. Gradually, my two lives pulled apart. I constantly needed to maintain dual running ledgers in my mind—who knew what about whom?—and be exceptionally cautious about permitting individuals to cross from one world to the other. Despite all the stress and fear of exposure, I continued down these two increasingly divergent paths. I began to think I was truly in control of my destiny—that I had become master of my universe. In politics, where perception is all too often reality and where image is a creation of polling, focus groups, and consultants, it can become easy to feel that way.

"The sadness of my closet was that love, friendship, and joy didn't matter."

As you probably saw on the nightly news in 2004, my political career didn't end well. I was blackmailed by my lover, a man I had wrongly placed on the state payroll in a sensitive position. I resigned as governor of New Jersey. My marriage to my second wife ended, badly, soon afterward.

Eventually, with the love of family and friends, and with psychiatric help, I pulled apart the tangled branches of my life and placed them all in plain view. Although my life has still too often been on the front pages, I am trying to start over with honesty and self-acceptance. I now believe being gay or straight are differences as natural as having brown eyes or blue. I believe being gay is a gift from God, the same God who grants identity to all of life. The closet is a terrible place. Ultimately, no one remains untouched by the deceit, and the price of deceit is formidable. I dream of a world in which people do

"I believe being gay is a gift from God, the same God who grants identity to all of life."

not have to—or believe they have to—stay in the closet in order to achieve their dreams or be right with their God.

Today, blessed with a loving, committed partner, I try to do God's will and simply ask of myself, as the Psalmist does, "Let the words of my mouth and the meditations of my heart be acceptable in thy sight, O Lord, my strength and my redeemer."

HOWARD BRAGMAN
Public Relations Consultant

Looking back on his outsider status during his childhood in Flint, Michigan, Howard Bragman now jokes, "I finally moved to LA because being gay and Jewish were two rungs on the ladder of success." But the jokes and his success hide real pain. "Sometimes it feels like somebody else lived the first part of my life," he confides.

He sold his first public relations firm in 2001, only to start a new one, Fifteen Minutes, four years later. Although he deals primarily with the entertainment industry, he is well known for helping golfer Rosie Jones, WNBA star Sheryl Swopes, NFL player Esera Tuaolo, and former hoopster John Amaechi come out of the closet.

His message to parents is direct and cautionary: "It's easy to believe you can dictate how the world should work, but that's not necessarily how the world really works. Ozzie and Harriet are dead." And his message to gay adults is equally emphatic: "Coming out is just about dealing with your secrets before they deal with you."

Somebody once asked me why there were so many gay people in entertainment, and I said, "Because we were actors before there were actors." We're always trying to blend in with everybody else, automatically changing pronouns from "he" to "she" in the seconds between when we think of a story and when it comes out of our mouths. From that kind of "creativity" can come either of two things: strength and resolve, or a pain and fear so deep that you have to find a way to make it go away. For many of us, that pain never goes away.

I always say I know what it's like to be a Martian because I was fat and Jewish and gay in Flint, Michigan, in the 1960s and 1970s. For me, Flint was not always a warm, wonderful place to grow up. It was, and is, a blue-collar town. Sometimes the kids who were cheerleaders and football heroes say junior high and high school was the best part of their lives. I had a tougher time.

Mom was a nice Jewish housewife. She went to the beauty parlor on Fridays and made brisket for shabbos dinner. My father owned an insurance agency. Compared to other people in town, we lived nicely, although my father didn't make more money than anybody else. We were hopelessly middle class; we just had a different taste level.

I never thought, *I'm gay*. I didn't have words for it. But I knew I was very different. And there were only one or two other Jews in my school, so I really was different very early on. I thought differently from other people. I read, and I liked old movies. I remember seeing *Bye Bye Birdie* about sixteen times. I went with everybody in my family who wanted to go—my grandmother, my aunts—anyone who asked me. That's how I knew: I liked Conrad Birdie. And in my early teens, when I started being sexual with myself, I realized I wasn't thinking about cheerleaders: I was thinking about the captain of the football team.

> **"I never thought, *I'm gay*. I didn't have words for it. But I knew I was very different."**

My mother and I have always been close. We've always understood each other intuitively. I helped her decorate the house. On her birthday or anniversary, I'd picked out my father's present for her. There were many times I wanted to burst out and tell her, but the fear was so great. Looking back, I can't even say what, exactly, I was afraid of.

I'm not a religious person, but I would pray to change. Everybody used the words fag and homo back then, and those were the worst, most emasculating things you could be.

In junior high I did a really wonderful job of compartmentalizing, of not dealing with it. But in high school, all you do is think about sex. And what the hell does a big heavy gay kid do about his sexuality in Flint,

> **"I was never more inauthentic and dishonest, and I cut off the people I loved, especially my family."**

Michigan, in 1970? The answer is nothing. He shuts up about it. My parents didn't pressure me to date—there weren't any nice Jewish girls in my high school anyway. But whenever I thought about it, I felt the pain. I was never more inauthentic and dishonest, and I cut off the people I loved, especially my family.

And then I got to college, lost a hundred pounds, and fell in love. I couldn't even carry my cafeteria tray, my hands shook so hard. More frightening than my lovesickness, however, was dealing with the implications of the object of my desire. He was a good friend of mine, straight, and lived in my dorm. He even had a fiancée. I went to my resident advisor and said, "I think I'm a queer," and broke down crying. Then I marched myself over to health services.

In 1975, the University of Michigan at Ann Arbor was not such a liberal place. Sure, smoking pot was okay, but sex with men definitely was not, although I'm sure it went on. Forty-five minutes into my classic fifty-minute session with the psychiatrist, I actually felt better for having finally unburdened myself. I said, "I feel ready to go on and really deal with my life, doc."

He said, "I'd like to see you twice a week." Thus began my attempt to become heterosexual.

Truth be told, I wanted to change. There were no positive role models, nothing that made it look good to be gay back then. We did not have TV shows like *Will & Grace* or *Queer as Folk*. We had Paul Lynde, Hollywood Squares' ambiguous man in the middle. And I read that hateful book, *Everything You Always Wanted to Know about Sex but Were Afraid to Ask*, which briefly discusses gay men's relationships as taking place in public bathrooms.

That's not what I was looking for. I wanted something meaningful. I'm a passionate guy. I had fallen in love, and I wanted to fall in love with someone who would love me back. I didn't know then if that were even possible.

It was the late 1970s, and I was living in Chicago. I waited until I graduated college to come out to my family because I wanted some measure of independence first.

I'll never forget the night I told my parents. My mother cried. I said, "There's nothing to cry about. I'm happy." She looked at me and said, "I'm crying for all the pain you had growing up that I couldn't help you with." I can't imagine a more empathetic or wonderful response from a parent. It took my father a bit longer to deal with it, but he has also embraced my life.

I look at my friends with young children today and revel in how accepting they are of their kids' sexuality. God bless parents who let their kids be who they are. How strong, how comfortable in their own skin those kids will be, especially if we can also get them the rights and protections they need to live comfortably in the world. They're going to live like so many of us didn't.

"God bless parents who let their kids be who they are."

When I finally did come out, I was socially stupid and ten years behind the curve. I made some really miserable choices in love. I didn't date in junior high school and high school and so didn't get a chance to learn, as some people do, how to take the measure of another person. Not that all heterosexuals get to learn this in high school, but I would have at least liked the chance to try. I'm a smart guy and I might have learned something and saved myself some time and pain later on when the stakes were higher.

Sex was always easy—so I went right to sex. And because sex is easy for most gay men, it was difficult to get beyond it to explore if something more might be there.

Today we know how AIDS is transmitted, but gay men continue to put themselves at risk, often because they don't have the self-esteem necessary to make self-preserving decisions. There but for the grace of God go I. As a kid who never felt attractive or even that there was anyone else like him who he could attract, whenever a good-looking guy hit on me, I was flattered. I think about my friends' kids today: how empowered they are going to be, how much stronger.

If somebody tells an antigay joke, my mother will call them on it. She wore AIDS ribbons for years. We have a very easygoing, natural relationship. Once, we were at Mizner Park, an outdoor mall in Boca Raton, Florida, and some flaming queen walked by. My mother turned to me and said, "Don't look at me, he's one of yours." I said, "When you take responsibility for every Jew in Florida, I'll take responsibility for every gay in Florida."

> **"Not everyone is as lucky as I am. But should you really have to be lucky with your parents and with your family?"**

I feel very lucky about my parents. Not everyone is as lucky as I am. But should you really have to be lucky with your parents and with your family?

In 2004, when Michigan amended its constitution to prohibit gay marriage, my uncle called me to tell me he voted with the majority. "None of your ex-wives or children even talks to you," I noted, "but you think it's okay to decide how other people should live?"

He admitted I had a point.

*Candace Gingrich as a high school sophomore in 1981, above,
and opposite, with partner Rebecca Jones (at left) in 2007*

CANDACE GINGRICH
Senior Youth Outreach Manager, Human Rights Campaign

Candace Gingrich does outreach on college campuses across the country, "helping folks go from being out to being active," and emphasizing voter registration. She knows the importance of political organizing—her older brother, Newt Gingrich, former Speaker of the House of Representatives and a conservative Republican, was a force to be reckoned with on Capitol Hill. His political career and Candace's lesbianism also became a source of conflict in a family that until then had been quite open about her sexual orientation.

When I first met Candace about a dozen years ago, I didn't realize who her brother was. She had this wonderful contagious smile, and the area of work she did interested me so we quickly struck up a friendship. When I did find out, my first thought was, "Wow . . . can't she convince this guy to be more fair minded to gay people and get his party off our backs?" It was actually an interesting political lesson for me. He was on the rise and very little would stop him. My hope with this book is that people like Newt Gingrich will read it and just take a deep breath—stop and understand that what they do is incredibly harmful to others. Full and equal civil rights for gay Americans has to be taken off the political table. It's a nonpartisan issue. Mr. Gingrich, will you help?

By the time I was six I was already pushing gender boundaries: always wanting to play sports at recess rather than jump rope, always resistant to wearing dresses. My first "wow" moment was at Girl Scout camp. We were living in tents in the woods of Pennsylvania, climbing trees and canoeing. One girl gave me butterflies: my first real physical attraction.

Growing up in a military family meant always leaving one place and starting over in another. I've always been quick to adjust to my surroundings, and I always had a sense of fearlessness and individuality: I was going to be who I was whether we were living in Kansas or California or Panama. So when I first had feelings for a girl, I didn't think it was a bad thing—although I sensed that other people would. After all, I saw no examples of what I was feeling around me. Sure, in books you read about crushes and getting butterflies, and you see it portrayed on TV—but not between people of the same sex.

So I ignored this newly discovered part of myself, pushing it down deep inside of me. I wasn't hoping it would go away; I just didn't have any way to deal with it right then. Instead, I became involved in everything else I possibly could. During high school in my hometown of Harrisburg, Pennsylvania, I played sports. I was in the choir, the band, and one of the musicals. I joined the journalism club and the yearbook club—anything so I wouldn't have to think about my feelings.

> "In books you read about crushes and getting butterflies, and you see it portrayed on TV—but not between people of the same sex."

It was through sports that I heard my first cautionary tale about being gay. During a pep talk, my high school hockey coach told me about two girls who used to be on the team. When people found out they were a couple, their teammates' parents called the principal. My coach spoke to them, and eventually they decided to leave the team. The coach never said, "Don't let this happen to you," but the message was there.

Going away to college gave me a chance to start with a clean slate. At Indiana College of Pennsylvania, about three hours from Harrisburg, I joined the rugby team—a stereotype, I know; and yes, there actually were lesbians on the team. Some were dating other team members, and they would hold hands and kiss. I realized I could live the feelings that I had been ignoring for a decade.

After that, things moved pretty quickly. Rugby practice started in early March. My first kiss was on April 16. Once that happened, it was like a tidal wave. In my women's studies classes, I would start my sentences with, "As a lesbian . . ."

My parents had always encouraged my individuality. I was very different from my siblings—a little jock playing ice hockey with the boys on the pond behind the house. But I just wasn't ready to tell them I was attracted to women. For the summer I moved back home to Harrisburg. The town actually had a lesbian bar. I was playing softball, going to the bar, and hanging out with people. It was heaven—I'd found my tribe. I was always smiling, almost giddy. My mom actually started getting concerned that I was on drugs because I was always in a really good mood. So she took it upon herself to get to the bottom of things: She searched my room. Instead of drugs she found a lesbian newsletter called *The Lavender Letter*. She brought it to me and said, "Are you trying to tell me something?"

My initial thought was, *Yes. Don't go snooping around my room.* I wasn't ready to come out.

She told me she had found it while cleaning my room. She had never cleaned that thoroughly before; I kept those newsletters hidden between the pages of a book. At first I was angry. Then I figured, now is as good a time as any, and I said, "Yeah, mom, I'm gay." There was no crying or hysterics. She just had pretty typical questions: What had she and Dad done wrong? What had made me gay?

I've since learned that one of the most difficult things for many gay people is giving their parents time to accept them. We expect unconditional love, and when our parents pull back, it hurts. But how long did it take us to get used to being gay? It can take parents a while, too, especially considering generational differences. Something my mom said underscored that: "When I was growing up, we didn't have gay people." Right, mom.

> "I've since learned that one of the most difficult things for many gay people is giving their parents time to accept them."

Toward the end of our conversation, Mom did try a little humor—we're all pretty dry wits in my family. She said, "Well, at least your dad and I won't have to pay for your wedding. I'm going on a shopping spree now." We had a good laugh.

Then she told everyone in the family. She called up Newt, and he, like the rest of my family, reacted supportively. It was probably what would have happened if I had actually come out at twelve. My sister still wanted me to babysit for her kids. My girlfriend was welcome at Christmas dinner and family picnics. I feel fortunate.

Growing up, my older sisters had been around, but Newt, who is so much older, was gone before I was born. So my interactions with him were limited to Christmas and occasional summer trips to visit him in Georgia. We were not estranged—he just didn't know me at all. One Christmas, he actually sent me—the world's biggest tomboy—a pair of pink leg warmers.

When I came out, Newt was a congressman from Georgia and I lived in Pennsylvania. It wasn't like his speeches were printed in my local paper. So I didn't know where he stood on things; I really hadn't been paying any attention. And he was still a backbencher, someone who does a lot of the political grunt work. My mom, on the other hand, ate, drank, and breathed what was going on in Newt's life. When his star really began to rise, she was, of course, very proud of him, and she also adopted his politics to some extent.

"As every gay person knows, there's out, and then there's *out*."

As every gay person knows, there's out, and then there's *out*. No one ever told me to keep my lesbianism hidden because of Newt or any other reason—no one had to. I definitely felt some anger when I first learned some of my brother's positions were antigay, but since it was clear his political career was moving well beyond run-of-the-mill congressman, I obligingly remained out of sight. I wasn't looking for things to change; I loved my life the way it was.

But it was just a matter of time before some reporter put two and two together. I wasn't embarrassed; it wasn't a secret. And I wasn't about to lie. So it got out that the youngest sister of the new Speaker of the House—the first Republican speaker in decades—was a lesbian. And my own political career was born.

When I went to my first Human Rights Campaign leadership training in Washington, DC, my mom told me, "Don't go dragging your brother's name through the mud."

I tried to explain to her: "This isn't about him. I have an opportunity to tell my story and talk about things that folks might not otherwise read about in their paper or see on the news, and I'm taking advantage of that. It's not a plot."

Newt and I were never best friends, but we had always been on good terms. The perception came to be that we were enemies because I'm gay. People thought we hated each other; that was never true. Our relationship continued to be amicable, even as I nudged him about his politics behind-the-scenes. He always said he was proud of me, and my being gay never affected his career.

> "More than anything, Newt's politics made clear to me the importance of every single fair-minded person standing up for equality for all people."

More than anything, Newt's politics made clear to me the importance of every single fair-minded person standing up for equality for all people. And that changed my life.

Polls today show that young people are more supportive of all things gay than any generation before them—I call them "Generation Equality." We've definitely seen a big shift in the past fifteen years, from the 1992 Republican convention and Pat Buchanan railing about the "culture war." But just responding to a pollster doesn't get legislation passed.

Back in the 1960s and 1970s, many students entered college wanting to work on political solutions for the issues of the day—the war, women's rights, civil rights. They couldn't wait to vote—they fought for the right to vote at eighteen. On campuses today, young people are busy studying and working toward the careers they'll have when they graduate or socializing and going to parties. They may not have time to watch a political debate or go to a rally.

But they will have a conversation: And that's the kind of grassroots work I do today on campuses across the country. Yes, it's one vote at a time, but each vote is important, much more than you might think. And people are much more powerful than they think. Today's students can still effect change if they want to. My goal is to help inspire them to do so.

> "Today's students can still effect change if they want to."

BOB WITECK
Cofounder and CEO,
Witeck-Combs Communications

Some kids are more resilient than others. Bob Witeck was one such teenager, reaching out across a hostile void of misinformation and silence, and holding up under the pressures of growing up gay in the 1950s. Sadly, those pressures—and that kind of misinformation—continue today.

Bob essentially got lucky. And his experiences raise important questions for twenty-first-century parents: How willing are you to risk how your own teenagers would hold up under that kind of pressure at such a sensitive—and often unforgiving—time in their lives? And do you want to play a role in providing information, guidance, and support for your children in this crucial area of life, as you do in many other areas—or leave them on their own, vulnerable to outside influences?

Today, Bob and business partner Wes Combs head a Washington, DC–based public relations and marketing communications firm that they started in 1993. In 2006, they shared their expertise in a book, *Business Inside Out: Capturing Millions of Brand-Loyal Gay Consumers.*

G rowing up in the suburbs of Arlington, Virginia, in the 1950s, simply thinking about another boy felt like a one-way ticket to lifelong shame and fear. It never once occurred to me that any of my early feelings and attractions had a real name or deserving place; I never even heard the words *gay* or *homosexual* until I was in high school. By that point I was, however, already well acquainted with the terrible power of words like *queer, fairy,* and *fag.* Those were the worst things you could be called when playing baseball in the parking lot, where I inevitably found myself terrified about catching a pop-fly ball. The unwritten rule was, never yell "fag" when a nun was in earshot. But during recess, there were plenty of opportunities for the bigger kids to terrorize the little kids.

I grew up in a large Catholic family with two older brothers and two older sisters. When I was born, my dad nicknamed me *Quintus Finis,* Latin for "fifth and last." However, he was better at Latin than practicing restraint: my parents brought home two more sisters after me. In a home with a dinner table set for nine and only two bathrooms, rules—and conformity—never went out of style. Fitting in, from the bedroom to the classroom, was a means of survival.

"Fitting in, from the bedroom to the classroom, was a means of survival."

So as a teenager, I followed my brothers into Boy Scouts. I don't recall even a moment of enthusiasm or enjoyment—it was simply an inevitable rite of passage, as well as my best option for acceptance, since I had long avoided organized sports. The troop was loosely organized in the same way champagne is loosely organized when uncorked. A pack of ten high-testosterone adolescents left almost daily without adult supervision, we transformed into a gang of wild animals, hanging out in the basement, practicing profanity, smoking cigarettes, and snagging an occasional beer.

Without an Internet of even wilder opportunities to explore, we were bound to push each other's limits with oddball games and contests, and before long, the sport turned on the youngest and weakest, the goal being to "de-pants" them. The larger boys would grab a younger boy and steal his pants and underwear, making him the butt of the joke, so to speak.

My fears and excitement were real. The game combined attraction and horror for me, since being even partially naked in front of other boys seemed as tantalizing as it was forbidden. Worse yet, at thirteen, my day had become roughly twelve hours of spontaneous erections broken up by moments of boredom. How would a prolonged woody in front of everyone go over? I imagined it would betray that I was up for a different kind of game. I would be an exile in my own neighborhood. My stigma and shame would become complete, not only with my friends and classmates but also with my parents and other adults. Unmasked as someone who got excited around boys, I had no idea what I would do, and agonized about it.

> "My stigma and shame would become complete, not only with my friends and classmates but also with my parents and other adults."

One afternoon in Danny's basement, it happened. An older scout decided I was the next sheep to shear. I jumped up and ran a few fevered laps around the basement. Seeing the basement stairs unblocked, I ascended with pants at half-mast. I zipped and buckled up safely, then ran the six blocks home: a narrow escape from self-discovery.

Of course, years of near misses still awaited me. In the 1950s and 1960s, television was the most powerful drug for gay boys, with nearly every show offering mesmerizing young male stars. I fell in love again and again with Robby on *My Three Sons*, Bud on *Father Knows Best*, and Wally on *Leave It to Beaver*.

By high school, I began to recognize these feelings as unchanging (even as I wished them to disappear), which heightened my fears, as did the increasing probability of discovery. Each day, I felt a growing need to read more and talk safely with others about my feelings—and to express myself. At a time when friends were beginning to date and obsess about girls, my lack of interest became suspect. So I went through the motions. I dated girls when it seemed the right thing to do and attended my senior prom. But mostly, I coped by focusing on schoolwork, which gave me a safe place outside sexuality to succeed. And as one of seven kids, it

> "By high school, I began to recognize these feelings as unchanging (even as I wished them to disappear), which heightened my fears, as did the increasing probability of discovery."

was probably a huge relief to my parents that at least one of the tribe wasn't wild-eyed and harebrained about the opposite sex.

In the public library, I clandestinely found the three or four books that described homosexuality in a clinical way, or worse, as a social pathology. And of course, being Catholic, I believed my deepest thoughts were sinful—errors I avoided ever mentioning by name, even in confession.

Ironically, the Catholic Church's teachings on sexuality were probably more of a bulwark than a bludgeon for me in those years. What was clear to us in Catholic school was that any kind of sexual pleasure was entirely off-limits. This meant that avoidance of physical contact with the opposite sex was a virtue, and that same-sex friendships were more likely to be overlooked or thought unremarkable.

Still, no matter where I looked in a library or on a bookshelf, and I looked often, I never stumbled upon so much as a pamphlet that revealed there were normal, happy, healthy boys who also were attracted to other boys. I believed I had never met one, talked to one, identified one—how could I but feel alone, strange, odd, twisted? I never imagined meeting anyone who felt as I did.

> **"I never stumbled upon so much as a pamphlet that revealed there were normal, happy, healthy boys who also were attracted to other boys."**

But as luck would have it, when I was sixteen, I read a newspaper story about a group in Washington, DC, that advocated for homosexual rights (though I wasn't so sure what "rights" they were advocating). I was amazed to learn that there actually existed a group of responsible adults who were unashamedly and openly gay and lesbian and actually wanted the world to know. It was boldness beyond my imagination, and its name was the Mattachine Society, named for a medieval French secret society of masked performers.

I looked up the group in the phone book, and there it was, plain as day. I was convinced the people in this group would be safe to connect with if I could make a private telephone call to them. One afternoon, with a couple of dimes burning a hole in my pocket, I walked to our neighborhood shopping center and found a phone booth. The number of the society was scrawled on a paper in my pocket.

A man answered politely. He was kind and helpful and smart and sensitive to each question I asked. I had been hoping that it might also be an informal social group—that I might be able to find other teens like me. But during our brief talk, it became plain that it was a group for adults. He mentioned the names of several gay bars in the city, but they would be off-limits because of my age. Anyway, I could not imagine socializing with strange men in a bar and trying to meet someone with whom to form a friendship, or even to date. I presumed bars were intended entirely for sexual encounters, and worse—that others would find out about me and destroy my reputation. Like many of us, I wanted it both ways—to find real friends, while also keeping my attractions and identity secret.

> **"It was the very first time an adult had ever spoken to me honestly and intelligently about who I was, and about who I hoped to become, without fear."**

That furtive phone call, however, was not pointless. It was the very first time an adult had ever spoken to me honestly and intelligently about who I was, and about who I hoped to become, without fear. He was caring and truthful and gave me a tiny bit of real hope that I would not be doomed to self-hate, fear, and rejection by everyone. He made me realize there were many others like me, and that we are not alone. He also told me about the *Washington Blade* and the *Advocate*, new publications by, for, and about homosexuals (a word I found impossible to use to describe myself). He suggested I get my hands on them.

That phone call changed my thinking. It not only helped me begin to believe that I was healthy and normal but also that I could find the community, friends, and loved ones I wished for. It gave me the courage to eventually admit to myself that I was gay and that I needed to talk to other gay people. In college and after graduation, I found out that many of us had the same fears, aspirations, and needs for reassurance, self-fulfillment, and love.

Years later, I discovered more about that phone call. The man on the other end of the telephone had been Frank Kameny, one of America's gay pioneers and the cofounder of the Mattachine Society—an individual who struggled for decades to help us achieve equality, respect, and inclusion.

> **"Without anyone to reassure me and give me hope, I might have made very different choices growing up."**

Without anyone to reassure me and give me hope, I might have made very different choices growing up. Some isolated, lonely gay kids became alienated and self-destructive and considered suicide. I probably would have tried even harder to fit in and become the person my parents, community, and church wanted me to be. All that acting each and every day—just so I could be loved and respected and trusted—would ultimately have been soul smothering.

Fortunately, someone reassured me it was okay to be myself at the time I needed to hear that most. And for that, I am indeed lucky.

*Donna Red Wing in her college days, above, and,
opposite, with her partner, Sumitra Red Wing
(seated, center); her son, photographer Julian Russell;
and dogs Doc Watson and Cinnamon*

DONNA RED WING

Senior Advisor,
The Interfaith Alliance

Donna Red Wing has spent most of her life as a grassroots advocate for fairness and equality. In 1999, she was the first recipient of the Walter Cronkite Award for Faith and Freedom. Today she is senior advisor for program and development at The Interfaith Alliance, in Washington, DC, founded in 1994 to challenge the radical Religious Right and protect both the sanctity of religion and the integrity of government. She also served with the national Dean for America presidential campaign as liaison to the gay community. I first met Donna when she gave a speech in Raleigh, North Carolina, in the late 1990s. I was mesmerized by her speaking abilities: "Here I am," she kept pronouncing as she told the audience to be who you are and be proud. I remember thinking she was one of the most beautiful and powerful people I had ever met. Donna has told me many times she will not give up the fight for equality. Gay teens today are lucky to have her.

O ne of the first things I remember was the Worcester, Massachusetts, tornado of 1953. With winds above three hundred miles an hour, it destroyed everything in its path in the eighty-four minutes it roared through central New England. I remember the sounds, the fear, and the stories: a bus picked up and tossed into a building, children pulled out of their mother's arms.

My mother walked home to my brother and me from work that day, all the way from downtown, through the carnage and debris. When she told us her story, I thought my heart would explode; she was the bravest person I knew. But as she described walking for miles in her heels, with stockings torn, pencil skirt hindering her gait, and blond pageboy mussed beyond belief, I could not understand how this astonishingly brave woman could be such a girly girl.

I was a tomboy. And that had to be my first clue. In the 1950s, there were not even words to describe how I felt. Tomboy was a code word, and had been for centuries if the dictionary is any indicator: Its definition—"a girl who acts like a spirited boy"—was first recorded in 1592.

We lived on the top floor of a three-decker house in Worcester. My twin brother, David, was my best friend. He was smart and shy and sweet. I was smart and bold and fearless.

My favorite outfit included a green jacket with a red flannel lining. It looked like a gas station attendant's jacket. I had my Roy Rogers six shoot-ers and my Daniel Boone coonskin cap. The only spanking I ever remem-ber getting was for refusing to change out of that outfit into a stiff, starchy dress to visit family friends. I understood that school and church had a uni-form—dress, frilly socks, pinched shoes, barrettes in my hair—but at my core I believed I had the right to dress like a boy in every other situation.

My mother and my grandmother were modern ladies who had their hair done at Carol's Hairdressing Salon. One hot sticky day in 1955, they decided to have Carol cut my hair. They dropped me off at the salon and went next door to the five-and-dime. Somehow, probably because of the heat, I con-vinced Carol I'd look really good with a DA, a ducktail haircut that was the rebel look of the 1950s: sides slicked back so they overlapped in the back of the head and the front a little mussed. Carol put pomade in my hair to make it shine. My grandmother cried when she saw me. My mother made Carol put multicolored sparkles in my hair in the hope that the glitter would magically feminize me.

We moved around a lot over the next few years and finally moved to Great Brook Valley, one of the largest housing developments in Massachusetts, in 1959. More than a thousand families lived there, most headed by single mothers. None of my friends had a father living with them. As it turned out, in the rough-and-tumble world of the projects, my "tomboy ways" were acceptable, a benefit even, because they helped me to take care of myself and my brother and my friends.

The first time I fell in love was as a kid at summer camp. A friend of the family decided to pay for me to go to the Girls Club camp instead of the horrible welfare camp my friends went to each summer and came back from with lice and sunburns. The Girls Club camp was great. We learned to swim, hiked the woods, ate s'mores, and sang silly songs around the campfire. At night, our counselor, Sparky, read us Nancy Drew mysteries. She would let me sit next to her and hold the flashlight. When she spoke to me, I would turn bright red and stammer. Sparky was smart and strong and funny. I signed up for every single activity she was involved in. I wasn't frightened about having this "crush" because I had no context or language or understanding of what it meant.

Later, when I was eleven, I met Pat. There was no library near the projects, so I would visit the Bookmobile in the parking lot every Tuesday evening. Pat and her friends would be hanging out in the lot. I could sense she was "different"—strong, athletic, a no-nonsense kind of gal who no one pushed around. But I still didn't understand what I was feeling.

Pat always had a basketball, and one day she tossed it to me. I dropped it, of course, and she laughed. I was so embarrassed.

It was near Christmas, so I asked my mother for a basketball. She just shook her head. Christmas morning, I saw no package that could possibly be a basketball. So I opened the obligatory pajamas and socks. My brother, meanwhile, got a chemistry set. I was so jealous. All that was left for me was a large, flat package.

At least it's not a doll, I thought. Previous Christmas dolls had become part of Man Ray–like sculptures I created, and I think Mum was a little creeped out by them. With underwhelming enthusiasm, I opened the flat package, and there it was: a deflated regulation-size basketball. That day, I walked a couple miles to the air pump at the nearest gas station and walked home with my very own basketball. I practiced and I practiced.

A few months later, as I was walking into the Bookmobile, I passed the ball to Pat and asked her to take care of it while I was inside. When I came out, she shot it back to me, and we began passing the ball to her friends. One of them tossed it really high and it sailed over the cyclone fence and into the street, where it was hit by a car and smashed flat. Pat was the one person in the group who tried to help me buy a new ball. It made me like her even more.

I didn't come out until I was in my thirties, in part, I think, because I had no context for what it meant to be gay. When I was growing up, homosexuality was not a moral, political, or legal issue. It was as if we didn't exist. The only time you might hear mention of gays was when you read in the local paper that the police had raided a gay bar.

> **"When I was growing up, homosexuality was not a moral, political, or legal issue. It was as if we didn't exist."**

The only lesbians I knew of were the big manly gals at the carwash in the industrial area. They scared me. The fictional characters in the lesbian pulp novels I read while babysitting for my next-door neighbor were "fallen women" who "just needed the right man." I'm sure my counselor Sparky was gay but didn't know it. I actually met Pat again thirty years after the basketball incident. She was a very successful athletic coach at one of the best private universities in Massachusetts. Sadly, she was not really out.

We were raised to accept strict gender roles. That's all we saw around us and absorbed from TV—even though *Father Knows Best* and *The Donna Reed Show* showed an American family image I'd never known. However, I do remember from my earliest days of watching *The Roy Rogers Show* that I always wanted to be Roy, not Dale Evans.

As I came of age, so did the Age of Aquarius, a time of experimentation, music, drugs, and happenings. I did not know who I was. How could I? So I volunteered at the draft-resistors bureau, marched against the war, and got involved with the most radical politics I could find. I smoked weed and dropped acid. I lived on a commune.

In 1969, I met my future husband, got pregnant at Woodstock, moved to his small family farm, and began raising my son, as well as goats and vegetables. Just nineteen at the time, I had done what so many young women of my generation did—married and started a family. No other option had occurred to me. I had never had a single conversation about sexual orientation with anyone. In my parochial world, even the concept of being a lesbian was silenced.

> "I had never had a single conversation about sexual orientation with anyone."

And still, I was searching for who I was and who I could become.

It was not until I went back to college in the 1970s and became involved in feminist politics that I began to have a glimmer of what my possibilities were. And in that work I eventually met my life-partner, Sumitra, who hosted a lesbian radio show, "Face the Music."

Like so many lesbians who came out in their thirties, my teenage "coming of age" never allowed me even to consider the reality of my emotions. To go through that is like dying a little bit every day.

* * *

It may be hard to believe now, but even in the free-spirited 1960s in Massachusetts, we had no gay icons, no lesbian role models. There wasn't a newspaper, magazine, or TV show that realistically portrayed us. I looked up homosexuality, once, in the downtown library, and the books were in the "special" section, under lock and key with the other prohibited material. Our churches never mentioned it, nor did our parents or teachers. Once in a while you heard someone was "that way," and everyone would laugh a nervous kind of laugh. The message was clear.

So some gay kids drank too much, others did drugs. Some ran away from home. Others lived in shame and guilt and led the "straightest" lives they could. Some took their own lives. The only option not available to us was to be who we are.

Today in my hometown of Worcester, same-gender people can marry. There are gay organizations and gay bars, gay cops, ministers, and politicians. I have spoken at Worcester Gay Pride and preached from the pulpit of a mainstream church there. I have come home.

> "And yet, there are still children coming of age, there and across the country, who cannot tell their parents, who are ridiculed by their classmates, and who are the victims of violence. My heart aches for anyone who cannot be who he or she is."

And yet, there are still children coming of age, there and across the country, who cannot tell their parents, who are ridiculed by their classmates, and who are the victims of violence.

My heart aches for anyone who cannot be who he or she is. It aches for those children whose spirits will be crushed by a society that still sees them as "other." And my greatest sadness is for a nation that is less than it could be because it does not yet value its gay, lesbian, bisexual, and transgender citizens, and it does not protect all its children.

JIM HORMEL
Philanthropist and
First Openly Gay U.S. Ambassador

Through individual giving and two small family foundations, Jim Hormel supports a diverse array of progressive causes, particularly those affecting the gay community. He is also a key funder of several cultural institutions and community organizations in San Francisco, where he resides. The James C. Hormel Gay & Lesbian Center at the San Francisco Public Library is named to honor his financial help in its construction.

In 1999, when Jim's nomination to the post of Ambassador to Luxembourg faced resistance from the Republican Congress, Jim's family, including his ex-wife Alice Turner and their five children, publicly lent their support. His son James C. Hormel, Jr., for example, wrote articles and gave interviews in which he shared the experience of having a gay dad and explained the impact of Congress's discrimination on their whole family.

In becoming our first openly gay ambassador, Jim broke barriers, refuted stereotypes and myths, and inspired many young gay people to have the courage to be themselves. I am honored to know him.

I was born in 1933, the youngest of three boys, in Austin, Minnesota, a small town about a hundred miles south of Minneapolis near the Iowa border. Even then it was a company town. My grandfather started the company, now known as Hormel Foods, which is still headquartered there.

Small towns are like fishbowls, and our family's prominence heightened the scrutiny. Everything was under observation. About a year after the Lindbergh baby disappeared, when I was just six months old, the FBI informed my father that I had been a target of kidnappers. After that, we were never left alone. An armed guard was always present at our home. I hated the security—it was isolating. We were already separated socially, by virtue of the company, and physically, because we lived on the edge of town, far from the neighborhoods where all the other kids lived. When I turned thirteen, and had the chance to go to boarding school, I couldn't wait.

"There were examples of heterosexual relationships all around me, and the dearth of examples representing what I was feeling underscored its taboo."

Religion's influence on my family was greater than nothing but less than substantive. My father was nominally Presbyterian; he seldom went to church. My mother was Roman Catholic, but she sent my brothers and me to a Protestant Sunday school. She was excommunicated for marrying outside the faith. She spent many years trying to get back in the good graces of the church, which she eventually did. But neither she nor my father ever attempted to influence our religious thinking. Nobody ever said homosexuality was terrible, or that it was against God's will. In fact, no one said anything. Today, people talk about sexuality all the time, but nobody talked about it at all then. There were examples of heterosexual relationships all around me, and the dearth of examples representing what I was feeling underscored its taboo. Then there were the accusatory or disgusted comments boys made about other boys. Fairy was the word they most commonly used.

Apart from the isolation of my family circumstances, I had a specific sense of otherness. My dreams and fantasies had always been about other boys, which made me feel different. I didn't want to be different; I wanted to be one of the boys. I would never be one of them, but I didn't understand that at the time. I tried to compensate by going out of my way to do or be things that I thought people expected of me.

At boarding school, I never had crushes or fell in love. I was too terrified—it was the 1950s, after all. The risk of public disgrace and expulsion were always in the back of my mind. One of our teachers had left the school under a cloud of rumors about something he may have tried to do—or had actually done—with a student. I certainly didn't want that.

> **"I thought that nobody in the universe would ever understand me."**

I did allow myself to have sexual experiences with other boys. They were meaningful to me, but afterward, the other person always pretended it had never happened. That left me feeling anxious and afraid, as if I'd done something illicit. I thought that nobody in the universe would ever understand me. I fantasized about having a twin brother so that I'd have somebody with whom to share my confidence. The first time I talked to someone who shared many of my feelings, I was relieved to discover I wasn't the only person in the world who felt that way. By then, I was already in my twenties.

The burden of carrying those feelings, without being able to express them, affected me more and more. Through my high school career, my straight As turned into mediocre grades and poor study habits. I managed to get into Princeton, certainly not because of my grades, but probably because my father went there. I flunked out after one semester. Obviously, I was in crisis, though no one could see it then. I wasn't unintelligent; I was unmoored. I was only seventeen. I could concentrate on nothing beyond what weighed most heavily on my mind.

As I was growing up, my parents' expectation of what I should do as an adult was very clear: get married and have kids. I had hoped that growing up meant growing out of this "phase," despite the fact that it never felt like a phase to me. When I did have the opportunity to have sex with a woman, it was an emotional disaster, which made everything much worse.

In 1952, my interest in learning renewed, I went to Swarthmore College. There, I met a woman with whom I felt compatible, whom I truly loved, and with whom I felt sexually comfortable. I thought marriage would lock out my desire for men. I married Alice in 1955. I was twenty-two.

I'm sure people would have told you that we were an ideal couple, and In many ways, we were. At minimum, we were very good at portraying the ideal couple.

In the early 1960s, there was a spate of movies about how homosexuality ruined careers and put one at risk of bribery, extortion, blackmail, and suicide. Lillian Hellman's *The Children's Hour*, with Shirley MacLaine and Audrey Hepburn, was set in a girls' boarding school. *Victim*, starring Dirk Bogarde, followed the career of a married barrister in London. In both films, the accusations of homosexuality were fabricated, and yet both films ended badly for their protagonists. What could I hope for?

And then there was *Advise & Consent*, a movie with an all-star cast, led by Henry Fonda, based on a novel by Allen Drury. It had a powerful impact on me. Set in Washington, DC, the movie focused on a young Mormon senator from Utah. Its message: When it comes to politics, the only thing worse than being a communist is being gay.

Even in Chicago, where I lived at the time, I found myself thinking, *It's not safe to be gay*. The gay bars were scary. The mafia owned most of them. They were raided constantly. And the *Tribune* published names on the front page after a raid of a bar or a bathhouse. I was just starting to get involved with politics, even considering a run for Congress. My fear of exposure, however, undid my plans.

Over a ten-year period, my life with Alice became progressively more difficult because our marriage was based on a pretense. By then, my fears were not enough to keep me faithful to my wife. I felt terribly guilty about violating my commitment to her, but I had all this pent-up sexual energy, which I sometimes could not contain.

Communication between Alice and me broke down terribly, and she, naturally, did not understand why. I wanted desperately to open up to her, but I didn't know how. I remember visiting Alice's mother in Virginia and hearing her story about a man just back from World War II who had told his wife that he was gay, shattering their relationship and her life. In the way she told the story, there was nothing but antipathy for the man. How could I possibly hurt my own wife like that?

"She blamed herself for the divorce, thinking she'd made me gay."

So I let our marriage fall apart, and Alice eventually left me. I was thirty-two.

I didn't come out until after I was divorced. By then, I couldn't keep things inside anymore. I didn't tell Alice right away, but I did come out to my two brothers; I felt I could trust them. I also learned that I could trust myself—I wasn't the devil after all. I know I was lucky—it was relatively easy for me. I didn't have to worry about losing a job. Most importantly, nobody in my immediate family turned away from me.

After we divorced, Alice and I had a few terrible years. I felt like a complete failure. She blamed herself for the divorce, thinking she'd made me gay. Eventually, we both came to terms with our grief, and she let go of her anger over my deceit. She went on to get a doctorate in psychology, and did her thesis on homosexuality in the Episcopal Church. Over the years, Alice has been very supportive of me. We realized at some point that we really did love each other, and that there was no reason to act as if that wasn't so.

I told my eldest child, Alison, when she was about thirteen, and I later talked to each child individually. (But after I told one, I'm sure word got around.) Today we have normal relationships. They all have children: I've got fourteen grandchildren and a great-grandchild.

Coming out is a process. Once it begins, it doesn't end—it just keeps going. I had always been involved in the political careers of others; then, in 1994, during the Clinton administration, I was under consideration to be the United States ambassador to Fiji. I got involved with the full knowledge that it would mean coming out all over again—this time, to a national audience—but I felt I had nothing to lose. When the Government of Fiji objected to having a gay ambassador, President Bill Clinton decided not to nominate me. Over the next few years, I pushed to be nominated as an ambassador, and was instead given appointments as a U.S. delegate to the United Nations' Human Rights Commission and a U.S. alternate delegate to the UN General Assembly.

Although some people hoped I would go away after serving out these appointments, I continued to push for an ambassadorial post. I knew that becoming the very first openly gay ambassador would break a barrier and make it easier for subsequent gay nominees to serve in the highest government offices. In October 1997, Clinton nominated me to be ambassador to Luxembourg. During a bruising two-year fight, three antigay senators blocked the appointment. Clinton made a recess appointment in 1999, and I was off to Luxembourg, where I was received warmly. Although being an ambassador was wonderful, what really meant a lot to me was making a difference in the lives of gay men and women in the government. There wasn't a time that I visited the State Department when somebody didn't come up and thank me, or say something about what my appointment had meant to them.

Back in the 1960s, when I came out, many members of Congress would tell you that there were no gay people in their districts. Today, only despots in certain foreign countries make those sorts of statements. The point of my ambassadorial fight was to be out, to be open, and to let other people see that I am no different from the other human beings who walk the earth.

Every time a gay person comes out, he or she helps break down myths and misconceptions. There's a totally counterproductive idea that gay men come from families comprised of a strong mother and a distant father—that parents make their children gay. This myth must be dispelled. So must the notion that God somehow created a universe intended exclusively for heterosexual beings, and that it's not natural to be gay, in spite of all of the evidence in nature to the contrary.

Coming out, and being out, is the single most important thing any gay person can do to make it easier for kids today to be who they want to be, and not what people expect them to be. And all of us can play a part in making the world a safe and comfortable place for gay people to come out.

BRANDON ROLPH KNEEFEL
Student, Pennsylvania State University,
Point Foundation Scholar
Age: 21

Brandon Kneefel was raised in an evangelical Christian household in Detroit. At sixteen, his parents disowned him because they could not accept his sexual orientation. Despite this, Brandon finished high school, breaking track records and playing leads in the school plays along the way. He stayed at the homes of friends, finally landing at the home of his best friend. His parents signed over power of attorney to his best friend's parents, which enabled him to stay in school and not become a ward of the state.

Brandon has served as media director for Soulforce Equality Ride—a two-month nationwide mission of young adults working to end religion-based discrimination against gay people. He is currently an organizational leadership major at Penn State. Refusing to limit himself, he plans to publish fiction and nonfiction; break into the entertainment industry as an actor, writer, and producer; and help the gay community achieve global affirmation and celebration. Brandon's parents still do not speak to him today.

I once knew someone better than I had ever known anyone. I haven't seen him since the winter of 2004. His name was Brandon. For several years, I thought he had been pulled from my life in one quick yank on a night of sadness and screeching finality. Now it seems as if he simply faded away.

You're probably wondering who I am. My name is Brandon, too. The same Brandon I speak of? No, he is gone, and I am who is left. You see, on that sad night we became two separate beings: Brandon Who Feared and Brandon Who Hoped.

Brandon Who Feared worried from an early age that society hated him because he was attracted to boys, dreaded spending time with most boys because of their awkward and incessant references to girls, was called "faggot" from elementary school on, and felt piercing shame because he was the very thing everyone thought was disgusting and wrong. This Brandon imperiled his integrity, lying about who he was because he knew if he did not somehow reject being gay, he would be rejected not only by his family but also by Christianity itself.

I am Brandon Who Hoped. This is the story of the night we separated.

The evening began typically—I came home from hanging out with friends after school. My mother and father were in the kitchen and wouldn't even look at me when I entered the room. I walked toward them and saw my backpack in my mother's hands. In that moment, the world stopped. Acid churned in my stomach. I realized I would be tried that night in two different senses of the word—my mettle would be tested and my guilt or innocence determined.

"Do you want to tell us what we found in here?" she asked as she clutched the backpack.

"No."

Why would I? Inside the backpack was my journal, in which I'd confessed my deepest sentiments about my current boyfriend. The journal held my most intimate thoughts—reading it would be like invading my mind. She pulled it out and began to read aloud.

My primal emotions took hold and I lunged for what was mine. I angrily grabbed the journal and backpack from her and ran to the living room, where I slept on the couch. I was not allowed a bedroom for reasons I still don't understand; maybe they thought it would be easier to keep track of my "homosexual behavior" that way. They followed me into the living room, and the threats began.

"We agreed to let you back in the house if you gave up this lifestyle. Is this how you repay us?"

How could she think my having a boyfriend had anything to do with repaying her?

"You need to leave," she said in an eerily calm voice.

She turned to my father. "Rolph, we can't have him in the house anymore."

In past moments like this I had sat there, not believing it was happening, overwhelmed by the ridiculousness of it all. This time I sat calmly on the couch in the dark with my eyes closed, clutching my journal, and hoping and praying they would just leave.

This would be the third time they kicked me out. Twice before I had come back, begging to reconcile. But now I was tired of fighting and of not being able to be myself. I was exhausted from having to lie about who I was hanging out with, of hearing suggestion after suggestion of how I could "fix" myself. I was sick of having pastors leave voice mails on my cell phone wanting to talk about my "afflictions" or how God just wanted me to be celibate. I no longer had the desire to talk back when someone called me "fag" or to object when my parents prayed over me in the middle of the night. I wasn't sure I could bear the weight of the words *disordered, diseased, abomination,* and *unnatural* anymore; they had sapped my strength, and I could feel my defeated heartbeat slowing to a halt.

> **"She turned to my father. 'Rolph, we can't have him in the house anymore.'"**

"Get out of our house," she said.

"No."

"Get out or we'll have the police escort you out," she said, extending her arm and pointing a wicked finger toward the door.

I chuckled nervously. "What are you gonna tell them? Our son's gay, and we want him out?"

"We have things to tell them." Her eyes burned into me, and no matter how hard I tried, I could not see the mother who had read *Harry Potter* to me in our exclusive book club.

For the first time ever, I rooted my feet and refused to be rejected. I knew I had done nothing wrong.

"We will not have someone with a sinful lifestyle living in our house!" my mom screamed. She turned to my father and demanded, "Rolph, get him out!"

Like a Southern Baptist preacher's condemnations from the pulpit, my mother's words froze my heart. Instead of fear, I felt a strong resolve. The Brandon Who Feared began to whither. I surrendered and allowed myself to be disowned. I did not belong to anyone anymore.

"I was sick of having pastors leave voice mails on my cell phone wanting to talk about my 'afflictions' or how God just wanted me to be celibate."

In time, I became fully disassociated from the Kneefels—my parents and my two older sisters. And I began to travel spiritually all the way to where my soul is now—reestablished in a place where anyone is welcome to be my family.

As for Brandon Who Feared, he still haunts me. Not in a Ghost of Christmas Past way, but in the way the death of a child would sting the memory of a devoted parent. I sometimes wonder what he would be doing if he were still alive. Aimlessly searching for someone to tell him he has worth and goodness? Needing someone to take him in his arms and hold him until he was ready to let go? Maybe he'd be out there, cold and lost and believing he wasn't strong enough to go on without his family . . . yet knowing he couldn't go on with them.

I think of him as in a dream: He's at the bottom of a confusing, lonely well. He needs to get out, so he climbs. As he nears the top, he sees his parents looking down at him. They reach out to him and he stretches out his arms to meet theirs, letting go of the walls. He holds onto them, trusting they will help him out . . . but then they let go and he falls.

That Brandon died. May his lonely, terrified, and struggling soul rest in peace. I am free.

Robert Wrasse, with his sister

ROBERT WRASSE
May 2008 Graduate,
University of Michigan
Age: 21

Robert Wrasse never wants to be separated from the people he loves and the Chaldean American community in which he was raised. And despite the condemnation of homosexuality by the Catholic Church at the heart of his culture, he feels hopeful that someday his family will accept him for who he is. Based on what Robert tells us about his family's heritage, I share his hope. His grandparents know the pain of not being accepted: They left their homeland to avoid religious discrimination.

A newly minted graduate of the University of Michigan, Robert plans to attend law school in hopes of one day making a difference in the fight for equal rights; whether it be working to reform hate crime laws or challenging discriminatory employment practices. He wants his work and writing to inspire young gay people to educate those intolerant of homosexuality by positive example.

26.

Twenty-six is the number of lockers that I counted as I meandered to the last hour of my school day in middle school. It was twenty-six moments of shifting my eyes over the carpet below me, nervously thinking and tightening my hold on the straps of my backpack. With each locker I passed, my mind would frantically search for another excuse to turn back. Around the corner was always a reliable arsenal of epithets waiting to be shouted and crumpled papers waiting to be thrown. Although bullying by the older students was common practice, their weapons of choice—words— preyed on the insecurities that by age twelve had already weakened me. Fag! Queer! I distinctly remember both those words—and not because they were only directed at me, but because of how venomous they were to a boy already hopelessly battling a sexuality he didn't want to admit.

Constantly anticipating the bigotry that awaited me in the halls was an exhausting distraction during my classes, one that could never be calmed by a friend, a teacher, or my parents. Many of my male peers also experienced what some administrators and parents would call standard teasing, or "boys being boys," but the effect on me was different. I was different. While I doubt the older boys actually knew I was gay, as sexuality was about as unpracticed as political affiliation at that age, it caused me to internalize pain that a young boy should not have to deal with alone. But the daily bullying was something I had to leave in my locker at the end of the day. It was not a problem I could bring home for homework.

I grew up in the suburbs of Detroit in a home ideal for a 1950s sitcom, although it was the late 1990s. When I was young, my mother stayed home with my brother, sister, and me, while my father worked. Part of the glue that bonded my family together throughout my childhood was religion. In fact, being Chaldean-American, religion is as important to our culture as our language and traditional foods. My grandparents emigrated from Iraq to escape the religious discrimination and persecution that Christians still face in that predominantly Muslim country. The pursuit of a life in which one can be who one wants to be without adversity is at the heart of Chaldean-American culture—but it has yet to apply to sexuality. "I am gay" may be spoken, but is simply not understood within the community as a possibility.

My declining to meet Middle Eastern daughters whom my grandparents discover among their friends' progeny will always perplex them. My disinterest and escapist declaration that, "I'll deal with that when I'm done with law school," deeply hurts me as well. Not only does the dishonesty leave me feeling hollow, but the feeling that I'm disappointing my grandparents' genuine attempt to secure a wholesome future for me lingers. In reality, I desire a large family. I desire to be with one person who I will love for the rest of my life. I would love raising children, and I feel two men are no less qualified to love and support a child than a heterosexual couple. However, I am living a life that does not allow my desires to come to fruition. I have human desires that Christianity, and by default my culture, sees as a choice and punishable. I constantly ask the question, "Why would I choose this?"

My mother and father hung the crucifix above my crib months before I arrived. When problems arise, they respond not only proactively but also biblically—this is what has made me fear them finding out about my homosexuality the most. In our home, rarely has a problem gone unaddressed without a prayer or quote from scripture. I fear the

> **"Unlike a bad grade or a poor decision, my interest in men is not something that can be corrected or forgotten."**

quotes from scripture that are available when dealing with "the gay question." I'm saddened that my family would in fact see my sexuality as a problem. The worst part is feeling like I have failed my family, a feeling that largely stems from my sexuality's disconnect from my parents' strong religious convictions. Unlike a bad grade or a poor decision, my interest in men is not something that can be corrected or forgotten. I am just now, at age twenty-one, beginning to accept that my interest in men does not need correction. Those who use Christianity to dehumanize gay people need correction.

Growing up, I was always aware of Christianity's condemnation of homosexuals, and on many occasions I witnessed my parents' own reaction to the gay community. The city where I was raised in Michigan has, ironically, become known for its growing population of homosexuals, which often clashes unfavorably with the older, less-accepting generation of residents there. My mother's infamous, "They'll be judged," was always a reminder of the pending condemnation that I so feared, and because of that, her words devastated me.

I often thought about the idea that I would not be joining my family in heaven. The notion of one day being separated from the people I love most because of a sexual orientation I did not choose caused me a host of insecurities. Throughout high school I often felt guilty for being gay, like it had been a decision I subconsciously made in my life and was actively suffering the consequences of. At times the feelings of guilt and uncertainty tore me away from my family, causing me to resent my parents and God. I began feeling a disgust for myself that mirrored the feelings I perceived society to have about homosexuality. Much like those afternoons in middle school, though, I still couldn't voice my emotions. I had no release. I feared that my family's love and support were conditional on my being a heterosexual.

Then came February 5, 2006—the day I came out to my sister. We both went to the University of Michigan. It was my sophomore year, and I had begun making gay friends who were supportive and empathetic toward my situation. For the first time, I could talk to people about my life without censorship. However, this required building a double life strong enough to protect against infiltration by my family—including my sister—and anyone with even the slightest connection to them. These were friends I couldn't be seen with publicly unless at a large gathering that would allow me to disengage from them the moment my paranoia activated. It was unfair. I admittedly used them as the therapists I could never seek, making up for all my years of silence. These friends were training wheels, the kind helpful for a gay man practicing for a possible coming-out experience.

Because we were so close, however, my sister could not accept the mysteriousness I had to maintain in order to see my gay friends. Eventually, because of my evasive answers to where I was going at night or whom I was with, she came to believe I was involved in something perilous like drugs. I will always remember the conversation we finally had that February night, the hardest one I have ever had. I remember hours of her expressing concern for my health and my future. Amid tears and hysteria I remember asking her, "Will you always love me?" There is no moment more insecure and humbling than the one in which you must genuinely prepare to lose one of the largest sources of love in your life. Thankfully, my sister opened her arms to me. For the first time, I tasted a family member's acceptance without the bitter sting of my religion's condemnation. She remains the only family member who confirmedly knows that I am gay.

Today, I never question my family's love for me. Although my parents have yet to seek confirmation of my homosexuality, I've mustered enough hope to believe that when my parents are ready to accept that their son is gay, the stability and love that I always felt as a young child will still be available to me. However, waiting for that day is exhausting, and arriving at my level of self-awareness has been a road that I doubt any parents would want their son to travel alone. I do not blame my parents for the years of inwardness and denial that too many times left me depressed. It's something they do not understand. It's something the world fails to universally understand. I would assume they would think homosexuality is a rebellious choice that enough fear in God could remedy, like all other immoral decisions. At times I feel as though I'm wearing a scarlet letter, other times like my family could surprise me. I am left with hope.

I am fortunate for my family's unconditional support for my education and professional future. I have graduated from the University of Michigan with a bachelor of arts in political science, a strong proficiency in the German language, and enough coursework to fuel my love and enthusiasm for modern art. I think of the other roads young gay males have chosen and I cringe. The activities available to young men unsure of themselves and their sexuality are destructive and luring. There is vulnerability and risk in the double life that some men create in order to be themselves and be accepted by family and friends. More pressing, the appeal of suicide to those who are dealing with being gay in a society that is far from accepting is real.

In Christian homes, collectively dealing with the homosexuality of a family member or attempting to understand it could end years of insecurity, depression, fear, confusion, and guilt. Even more optimistically, it could put an end to the carelessly expressed "Fag!" and "Queer!" that still hiss from the mouths of not only middle school children but also adults. I still look to the Bible because I believe its stories, once interpreted, are in most cases applicable to my life. However, there is a need to stop looking at the Bible and start looking at the person, at a fellow human being. One's religion should not disable one's ability to empathize with others, as I believe Jesus was able to do. My sincere hope for the future is that Christian families like mine will look past their religious convictions and realize that, along with Jesus, they too have the power to save.

PART 3
School and
Social Discrimination
How Good Would You Be at Pretending?

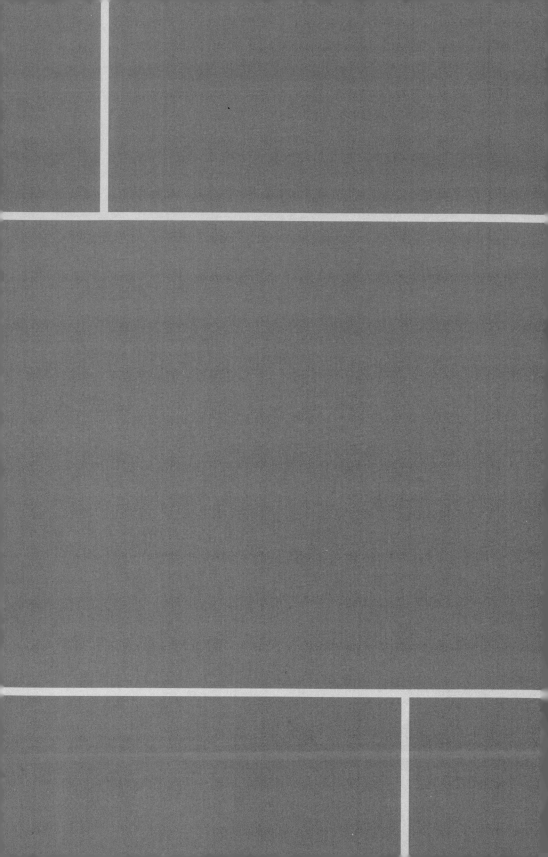

HOW GOOD WOULD YOU BE
AT PRETENDING?

BY KEVIN JENNINGS
Founder of the Gay, Lesbian and Straight Education Network

For Nick

Thompson was the kind of kid I always liked. A slight, sandy-haired sixteen-year-old sophomore, he was funny, smart, and irreverent. He wasn't the best student—he was a little too cool to be bothered with quotidian tasks like homework, and getting to class was sometimes a bit of a struggle for him—but his charm and innate intelligence allowed him to get away with manslaughter, if not outright murder, academically. Even though I would never have admitted it publicly, the offbeat kids always interested me more than the A students in my class. They presented more of a challenge.

Not that I needed more challenges as a third-year teacher in Concord, Massachusetts, in 1988. I was just twenty-four years old, and my undergraduate studies in nineteenth-century French history hadn't exactly equipped me for what I was facing as a high school history teacher. I was often daunted by the complexity of the needs students brought to me: conflict at home, struggles with substance abuse and eating disorders, and the feelings of inadequacy that plague almost everyone's adolescence. I struggled to be the wise adult they clearly thought I was.

Apparently, the years I had spent honing my acting skills in undergraduate theatricals paid off, because they kept coming to my office to talk. Having lost my first teaching job because I was gay, I had never made a public statement about the subject to my students. But the glass closet didn't fool many of them, Thompson in particular. He came out to me during the second half of the year, and soon our conversations turned to his struggle to accept his homosexuality. His bubbly, self-assured exterior hid the feelings of self-hatred that inevitably come from internalizing society's message that gay people are literally "worth less" than others.

One morning, Thompson sat in my office and confessed that at times he had thought about ending it all rather than struggling to be gay in a homophobic world. Startled, I immediately launched into a lecture about how much he had to live for, about the promise his future held. He cut me off: "Why shouldn't I? My life isn't worth saving anyway."

Suddenly, I was his age again.

Growing up gay in the rural South, I had often felt the way Thompson did. School was hell for me, a place where, starting in sixth grade, I was called "faggot" regularly while teachers looked the other way, where my difference was held up for all to see. My mom noticed (without ever knowing why) that I always developed what she called my "funny feeling" on Sunday night, which was really nausea induced by fear of heading back to school and another five days of torment. Despairing that I would ever escape, I had tried to take my own life in my junior year of high school.

"School was hell for me, a place where, starting in sixth grade, I was called 'faggot' regularly while teachers looked the other way, where my difference was held up for all to see."

When I looked at Thompson, I saw myself just a few years before. And I thought, *This has got to stop*. I didn't know how, but I knew that I would from that day forward dedicate myself to trying to make sure no kid ever again felt like I had felt in high school.

A few months after my conversation with Thompson, at an assembly, I came out to the entire student body. A few weeks later, I helped students start the nation's first Gay-Straight Alliance (GSA) student club. Eventually, my journey would culminate in founding the Gay, Lesbian, and Straight Education Network (GLSEN), a national education organization working to make schools safe for all students regardless of their sexual orientation or gender identity. Today GLSEN has a network of more than thirty-six hundred GSAs, with at least one in every state. It has helped make the kind of bullying and harassment I suffered in school illegal in ten states and has created groundbreaking programs like No Name-Calling Week, which adds a fourth R—respect—to the reading, 'riting, and 'rithmetic that schools have always taught.

We have come a long way. But not far enough.

I learned this the hard way a couple of years ago when we had a young man in our National Student Leadership Program who I will call Nick. Nick hailed from the rural South—like me—from a deeply religious family—like me—and struggled to find acceptance in his intolerant community—like me. My heart went out to him, especially when he shared the heartbreaking news that his family had given him an untenable choice: stop being gay or get out of the house.

Nick moved into a friend's home. But he missed his family and wanted to go home, so he decided to accept their terms and try not to be gay. This struck me as an impossible position. How long can you not be who you really are? For Nick, it turned out to be a year.

About twelve months after Nick moved back home, I got an e-mail from his older brother asking us to take him off our mailing list. Nick had taken his own life, and his mother was upset by mail that had his name on it. He asked us to spare her that pain by taking him off our list.

I was stunned. Despite his difficult situation, Nick had seemed so strong, so vital, so full of life. How could this have happened? I related the story to a friend, who replied, "You should call his mom and tell her: 'You didn't want to have a gay son and now you don't. Happy now?'"

I am not proud to admit that making such a call was tempting, that on one level, it would have been satisfying. But I also knew from my own experience that Nick's mom was a victim, too—of a society, a church, and a community that had told her not to accept her son. She had done what she had thought was best based on the misinformation and prejudices she had been raised with—misinformation from a church that probably taught her

> **"Nick's mom was a victim, too—of a society, a church, and a community that had told her not to accept her son."**

she could somehow hate the sin but not the sinner (as if her son could tell the difference), from an education system that never gave her accurate information about the nature of sexual orientation and allowed her to be deluded by the notion that her son could "change," from a community that made her intolerant of difference and afraid to accept her son as he truly was. In the end, it was not her fault alone.

So who else is to blame? Every single one of us. Everyone who has not taken the time to learn more, who has not taken the time to get involved, who has not taken the time to do something. Martin Luther King, Jr., said, "History will have to record that the greatest tragedy of this period of social transition was not the strident clamor of the bad people, but the appalling silence of the good people." We good people would like to pretend that Nick's blood is not on our hands, that we weren't involved, that it had nothing to do with us.

> **"We good people would like to pretend that Nick's blood is not on our hands, that we weren't involved, that it had nothing to do with us."**

But it is our silence that allowed him to die. As Elie Wiesel said, "Silence encourages the tormentor, never the tormented."

So stop being silent. Read stories in this section to more fully understand the impact of the torment. Demand that your school board and your state make bullying and harassment based on sexual orientation and gender identity illegal in the same way that bullying based on race and religion already is. Contact your local high school principal and ask if the school has a GSA (and offer them GLSEN's guide to how to start one if they don't). Make sure your local elementary school is conducting No Name-Calling Week. Offer teachers and librarians resources from GLSEN's BookLink list of education resources (www.glsen.org/cgi-bin/iowa/all/booklink/index.html). Get involved. You owe it to Nick. This has got to stop.

For more information on GLSEN and how to get its guides, please visit www.glsen.org or see the resource section at the back of this book.

*Alec Mapa in high school, above, and with his partner
Jamison Hebert (on right) in their wedding photo, opposite*

ALEC MAPA
Actor and Comedian

You may have enjoyed his work as scandal-seeking fashion reporter Suzuki St. Pierre on *Ugly Betty* or as Gabby's friend Vern on *Desperate Housewives.* In 2008, he hosted the premiere season of Logo's *Transamerican Love Story*, a reality dating series in which a transgender bachelorette chose from eight eligible bachelors. In December 2007, Alec appeared in classic form on *Ellen*—you can catch that appearance and get a sense of his great warmth and brilliant humor via YouTube.

But actor and comedian Alec Mapa learned the painful difference between being laughed at and laughed with as a teenager, growing up in a strict Catholic Filipino-American home in the 1970s. Looking back, he notes how caring words from special individuals—a high school teacher, a waiter at the restaurant where he worked—saved him by helping him to see he had a future. In addition to appearances on Broadway, TV, comedy specials, and in movies, that future has included supporting organizations that benefit AIDS research and the lesbian, gay, bisexual, and transgender community, including Project Angel Food and AIDS Project Los Angeles.

Whoever said, "Sticks and stones may break my bones, but words may never hurt me," was never called "faggot" in front of the entire eighth grade. Words hurt like hell. Just think of the words *paper cut* and try not to wince as you visualize that razor-thin memo slicing through the meatiest part of your thumb.

I'm thirteen years old and carrying my tray of Thursday sloppy joes across the cafeteria. I'm wearing rainbow suspenders festooned with colorful ceramic pins, just like Robin Williams on *Mork & Mindy*. I knew wearing them to school wasn't a good idea, but I had just bought them from a thrift store on Haight Street in San Francisco with my paper route money, and the thrill was simply too big to suppress. Someone yells, "Nice suspenders, faggot!" and the entire cafeteria laughs in unison.

The laughter isn't the fun we're-laughing-with-you kind. It's the I'm-so-glad-I'm-not-you kind. The word *faggot* sears my skin like a branding iron. Throughout elementary school, middle school, and high school, I am continuously teased and bullied, and I never fight back because I know they are right. I am a sissy. It's shameful and I deserve it. I was taught this at home.

When I was four, I had gathered up all my sister's plush toys, put them in a cradle, and rocked them to sleep because that's what four-year-olds do. They role-play and mimic adult behavior. The only problem was that I was supposed to be aping a fireman or an astronaut, not Florence Henderson. I was rocking the cradle when my father spotted me through an open doorway and snarled, "What are you? A girl?" The disapproval and menace in his voice stopped my heart. I never touched that cradle again. I passed by it; I thought about it, but any urge to mother a koala or the bunny I got for Easter was henceforth quashed. In the blink of an eye, his words taught me that how I was behaving was displeasing—and the lesson stuck. That day, my authentic self got a thumbs-down, and my neurotic self was born. I existed in a state of constant anxiety. I was the only preschooler with a Partridge Family lunch box and an ulcer. Everything was wrong because I was wrong.

> "That day, my authentic self got a thumbs-down, and my neurotic self was born. I existed in a state of constant anxiety."

Luckily, I grew up in San Francisco. We had a gay and lesbian teen support group in our school—only back then, we called it "drama club." I loved drama club because it was full of misfits. I made them all laugh 'til milk shot out of their noses, and that felt like love. I had a boyfriend: Darnell. He was stunning—African-American, six feet three inches tall, and a senior. After rehearsal for the spring musical, *Bye Bye Birdie*, we got drunk on a cheap bottle of Cold Duck and made out. We had sex nonstop for three weeks; he left daily love letters and poems in my locker; he couldn't keep his hands off me. Then one day he completely refused to acknowledge my existence. He wouldn't talk or make eye contact, and when I waited for him outside biology class, he walked right past me. He hung up whenever he heard my voice on the line. I passed him a note in class ("What happened? What did I do?"), and he dropped it in the garbage right in front of everyone. It felt like a swift kick in the stomach. I could only arrive at one reasonable conclusion: It's because I'm a big fag. He's too embarrassed to be seen with me. If I were butch, or tall, or had an amazing body, we'd still be together. Before that moment, I had just been ashamed. Now I absolutely hated myself.

I dealt with this heartbreak the only way I knew how: I got stoned every day before school. My grades were catastrophic. When I wasn't high, I'd cry nonstop because I wanted to look like Christopher Atkins from *The Blue Lagoon* or Maxwell Caulfield from *Grease 2*. I never would, so of course that meant no one would ever find me attractive. I started taking quaaludes before school because they were easy to swallow and they didn't make my clothes and breath reek.

Pilled up, I stumbled through a scene from *Richard III* in drama class. Drooling and incoherent, I was Foster Brooks trapped in the body of a little Filipino boy. I was supposed to say, "Vouchsafe, divine perfection of a woman." It came out, "Vowshafe divine prefectionuvawoman!" Infuriated, my drama teacher pulled me aside before the bell. She gripped me by the shoulders and hissed through clenched teeth, "You're throwing it all away. You're gonna graduate with no place to go. You'll be nowhere doing nothing. You come to my class high one more time, you are out. I mean it."

Her words yanked me off a ledge. I got myself together and applied to NYU because I thought if I could just get to New York City and study acting, my life would be infinitely better and I would never have any problems.

I worked as a busboy at a restaurant in Pacific Heights after school. All the waiters were flamboyantly gay. To me, they were the epitome of glamour.

They all had cool clothes and outrageous sex lives. My favorite was Billy. He was completely unashamed, and I was in awe of his fearlessness. It baffled me. He was girly, but he was never punished for it. He was gorgeous, sexy, popular. People lined up outside the restaurant just to be waited on by him because being served by Billy was the single most hilarious evening you'd ever spend in San Francisco. I worshiped him.

Near the end of my senior year, I still hadn't heard from NYU. I knew I wouldn't get into a reputable university based on my grades alone, so I felt sure that if NYU didn't accept me into their drama program, I'd end up at city college with the rest of the stoners. One night, right before my shift started, I told Billy this, and before I knew it, I was sobbing and saying, "I just want to be somebody. And now I know I never will be. I'm nobody. I'm nothing."

> **"I never deserved to be punished or humiliated for being gentle and kind. No one does."**

Billy hugged and shushed me, saying, "Don't cry. Not now. You are somebody. You are a wonderful, funny, sweet, talented person. Someday you'll be living in New York or Los Angeles, and you're going to be a terrific performer. And there isn't going to be any work. Cry then."

* * *

Back when I was four, my heart was wide open. I was loving and affectionate. I took genuine delight in everyone and everything. I wasn't ashamed of anything. And over the years, no matter how much I was teased, rejected, or bullied, somehow that part of me managed to stay intact. It has taken me years to retrieve and champion that part of me. The only way I have survived as a gay man is by embracing everything I was taught to hate about myself. It takes enormous strength to be vulnerable and open in a world that rewards toughness and cruelty. I never deserved to be punished or humiliated for being gentle and kind. No one does. It took years of therapy to interpret events differently: My father was only trying to protect me. Darnell had to reject me in front of everyone to cover his own guilt and shame. I was never going to be blond, but that didn't mean I wasn't beautiful.

Years later, I returned to San Francisco, long after I had graduated from NYU and been on Broadway, long after that Pacific Heights restaurant had been torn down, and long after I had lost touch with Billy and learned he had died of AIDS. I ran into a former classmate downtown—at seven miles by seven miles, San Francisco is essentially

"The only way I have survived as a gay man is by embracing everything I was taught to hate about myself."

a small town. She said, "We always knew you were going to be somebody. You were such a badass in high school. You were out, and you didn't care what anyone thought."

I gasped because the exact opposite had been true. I cared deeply about what everyone thought. I desperately wanted to belong, but it simply hurt too much to let it show. I covered up my pain with the jaded, half-lidded gaze of a stoner.

Now my eyes are wide open. I know firsthand that words are extremely powerful. They can hurt or heal, and therefore must be chosen with extreme care. In this age of conformity, I wonder how many of today's gay youth feel safe to be exactly who they are. Are they being respected? Celebrated? Encouraged to be their genuine selves? Would it even be safe for them to do so? In a perfect world the answer would be yes. Wouldn't that be the most wonderful word you could ever hear?

NEIL GIULIANO

President of the Gay & Lesbian Alliance Against Defamation and Former Mayor of Tempe, Arizona

Like many people in this book, Neil Giuliano dealt with his fear of people finding out the truth about his sexual orientation by "hiding in plain sight"—becoming a student leader in college and eventually the mayor of Tempe, Arizona, from 1994 to 2004, the job he held when he came out publicly. However, as a college student, Neil literally teetered on the brink of suicide because of societal attitudes toward gay people. He now uses his experience to fight that kind of prejudice, heading up GLAAD, one of the country's most high-profile gay organizations, dedicated to ensuring fair and accurate representation in the media as a way to eliminate homophobia and discrimination. GLAAD's work has helped change the ways gay people are portrayed, educating the heterosexual community as well as giving gay teenagers and adults hope. His chapter is an excerpt from his forthcoming memoir, *The Campaign Within*.

He was riding a lime green Sting-Ray bicycle with a white banana seat and chopper handlebars. I knew who he was, but seeing him this time was different—I sensed something going on inside me. Just an inner stirring I had never felt before. It was late afternoon after school on a crisp fall day. The sun was throwing long shadows on the changing leaves, and I was in the backyard hanging out with some neighborhood kids. Just beyond our yard was a vacant lot where kids would gather to hang out. From my yard, I watched the boy stop to talk to his friends, who were also on bikes.

The boy, who had whitish-blond, shoulder-length hair, was wearing a tank top. At thirteen or fourteen, he was older, and I remember looking at his shoulders and arms; I was fascinated. There was something about him drawing me in, and I wanted to be closer to him.

That was when I first started noticing my attraction to guys. I was around ten years old. I began looking at their chests and shoulders, just to see if the feeling was the same as when I watched the boy on the lime green Sting-Ray. More often than not, it was. I had no idea what it meant.

As I headed into high school, I got a better idea, and what it meant was not good. So I ignored it and told myself it was not what it was. It scared me to think something was very wrong with me inside, that I was not like my buddies. I hoped it would go away.

It didn't.

So when I looked at my first *Playboy* in Tommy Debold's garage where we hung out, I knew I had to pretend to like what I was seeing, even if it did nothing for me. I knew I was not interested in all the talk of touching girls. Yet I didn't seem or act like those queer guys in school who people said wanted to touch other guys. I had no idea what I was, but I knew I had to act like my buddies. People did not make fun of them, laugh at them, or taunt them. True, I wasn't yet like them, entirely, but I couldn't possibly be a queer. Some of them were already shaving and I wasn't, so I told myself there was still time for me to become like them.

I hoped.

But after shaving for a few years, I was even less like them, and I drifted away. I couldn't be part of their social world; I didn't really jibe except on the soccer field, and I was an average athlete at best. The only way I fit in with my peers was as a leadership geek—one of the socially awkward kids who could nonetheless organize events and activities and get people to show up. That was me.

And so I had a ton of friends throughout high school, but never a date. My world was neither like my buddies', who were dating the cheerleaders and class officers, nor like that of the very few queer guys who hung out near the north hall stairway during lunch. I was very active, a leader in the school, but socially very alone, terrified that those feelings about the boy on the lime green Sting-Ray had never gone away. Something in my wiring was wrong. I seemed normal on the outside, but I really wasn't like everyone else.

During my sophomore year in college, I was in a huge communications class that involved weekly breakout groups of fifteen students. One day we did an exercise in using senses other than sight that required us to be blindfolded while other students gave instructions. When my turn came, I put on the blindfold.

Two guys in the class had that macho confidence and 1970s style to which I had always aspired, right down to the long sideburns, muscular bodies, and shiny blue polyester shirts unbuttoned halfway. I was now standing in the middle of the group and, although blindfolded, I could see just a bit of daylight. One of the cool guys pointed at me. He couldn't see my eyes, but I saw him mouth one word repeatedly: "Fag. Fag. Fag."

His buddy raised his pinkie finger and flicked his hand back and forth. The other students were smiling and suppressing their laughter. A burning heat flashed through my body that quickly turned to sweat. I couldn't breathe. I felt numb.

What had I done? What had I said? How could they possibly know? I was terrified. The professor said something about the exercise, and my turn ended. I handed the blindfold to the next person.

The two guys were now standing nonchalantly and acting interested in what the professor was saying. I looked at them and thought, *I know what you just did.* I also knew I would never say those words aloud. I wanted to confront them, but I didn't know

> **"What had I done? What had I said? How could they possibly know? I was terrified."**

how. I was silent in my humiliation. Always silent. They were right. I was a "fag." My confusion and depression and unresolved angst worsened. I should have been angry at them, but instead, I was angry at myself. I lacked any self-respect. The numb feeling lasted the rest of the day. To this day, I can still feel a burning humiliation whenever I recall that moment.

From the afternoon I had seen that kid on the Sting-Ray, I had known I was different. And because of that difference, I liked myself less and less. I had no courage to face what I had come to know was the truth. I lived alone and in fear of others learning the truth about me.

My leadership activities and classes became my means of survival. Waves of despair continued to wash over me, but these things, at least, served as a life raft that kept me afloat.

One Friday night I will never forget started like so many others. I went to yet another campus party with guys and girls drinking and socializing while I drifted around the perimeter, an alien who knew neither the language nor the customs. The stress was cutting into my sleep, and I had lost my appetite. I simply didn't have the energy for the charade this night. I left the party and walked east on University Drive back toward the Terrace Road Apartments, where I lived. Then, without warning, the tears started to roll down my cheeks. I would never fit in either world. I wanted to be like the straight guys, but I wasn't. I didn't want to be different, but I was. My pace slowed the more I cried, until I stopped completely at an intersection. I

"I wanted to be like the straight guys, but I wasn't. I didn't want to be different, but I was."

would be alone my entire life. My friends would never accept me if they knew I was a queer, and I would never be a true leader, no matter how good I was at organizing things. Even if my ideas were the best, no one would think so if they knew. Who would want to be around some fag, a queer, a deviant by society's standards? There was no one else like me.

It began to make perfect sense: No one ever had to know I was gay. I could be remembered for all the good I had done up to that point. The burden of being different would be forever lifted.

I sniffled and felt the rush of air as cars flashed by at forty and fifty miles per hour. A pickup truck rumbled by. Then a smaller import car. The walk sign turned green, but I just stood there like a *Night of the Living Dead* zombie, alive but vacuous. The walk sign flashed red. Then solid red. Cars began whizzing by me again, and I inched closer to the curb. The light changed again, and I knew I could cross the street. But I didn't. Was I ready to do this? The light changed again, and the cars started up. I was standing so close to the street that half of each foot hovered off the curb.

"It began to make perfect sense: No one ever had to know I was gay. The burden of being different would be forever lifted."

Cars were visibly moving left to avoid what I'm sure they thought was another drunk college student.

Then I saw my liberation: the approaching high beams and red-and-yellow running lights of a large delivery truck. I started counting in my head for the moment I should step off the curb. I shifted my weight. The truck closed in. A switch clicked in my brain. An accident would be okay. I started to lean off the curb. In an instant, the pain and confusion would finally stop. Just a white space of calm where being different would no longer have any power to torment me.

Then, in a brief flash, I froze, and the truck barreled past, blasting its horn and whipping wind across my face in a wake of diesel exhaust. I started shaking, heaving. When the intersection cleared, I darted across and ran all the way back to my apartment. I can't remember anything else about that night.

I didn't wake up the next day until around 11 a.m. I went into the bathroom, and while washing my hands, I caught a look at my face in the mirror, just as I had a thousand times in my life. I was a mess. And staring at myself, acknowledging what I had been through, I said it for the first time out loud: "This is the way it is. I'm gay."

A week later, I called a friend who lived out of state and told him about being on the brink of suicide. I was just completely lost, and he was the only person I knew who might understand.

"How could you do that?" he yelled.

"I can't live this way," I said. "I will never fit in anywhere."

He reprimanded me once more: "Don't you ever do that again. I care about you."

That someone could care, even knowing that I was gay, was what I had needed to hear all along.

*Brian Graden (second from left) with
his parents and younger brother*

BRIAN GRADEN
President of Entertainment, MTV, VH1, and CMT, and President of Logo

If you live with anyone between the ages of twelve and twenty-four, you are no doubt familiar with Brian Graden's work. As an executive at MTV Networks for the last decade, he has green-lighted pop-culture icons including *Laguna Beach*, *The Osbournes*, *Punk'd*, *My Super Sweet 16*, and *Jackass*. Earlier in his career, he helped bring Emmy-winning animated comedy *South Park* to fruition. In all the programming he has been involved with, he has worked to ensure that gays and lesbians are included and accurately represented—and in doing so, has helped viewers become accustomed to seeing gay people in all areas of life. Brian was also key in the launch of Logo, the world's first TV network for the lesbian, gay, bisexual, and transgender community. And as he tells it, the network's tagline—"See yourself, be yourself"—is no coincidence. It wasn't until he was twenty-one that images from a movie helped him understand himself. Brian has run such movies on Logo in the hope that other gay teens will see positive reflections of themselves.

Nothing is wasted, nothing is in vain: The seas roll over but the rocks remain.
—A. P. Herbert

Sunday nights, at home in the Hollywood Hills, my boyfriend, Jimmy, and I watch *Extreme Home Makeover*, one of the many small rituals that, when taken together, create the domestic cocoon we call a life. On each episode, a victim of unfortunate circumstances gets very lucky in the form of a new home. Today, I believe in the possibility of such miracles, and in the miracle of possibility. Twenty years ago, my life was as good as over. I'll get to that.

On the show, we hear the invariably sad story. And here's the embarrassing part: I sit on the couch and cry, more than a little, though I try to hide it. Jimmy laughs at me. Then he hugs me and says, "Hey, I fell in love with you for your big feeler," a mostly complimentary observation of my overdeveloped reflex to empathize.

And it's true: The notion of people hurting hurts me. The notion of people silently hurting hurts me more. And the notion of people hurting silently for unjust reasons undoes me completely. And that, in essence, is my story and my cause. I grew up hurting because I was so obviously different, burying my truth in silence and yet cultivating a quiet defiance against injustice that would save me later in life.

My childhood involved fantasy worlds in the sandbox, all rather typical. Granted, I also played with paper dolls, drew *Josie and the Pussycat* cartoons, and at Thanksgiving caucused with the women in the kitchen. Easy-Bake Oven? Check. But hey, at age seven, that's "creative."

In sixth grade, we moved into a neighborhood full of guys my age who today are lifelong friends, bonded by a shared interest in music. They were popular, and I was happy to be included. We'd hang at the basketball court down the street; my friends dribbled that silly orange ball, and I circled happily on my bike.

That is, until the perpetually rabid neighborhood bully started railing at me, first on a weekly and then daily basis, calling me "giant-ass sissy," "faggot," and "cocksucker." The less I reacted, the louder and angrier he became. All the while, I wondered, *What do these things mean?* I honestly didn't know.

Until then, I had never felt separate. But I learned the rules of the playground fast: sissy faggots get mocked and treated like social lepers. All these years later, I still can't paint that picture without feeling it all over again, tidal waves of shame that would overwhelm

"But I learned the rules of the playground fast: sissy faggots get mocked and treated like social lepers."

me and then recede, leaving in their wake lifelong pools of suppressed sadness. Not so surprising that the tears are near the surface.

At the beginning of eighth grade, Gwen shocked us all by showing up as a hot chick, having lost seventy pounds over the summer. (This was before the age of dramatic television makeovers, so imagine our surprise.) *If she can change her image,* I thought, *so can I.* So I created many masks designed to ingratiate me to my tormentors. It was a conscious decision, made in the moment, in the hallway near the principal's office, as a matter of survival.

My yearbook says, "Football player, tennis player, class president, Boone's Farm drinker, popular kid with girlfriend"—these were my lines of defense, my accumulated evidence I wasn't "that." I belonged in the drama club, but when offered a lead in *Little Women,* passed. The setup for the inevitable punch line was too obvious, even to me. I chose conformity at any cost, and trust me, football practice was too high a price—although the showers afterward weren't so bad. Yes, that's when I realized what *gay* actually meant (damned hormones). It seemed natural; the rest of the world seemed upside down.

Did the masks work? Well, here are some of my high school greatest hits: Bobby berating me for being a "homo" on the football field every time I fumbled a pass (this happened a lot); Jake keying *faggot* along the fender of my baby-blue Trans Am; and my best friend, Jerry, turning on me at a keg party for fear of losing his own social status. Every incident caught me off guard, leaving me suddenly submerged in self-hatred until, over time, I resolved to feel nothing, suppressing my "oversensitive" side in every way.

My aforementioned neighborhood friends were my salvation. We formed a band called Ace Oxygen and the Ozones (seriously); I was Nicky Nitrogen, keyboard player. And yet, that salvation led to my most hurtful memory. The Ozones played a hot gig at the local Moose Lodge, treating the audience to Loverboy and Foreigner covers. The local newspaper gave the Ozones a full photo feature. Well-meaning high school teachers posted our pictures on hallway bulletin boards. And a very proud moment turned into a stomach punch when fellow students altered the shot and turned my microphone into something obscene.

"Please God, let me find the imaginary switch that can flip me from gay to straight."

On a relative basis, I realize people all around the world endure far greater suffering. But try telling that to a devastated seventeen-year-old stranded in small-town Illinois. My instinct was to run and hide. And in effect, I did go on to hide my true self from the world for many years—ironically, through faith. A good Methodist boy trusts God to change any circumstance, and so I prayed—hard: "Please God, let me find the imaginary switch that can flip me from gay to straight." I kept up my end of the bargain, going to church and leading the youth group, even attending Oral Roberts University. But God let me down; my crush on Burt Reynolds continued unabated. It's a fine line between faith and delusion.

This was the late 1970s, and every media image reinforced the notion that gay was evil: Al Pacino in *Dog Day Afternoon*, Anita Bryant berating leather queens on Gay Pride floats, and those bitchy *Boys in the Band*. Even those two old Muppets in the balcony were probably gay (think about it: two cranky queens who were always at the theater). Not an inspirational figure in the lot.

Finally, at age twenty-one, I snuck into a movie theater in Tulsa, Oklahoma, to see a film called *My Beautiful Laundrette*. The protagonist, Omar, was trying to be true to his South Asian roots, yet he couldn't help but fall in love with Johnny, the outsider rebel played by Daniel Day Lewis. In those characters, and in that story, I saw myself clearly for the first time.

If positive imagery opened the closet, love pushed me out. A couple of years later, I fell hard for a fellow Harvard Business School student. It lasted through four seasons, each more magical than the one before. It was beautiful—and secret. This was 1988. Reagan was president, and Harvard Business School was a bastion of future corporate starched collars.

That said, Steven Carrington had already come out on *Dynasty*. Things were changing, and so was I. The deeper in love I fell, the more absurd hiding seemed. My world was finally turning right side up. People could take me or leave me.

My boyfriend left me. The pressure of going public was too much for him. Though I couldn't understand it at the time, we were two tops spinning toward diametrically opposed destinies. He remains in the closet today; I'm free to write about our relationship in this book.

At the time, however, I was crushed. His rejection felt like a repudiation of my entire gay being, one more person echoing the callous chorus of my youth, affirming they were right about me, causing the issue to crescendo once and for all. What followed was a fog of hopelessness and desperation, a free fall. Today, it would be called clinical depression. Killing myself crossed my mind, as a remedy from the torment.

> **"My boyfriend left me. The pressure of going public was too much for him."**

Months later, on a trip to Greece, alone on a rock in Mykonos, something happened that I can't explain, except to say faith finally prevailed over delusion. When my emotional energy was spent and resistance was no longer possible, there was silence, and within it a voice declaring the absolute truth: that God made gay people, and that we are perfect. Alone in the brilliant Greek sunshine came the clarity that I hadn't lost love but rather, through love, lost my shame; the joyful realization that being gay is only and will forever be about love, its expression, and its simplicity. In that moment, I knew: No one was going to steal from me the possibility of miracles and the miracle of possibility. Not in this lifetime.

As for Bobby, Jake, and Jerry, and whoever sullied my Ozones photo (you know who you are), today I say thank you—for pissing me off. Once the tears stopped, my inner queen eventually waved her hands, threw down a finger snap, and said, "Wait just a friggin' minute. I deserve to be included and respected and even revered exactly as I am."

> **"What followed was a fog of hopelessness and desperation, a free fall."**

It was unimaginable then, there on that rock in Mykonos, that a megaphone called MTV would one day land in my lap, a grown-up sandbox where I would create worlds as they should be, liberally including gays in the fabric of reality programming. But it did.

In June 2005, twenty years after I first saw it, I watched *My Beautiful Laundrette* again, this time on MTV's newly launched, first-in-the-world gay and lesbian network, Logo. And I thanked God that a switch to turn me from gay to straight never existed, because I would have missed that moment.

At the age of forty, I went back to Mykonos with Jimmy, who, understanding me so well, insisted we find that rock. This time, I was humbled to my core by the utter magnificence afforded me on this ride through life. A framed piece of the rock sits on my desk today.

As for the one thing I vowed to suppress, that oversensitive side that caused me so much pain growing up, it turned out the ability to "feel" what America would respond to on television was my greatest professional gift.

I held on—and I pray that every young gay person who is unsure about what is ahead will have the strength and support to hold on, too. Today they can tune in 24-7 and see their brethren living full, rich, complex lives on Logo. I know this alone is not enough, but what I hope they take from it is that their lives can be whatever they dare to believe they can be—and that they should never give up.

And we established members of the gay community, along with the braver souls of angels who came before us, will keep the faith with them. After all, our generation knows a thing or two about faith. We walked through the fire and made it to the other side.

*Joe Solmonese in high school,
above, and today, opposite, with
his partner, Jed Hastings (on left)*

JOE SOLMONESE
President, Human Rights Campaign

Joe Solmonese is president of the Human Rights Campaign (HRC), an organization devoted to achieving equality for gay, lesbian, bisexual, and transgender Americans, with more than seven hundred thousand members and supporters nationwide. Before coming to HRC, Joe was chief executive officer of EMILY's List, overseeing one of the nation's most successful efforts to elect progressive women in every part of the United States.

When I first asked Joe to write for this book, he told me that he was raised to believe admitting you had a painful childhood was a sign of weakness, just as it was weak to be sick or unable to come to work or fired from a job—and therefore, something you never mentioned. But from this experience, both Joe and I have learned that being able to talk about the pain inflicted on you simply for being yourself takes great strength. And it is so important to do because much more than facts and figures are needed to illustrate the harm being done. So I thank Joe—in all the years I've watched him fight for equal rights, I've never admired his strength and commitment more.

Even though I'm president of the largest gay rights organization in the country, the thought of writing about the pain of growing up gay made me groan. I was raised in a family where you always persevered, no matter what. We never stayed home from school when we were sick. My father died on a Friday, and my sister, brother, and I were back in school on Monday. When you had a bad day, you put it behind you and never thought of it again. That's probably why in the twenty-five years since I've been out of high school, I've never really articulated what I experienced. I just put it out of my mind.

In 1979, when I started high school in Massachusetts, nobody was out. Even in 1983, when I went to Boston University in downtown Boston, I knew of only one gay student. I was having lunch in the student union, and someone at my table said, "There goes that gay guy." And everyone turned and stared at him—this big blond guy on the crew team. The guys especially were uncomfortable, but even the girls said, "Oh, that's weird."

Sitting there, I didn't feel anything. I still didn't think I was gay. You know what they say about young people needing good role models: You can't be what you can't see. Well, that's how it was for me. There were so few images of gay people. And the little I knew about being gay made it seem like something you didn't want to be. I read in *Time* about the mysterious gay cancer. The AIDS epidemic had begun. As a result of AIDS, people started coming out. I remember walking down Newbury Street and passing a gaggle of gay men—loud, flamboyant, screaming back and forth to each other. I had such a visceral reaction to them: "That is not me."

"The little I knew about being gay made it seem like something you didn't want to be."

Yet even early on there was something . . . I had glimpses of being different in sixth or seventh grade. But then my father died and things changed. My mom had three kids to raise, ages eleven, thirteen, and fifteen, and we all had to help out. There wasn't much time for thinking about such things—even if I had known how to process it.

At that age, I didn't know what to make of it. I'd have this innate reaction to a boy in class, and feel this attraction. I'd tell myself everybody was probably having that same feeling, and eventually it would all sort itself out.

There was no question in my mind that I would marry a woman and raise a family, and I kept moving right along that path. In high school, I was vice president of my class. I was on the student council. I was on the track team. In my junior and senior years, I had a girlfriend.

I wasn't generally a "target" in high school—I had my achievements and my girlfriend as a shield—but there were episodes, depending on who was in my classes. It wasn't everybody; it was a small group of boys. Despite the false reality I had created,

"My focus was on survival."

despite being on the track team and even finding someone I could call my girlfriend, these boys knew. It felt almost primal; it was like they could smell it. When I walked into class, they locked eyes with me, and I locked eyes with them, and I became the target. For me, that constant fear—"Can I get down this hallway without them seeing me today?"—was the hardest.

On the first day of each semester, I'd look around and know what I'd be up against. One year, two of them sat behind me in homeroom. Every time the teacher called my name during attendance, they would repeat it in a flighty, effeminate tone. The next year, they did the same thing in Spanish class until eventually the Spanish teacher stopped taking attendance. As a fifteen-year-old kid, it gave me great relief, but how humiliating that it needed to happen that way.

A big part of the problem was the dread. I knew what was going to happen and there was nothing I could do to stop it. It was knowing that at one particular moment of every single day I was going to be humiliated. And each day I'd dread that moment until it passed. The constancy of the taunting and humiliation wore you down.

I would lie awake at night trying to come up with any way to change the inevitable. I'd brainstorm how to get out of class. I'd pray for a snowstorm or for the school to burn down—anything to make it stop. But, of course, it never did. There were days when I'd wake up and think, *I can't get through those fifteen minutes of homeroom again. I can't go to gym.* But what choice do you have?

My focus was on survival. One highly effective technique was finding ways to get out of classes in which I was being harassed. By senior year, I was so busy with school activities that I was barely in class.

It's a full-time undertaking to figure out how to diminish what's happening to you. And for every young gay man like me for whom a cruel high school experience turns out to be a catalyst for success, there's another young gay man whose spirit is crushed by it.

At no point did I ever say to myself, *I'm going to talk to my mother. I'm going to tell her I can't take this.* My instinct told me I had to figure it out alone—to get through and never look back. And I did. And then I blocked it all out.

In college, I also had a girlfriend, a woman with whom I was intimately involved. And everything worked well, so I thought it would be doable. I told myself that everybody's sexuality fell along a spectrum, and mine was just a little more toward one end.

Then, near the end of college, my girlfriend decided to live in Europe. We both knew I wasn't going with her. In that moment, I felt the greatest weight of my life lifting from my shoulders. I remember telling myself, *Somebody has just given you a chance.* This was 1987, and I was twenty-two. A guy born ten years earlier might have married that woman. I got a break. And so did she. And in that moment I thought, *I will never do this again.* Right after she left, I moved into the gay neighborhood.

* * *

My mother and I have always been close, and her views have always been progressive. Yet I still waited until I had established a support system outside my family before I came out to her. It's not something I did consciously. I just created what I thought I needed: a group of people who would support me unconditionally. And if that's not going to be your biological family, who will it be? It's also a defense mechanism: If my family does reject me, at least I'll have somewhere to go for Christmas.

No matter how close you are with your family, there's always a deep-seated fear. You try to evaluate their response in advance. If, as in my case, you hear your straight brother and sister from Massachusetts say, "We're supporting Ted Kennedy because he's a champion of gay rights," it certainly gives you a great sense of where they stand on gay rights. However, that is still an entirely different calculus from knowing how they'd feel about *me* being gay.

It's common to see a really accepting mother burst into tears when her gay child comes out, and say something like, "I can't believe you didn't tell me five years ago." Even if all she's ever done was send supportive messages, the situation is still so hard to trust. And when it's your family, there's so much at stake. Even if kids don't ever hear anything specific about being gay, they still get a sense of whether it's "safe" to come out. Maybe they get scared off by a joke or passing comment, or they hide for years because of their family's religious beliefs.

> **"Even if kids don't ever hear anything specific about being gay, they still get a sense of whether it's 'safe' to come out."**

* * *

Today I know I wasn't the only gay person in my high school. I went to my twentieth reunion, and there were probably three or four of us in attendance. I wasn't totally out—I didn't bring my partner with me—but enough people knew, and I felt like it wasn't a big thing.

For decorations, the reunion organizers had put up high school photos of people in the class. My friend Cindy had been class president, and I had been vice president; so they put a picture of her on the ladies' room door and a picture of me on the men's room door. Later that evening I was heading to the bathroom, walking behind a woman and her friend. The woman, who didn't see me, looked at my picture, smirked, and said, "Oh, that picture should be on the women's room door; we should switch them," and they both laughed.

It felt like being fifteen all over again; it brought back all the bad feelings, the frustration and fear. I had forgotten how much it hurts to be hit with it out of the blue like that. And I had forgotten the frustration of being judged by people—mean people, bullies—who you know have no right to judge you.

I admit I'm no saint. It took all of my control not to make a comment about her outfit and her perm and fill her in on my great relationship and successful career. But then my anger dissipated, and I had a really sad thought: *Even today, some thirty-eight-year-old adults are still bigoted. And worse, this woman might have a teenage child who she's teaching her prejudices to . . . or perhaps she's hurting her own child by her cruelty toward who that child was born to be.*

BOB WILLIAMS
Cofounder and President of Design,
Mitchell Gold + Bob Williams

Bob Williams started as an art director for *Seventeen* before turning his talents to home furnishings and joining me in creating our company. But years before, in his native Texas, Bob was yet another conflicted teenager with a secret that nearly prevented him from realizing his potential.

Although we are no longer life partners, Bob and I remain business partners and best friends. We raised Lulu, our late English bulldog and company mascot, together, and nurtured a business we're proud is known not only for its comfortable furniture but also for its dedication to comfort—and equality—for all.

My aunt is a lesbian, and I remember growing up that her girlfriend would come with her to our family functions. Yet our family never talked about it, and I didn't understand their relationship until much later in life. It would have taken a grown-up's ability to read between the lines to figure it out—like knowing what people meant when they called a man a "confirmed bachelor." But I wish I'd been able to figure it out back then; it would have helped me understand myself and saved me years of feeling alone.

My father died when I was ten. He had been in the military, so we had always moved around a lot. After he died, my mom and my younger sister and I settled in a subdivision in Conroe, Texas, a rural corner of the state. Five years later, in 1976, my mom remarried, and we moved a few miles out to the country. It was much more isolated; there weren't any neighbors around. And all my friends from my old neighborhood went to a different school now—the new rival high school.

My high school was overwhelming: forty-five hundred kids. In Texas, they keep the high schools big to create the best odds of having winning football teams. At graduation there were kids on either side of me that I'd never even seen in school before.

Although I was eighteen before *I* was sure I was gay, other people were apparently sure well before then; so my high school days were not much fun. There I was, being myself, and the next thing I knew I was being called names. To get through, I decided invisibility was my safest bet. I went from classroom to classroom without talking to anybody. I didn't raise my hand in class. I tried not to do anything to draw attention to myself because if I did, I'd get ridiculed or picked on. Teachers didn't necessarily step in. I don't remember anybody being punished for being a bully.

"There I was, being myself, and the next thing I knew I was being called names."

Lunchtime was tough. I wasn't such a great student, but I started pretending I was a nerdy, geeky kid just so I could sit with a few of those kids and wait for the time to go by.

In those days, you rarely saw gay people on TV, and if you did, either they were drug dealers or hustlers who died or got murdered, or they were extremely feminine. I didn't see myself in any of them. I didn't even realize that gay people could be lawyers or doctors or judges until I got to college.

"I don't remember anybody being punished for being a bully."

The fact that my family didn't talk about certain things occasionally had its advantages. I never dated in high school, and no one ever asked why.

However, while it might sound great not to have to fend off nosey parents and siblings, it also meant there was nobody to talk to about myself, and it left me feeling very isolated. I thought the way I felt

> **"Mostly I kept hoping I would change—that something magic would happen to make me change."**

might be a phase I'd grow out of—I thought all kinds of different, crazy things. Mostly I kept hoping I would change—that something magic would happen to make me change.

My mom had been widowed at thirty, in the early seventies, and she had become very influenced by the feminist movement. She ingrained in my younger sister and me the importance of never being dependent on anyone, which, despite my struggles at times with academics, made me very goal-oriented and less concerned about my high school social life. And I wasn't a very social person to start with. I didn't need a lot of interaction, but a few close friends would have been nice.

I had felt so lost at my big high school that when it came time for college, I decided to go to a tiny Methodist liberal arts school: Southwestern, in Georgetown, Texas, about three hours from home. However, that meant I still couldn't be out. Everybody knew everybody else's business there. My frustration started to build. I was finally getting to meet people. In fact, I went from hardly going out to the other extreme, partying a little too much. But I still couldn't be myself.

One night when I was a sophomore, right before spring break, I got really drunk, flipped out, and wound up in a chemical abuse ward. Typically for me, I didn't explode—I imploded. I kept repeating, "You just don't understand." I didn't know if I could trust anyone, so I never even talked to the thera-pist at the hospital about being

> **"I didn't know if I could trust anyone, so I never even talked to the therapist at the hospital about being gay."**

gay—but I think he knew that was the issue. They usually kept people there for four weeks, but he made a deal with me that if I promised not to drink for the rest of the semester, I could go after two weeks. He realized alcohol wasn't the real problem.

That fall I transferred to North Texas State—a big university in Denton with eighteen thousand students. I changed my name from Bobby to Bob. I made friends. Five or six of us guys would always go to the girls' cafeteria to eat. I never met any girls, but neither did they—and they were trying.

I also started going to a gay bar. The first time really changed my perspective on what being gay was about. People didn't look at all like I thought they would—they looked like regular people. I met a lawyer from Dallas who was a little bit older than me, and we went out a couple of times. But still, nobody at school knew.

My father was the first in the family to go to college, and I always felt I had to raise the bar. I thought that meant becoming a doctor or a lawyer or a businessman—and that if I became an artist, I'd wind up poor. My father's mom had been an antiques collector; my mom was, too. I used to love to tag along with them to antiques stores and flea markets. When I found out I could pursue something more creative and still be successful, I decided to go to art school in New York. And there, for the first time, I met other students who were gay.

However, I got to Parson's School of Design in 1983, just as AIDS surfaced. Clubs and bars were closing down—it was the tail end of what New York had once been for the gay community. And yet people were hopeful, saying, "Oh, they'll have a cure for AIDS in two years." And now it's been more than twenty-five years . . .

* * *

I still remember the first Friday night of my college life back in Texas. I made a conscious decision not to repeat my high school experience, and so I purposely went out to socialize, meet people, and try different things. I was almost nineteen years old and hadn't ever gone on a date. But going out and pretending didn't work either. I still believed there was a side of me that no one could

"I knew I would always have to hide the fact that I am gay. That's why I had a breakdown—I couldn't keep things bottled up anymore."

know about. I knew I would always have to hide the fact that I am gay. That's why I had a breakdown—I couldn't keep things bottled up anymore. It's like a dam: When there's too much pressure behind it, it finally bursts.

But I don't dwell on the past. I try to learn from the negative things and go forward. It's like moving from one house to another. Part of what makes it worthwhile is throwing away all the old junk. Why bother to move if you're going to take the garbage with you?

When I was young, I thought there was only one path: you went to school, got married, and had two kids. Then you bought a station wagon and drove the kids around in it. But life is like a maze: You can turn this way and that, and you maybe get to a point that's a little bit different from where everyone else is—but right for you. Life is about navigating the maze to get to that point.

> "It's never too late to build a bond based on honesty and trust with the people you love."

My mom never asked me if I was going to get married and give her grandchildren. I think she always knew the answer and didn't want to confront it. We've only just begun to talk about my being gay in the past few years; since my stepfather and my sister passed away, we've been spending more time together. It still sometimes seems like it is the big pink elephant in the room that neither of us mentions. But I know we'll keep trying. It's never too late to build a bond based on honesty and trust with the people you love.

JACOB BRESLOW
Student, University of California
Point Foundation Scholar
Age: 21

For Jacob Breslow, hate speech and bullying at a school in the suburbs of San Francisco—perhaps the most gay-friendly city in the country—led to an all-too-common place: the hospital after a suicide attempt. Fortunately, he has been able to turn his own experiences into fodder for change, working for numerous gay rights organizations in his home state of California, including the Queer Youth Leadership Awards and The Trevor Project, as well as abroad. He also leads antihomophobia trainings in schools, correctional facilities, and community groups. "I want to make sure that people don't have to go through what I went through," he says. A senior at the University of California–Santa Cruz, Jacob is majoring in community studies and feminist studies.

I'm so tired of reading about the doomed gay teenager. Hopelessness is not tied to sexual orientation. It's tied to a lack of acceptance and a lack of visibility. I wasn't depressed because I was gay; I was fine with being gay. I just didn't understand why people were being so mean.

I grew up in the East Bay—in Walnut Creek and Lafayette, suburban towns outside Berkeley, California. When people hear "Berkeley" they think liberal, but Walnut Creek is fairly conservative. People there are not necessarily concerned with politics—they're more focused on being "respectable" citizens and getting their kids into top colleges. Being true to yourself and open about who you are aren't priorities.

My parents got divorced when I was four, and both remarried. I have four younger brothers from different families—two stepbrothers, a half-brother, and a biological brother. My dad traveled for work, so I mainly stayed with my mom in the Bay Area, although for a while I moved back and forth between my parents' houses.

When I was in middle school, everyone was always using the expression "that's so gay" to describe something bad or wrong. And yet they also used the word *gay* to describe guys who were attracted to other guys . . . like me. Prior to this, it hadn't crossed my mind whether I was gay *or* straight. As a little kid, I didn't have the vocabulary to describe my feelings. But in middle school, when I did start realizing I was attracted to guys, the words I heard in the halls told me it was unacceptable to feel the way I did.

Once I understood this, I got scared. I realized I couldn't let anyone know. One of my biggest concerns was my brother who was just a grade below me. With our parents' divorce, we were the constants in each other's lives, and we fought a lot, taking out our anger on each other and using whatever we could against each other. I was terrified that if he found out, he would tell the whole school, and I would become a joke or be tormented. To make sure that didn't happen, I went to the opposite extreme and became the school bully: I figured if I were the homophobic one, then I couldn't be the gay one.

* * *

I came out to my stepmom, who is bisexual, during the summer between eighth grade and high school. She and I were driving home from a family party, talking about why the Red Cross doesn't accept blood from gay men. This segued into whether there were gay people at my school, and she asked me if I knew any. I didn't want to tell her while she was driving—I thought for sure we would crash—but I ended up saying, "There's this one gay kid . . . me."

Her jaw dropped. Then she looked over and said, "We always thought your brother was the gay one." I started laughing and said, "So did I!" And it did turn out that my brother is gay, although he didn't come out for a few more years. My parents never considered there could be another gay person in the family.

My stepmom and I decided we should tell my dad; so the three of us sat down and had a

"That kind of acceptance was powerful."

discussion. A few weeks later they gave me some books about coming out as a gay teen which, ironically, we put away in my closet—and my brothers found. So my dad and stepmom called a family meeting and said, "We're not leaving this room until everybody's okay with this." Luckily, it was easy for my family to accept me.

That kind of acceptance was powerful. It was amazing. And people have said to me, "I don't get it. So why did you have such a hard time?" What they don't realize is that there's so much more needed than just family acceptance. You can go home to a supportive family or attend a supportive youth group as much as you want, but if you have to go to school every day and have people bullying you and pushing you around and making jokes, home is only a safe space to rest your head before the next day.

Teachers definitely see the bullying. But they feel it's too much to deal with. They're trying to teach a class. And a lot of teachers are terrified to say *lesbian* or *gay* or *bisexual* or *transgender* because they're afraid they'll get fired for talking about sex.

Think about all the pictures and posters we put up in school and all the stories we tell. Where are the images of different kinds of families? Where are the discussions of different types of people? There aren't any because we're terrified to talk about them. If we talk about them, then it proves they exist. And yet somehow we are able to talk about mothers and fathers without talking about what made them mothers and fathers. Sex only becomes an issue when we are talking about lesbian, gay, bisexual, or transgender people.

That's what really got to me—the complete lack of acknowledgment of gay people. There I was, a gay student having a hard time, but I was left to struggle on my own. Because my grades were okay, people assumed I was fine. But I wasn't. It clearly wasn't okay to be gay at school—and that's who I am.

> **"Because my grades were okay, people assumed I was fine. But I wasn't."**

I got so fed up with everybody either not mentioning it or saying something mean that I began pushing it in people's faces. I literally became a walking rainbow; my backpack had rainbow stickers all over it. This set me up to be an even bigger target and brought more bullying. But I kept making sure people knew.

The teachers and administration didn't know what to do. I wasn't attending school as much anymore, so I wasn't doing well in classes. School seemed like a place where only people who were straight and accepted could thrive and learn—so what was the point of me going?

It was also incredibly lonely. At first, out of twelve hundred students, I was the only out guy; later, there was one other person: my brother. There were a few other kids in the school, but most didn't feel comfortable being out. That probably had a lot to do with the fact that, unlike me, they didn't have a supportive family to escape to after a day of torment.

> **"School seemed like a place where only people who were straight and accepted could thrive and learn—so what was the point of me going?"**

Although I had the support of my dad and stepmom, I also wanted to tell my mom, but I knew it wasn't going to be easy. One day before school we were listening to the soundtrack from the musical *Rent*, and I asked her if she knew what the show was about. She said, "Those weird gay people with AIDS." Hearing that really made me hesitate to tell her.

It's really important to understand that it wasn't one specific incident that sent me over the edge. And that's the case for so many gay people. Every day becomes a battle. You get so tired of the harassment on so many fronts that you can't see why you should even continue. After a while, all you want is some peace. Even when the homophobic language isn't directed toward you,

you feel its effect. Hearing homophobic language go unchallenged at school every day makes you feel that you are in an unsafe environment.

The first time I attempted suicide, I tried to jump off an overpass near my house. My friends found out and told my dad, who came and grabbed me and locked me in my room for the night. The second time, I was trying to hang myself in my backyard and my friends called the police. They took me to the youth mental ward at the hospital.

It wasn't until I hit rock bottom that I started thinking, *Why am I doing this to myself?* What I needed was to stop accepting the bullying and stand up to it. It had to stop.

> **"The first time I attempted suicide, I tried to jump off an overpass near my house."**

With the help of my parents, friends, and therapist, I realized I needed some community outside my school. I went to a youth group called the Queer Youth Action Team in East Concord, and the former San Francisco/East Bay chapter of the Gay, Lesbian and Straight Education Network, now Ally Action. Along with other lesbian, gay, bisexual, and transgender (LGBT) students, I found out about my rights at school. Learning that it was illegal for people to bully me helped a lot. I began saying, "This is unacceptable. I won't be treated like this; I deserve better."

I started appreciating how lucky I was—not everyone I met there was able to go home and talk to their parents about what they were going through. It took a while, but I even worked things out with my mom—she finally found out about me after my first suicide attempt. Things between us are really good now.

* * *

Sometimes teachers, administrators, and parents tell kids who are bullied and harassed, "Once you leave here and get to college, it's going to be okay." But what are these kids supposed to do every day until then? Middle school plus four years of high school is a long time. That is a dangerous line of reasoning. We need to say that if this is an unsafe place, then we need to change it, not simply wait it out until the bullied students are able to leave. Just because one

LGBT kid made it through alive doesn't mean they all will. It is vital that we make schools safe places for all people to learn.

It's also dangerous for the friends of kids being bullied. If you're fourteen years old and the only line of support for your suicidal friend, it's a lot of pressure. How are you supposed to handle it? We need our counselors and educators to be prepared to support LGBT kids and their straight allies.

"It wasn't until I hit rock bottom that I started thinking, *Why am I doing this to myself?*"

After the shootings at Columbine High School in Colorado, the middle school I went to started holding a Day of Respect. For an entire day, classes stop and students take part in workshops about bullying and name-calling in an effort to change the way they behave at school. LGBT kids need this. It's important for them to see that their peers and teachers are invested in their well-being, just as it is important for gay adults to know that there are laws protecting them and that their government is on their side.

If we support these kids through their education, we won't continue to hear about them as victims. We need to start appreciating and celebrating them for their vast potential to contribute to our world.

KATIE BATZA

PhD Candidate,
University of Illinois at Chicago
Point Foundation Scholar
Age: 28

Point Foundation scholar Katie Batza is currently writing her dissertation on the history of gay and lesbian health activism in the 1970s. In the 1990s, she was engaged in a little health-care activism of her own: She insisted her Catholic high school incorporate positive discussions of homosexuality into its health classes—and she ended up leading the discussions.

I had always had crushes on girls, but I didn't realize my feelings were different from other people's until I was twelve. One day I was explaining my crush on Natalie, a girl in school, to another friend.

"Natalie is the best," I said.

She replied, "You really do care for Natalie, don't you?"

And I said, "Well, yeah!"

She stared at me and said, "No, I mean, you really *care* for Natalie."

That was the moment when I realized not every girl cares for her Natalie the way I cared for mine and thought, *Hmm, maybe I* am *a little different.*

I had heard the word *lesbian* before, but I didn't really understand what it meant. I looked it up, and it all made sense. Once I realized lesbians existed, it was clear to me I was one. I came out a few months later to a few people.

Marietta, Georgia, where I grew up, is a very, very conservative town—Newt Gingrich's hometown. In fact, my dad was a political fundraiser for Gingrich and would often have politicos over for drinks or dinner.

My parents divorced about six months before I came out. That fall they sent me to a new school, a private Catholic school in neighboring Atlanta, where I promptly got a crush on another girl—sorry, Natalie. She was a senior and I was in eighth grade, and I followed her around like a puppy. She was out—not at school, but in other aspects of life. She invited me to her folk music concerts, and I dutifully went along.

> **"Once I realized lesbians existed, it was clear to me I was one."**

One day I was on the phone with her at my apartment and she asked me if I was gay. My mom was home, in the front room. I went into the bathroom and shut the door. I got in the tub, pulled the shower curtain closed, and said, "Yes, but you can't tell anybody."

By then I had also told my guidance counselor at school. She knew my parents had gotten a divorce, so she tried to check in with my sister and me. It wasn't unusual for me to stop by once a day just to say hey. On one occasion, after a long, meandering conversation, she said, "It sounds like you're dealing with your sexuality."

I got very defensive and told her, "It's not a big part of my life. It's just this one thing about me."

Fortunately, she was very wise and supportive. She told me, "Actually, it is a really big thing. There's no need to kid yourself. This is going to change your life."

My parents were no liberals—the idea would probably offend them. Nonetheless, they were very open-minded. They made sure I knew I was loved no matter what, always supported me, and always encouraged me to do what I thought was right—and especially to always be truthful. So I didn't feel a lot of shame about being different. In fact, they had *taught* me that I was different—because I was so loved, so smart, so good at sports.

Still, what the guidance counselor said gave me pause. I was in a Catholic high school, after all—a Catholic high school in the Deep South, full of football players on a nationally ranked team. So I kept a low profile at school—well, until I started dating the captain of the cheerleading squad's older sister, who was in college.

Up to that point, I had always been a bit of an outsider. I didn't really have many friends, although people were generally friendly.

> "There were certain groups of people with whom I was afraid to be alone in halls or on the school grounds. Once, I got shoved down the stairs."

Then, all of a sudden, the captain of the cheerleading squad started talking to me. And her sister was picking me up from school, and everyone knew her sister was a lesbian. Soon they pieced it together—and I didn't deny it when asked.

After that, people began calling me names. And I started getting threatening notes in my locker saying things like "I'm watching you." I felt like I was under constant surveillance. Somebody slashed my tires. There were certain groups of people with whom I was afraid to be alone in halls or on the school grounds. Once, I got shoved down the stairs. The notes continued. Midway through junior year I stopped going to my locker entirely: I carried everything in my knapsack.

I was on the school volleyball team and became so concerned that my teammates felt uncomfortable around me that I stopped changing in the locker room. I was scared someone would accuse me of looking at her inappropriately. Eventually I quit the team. I wouldn't even go to the bathroom if other girls were in there. As the first out person in the school's one-hundred-year history, I felt I had to be beyond reproach. I took school seriously and did well academically. But the minute the bell rang, I was out of there.

The administration's support and concern went only so far because I could never match an incident of harassment to a specific person. Unfortunately, students call other students "faggot" in high school regularly, and they weren't about to kick out every single person who did it. This might have been why administrators at a Catholic school were willing to let me try to educate people about homophobia and homosexuality.

Many of the students and teachers were very conservative, and the feeling around the school was very homophobic. In class, homosexuality was not spoken about at all. But there was a handful of teachers, and the very rare student, who embraced a more liberal Catholicism. They were the kind of Catholics who believe judging is not their job. Like my best friend: when I came out to her, she said, "Jeez, is that all? I thought you were going to tell me you had been abducted by aliens."

I've wanted to be a professor and a historian since I was twelve, and I believe teaching does not always have to take place in an academic setting. So at lunchtime, instead of sitting alone or hiding in the library, I began cavalierly sitting down at a table full of people and forcing them to talk with me in the hopes they'd realize I wasn't going to infect them with lesbianism—that I wasn't the biggest freak they'd ever meet and that lesbians could talk about something other than homosexuality.

During the week we discussed sex in health class, I asked the teacher if I could talk about homosexuality—to make it a little bit more normal and to let people who might have been thinking about it know that they weren't crazy. There was some opposition, but in the end, I was allowed. So there I was: a fifteen-year-old teaching other kids about the Kinsey scale.

* * *

From the beginning, my parents were accepting and caring. And the truth is, they had other things to worry about at the time. They had just gone through a divorce. And I was the tamer of their two daughters. I wasn't doing drugs; I wasn't staying out late at raves. My sister was the party kid.

I did worry that my mom might flip out. But ultimately, she had her priorities straight: I was merely gay; my sister was in danger. My mom continues to be supportive: She always walks with me in the gay pride parades.

I was also nervous about coming out to my dad—he's so politically conservative. So I didn't actually come out to him. I was already out at school. I had cut my hair very short. I was dating a woman seriously, and she would come to dinner at my dad's house with me. She had a shaved head: There was no mistaking her for straight. But my dad never said anything. We just talked around it. Finally one day, he said, "I know, and I know that you know that I know, and everything's fine." And then I told him about the work I was doing with YouthPride, the organization for lesbian, gay, bisexual, and transgender kids I'd helped start.

Even though we don't necessarily share an ideology, he's proud of my sense of civic duty and my refusal to go along to get along. To know that he's proud of me, especially for my gay activism, really makes me feel good.

My sister, who is three-and-a-half-years older, has been wonderful, too. She took me to all those folk music concerts so I could see that girl I had a crush on in eighth grade, and she never once questioned why I was obsessed with her. She knew Atlanta so well that even though she's not gay, she was able to introduce me to lesbian-friendly places, and thus to some of the first lesbians I ever met—without my ever having to ask. She even gave me my first Indigo Girls CD.

> **"That I didn't struggle with my sexuality or doubt my self-worth is atypical, I know. It likely has much to do with what my parents taught me about myself, and how they reacted when I came out."**

I brought a woman to my Catholic high school prom. I was working for causes in the greater Atlanta gay community by then, and as a result, there was a lot of press around my decision—even my dad was interviewed. By that time I was a force to be reckoned with. I never threatened the school or gave them any kind of ultimatum; it was probably easier for them to let me bring my date than to try to put the kibosh on my plans.

That I didn't struggle with my sexuality or doubt my self-worth is atypical, I know. It likely has much to do with what my parents taught me about myself, and how they reacted when I came out.

But other people's reactions to my sexuality have been sadly predictable. That's why I've dedicated my life to education: I want gay people to know about their history and straight people to know that the earth will continue to rotate in spite of—or because of—that history.

Martin Luther King, Jr., said, "True peace is not merely the absence of tension; it is the presence of justice." My own activism was born out of a sense of inequality and injustice. I can't just sit on my butt and have fun being a lesbian.

It's sad that we have to plod along and fight tooth and nail, but change over time is often more long lasting. As a teacher, I already see rewarding signs of it in my own—straight—college students. To them, gay history is a source of interest. They don't see it as a threat to their sexuality or religious or political views. Education is making a difference, and if we can continue with it, by the time my own kids are in high school, gay kids in most places in America hopefully won't face the kinds of threats I did.

TONY MEYER

Student, Harvard University
Point Foundation Scholar
Age: 19

Support at home is priceless . . . but it is not enough. Being one of the biggest guys on your sports team offers some protection, but it shouldn't have to. To defeat discrimination, we also need schools to do their part. If administrators and teachers don't set an example with a zero-tolerance policy and full support of equality and safety for every pupil, what can they expect from their students? Even in a California community with many progressive people, Tony Meyer was surprised to find an open display of prejudice among his high school's staff.

The copresident of his school's Gay-Straight Alliance (GSA) student club, Tony served on the board of directors for the Gay-Straight Alliance Network and was a senior member of his community Youth Council for GSAs in Southern California. A government major at Harvard, he hopes to attend law school or medical school and pursue a career in public service.

I wasn't planning to pick any fights, but I wasn't planning to lose any either.

I was on the wrestling team all through high school—and I was out all through high school. If you're good at what you do, people give you a lot of leeway. Even people who thought gays were sinners (and going to burn in hell for all eternity) didn't seem to care as long as I was kicking butt on the mats every weekend—they needed me to win for the team.

It also helps that I'm six foot three and was 215 pounds back then. On the wrestling team, if trouble arose, the coaches let us resolve it with a fight to the finish. So no one said anything to me because there was a good chance if they did, they'd lose.

My two younger brothers and I grew up sixty miles south of Los Angeles in Mission Viejo, California, a city of one hundred thousand people—it was named the safest city in America in 2007. School always came naturally to me—I was my high school valedictorian. Wrestling was more of a struggle, but my parents encouraged me to play a sport so I would have a release for all the stress that comes with high school.

On the first day of seventh grade I walked into homeroom, sat behind a kid named Mitchell, and immediately thought, *Wow, he's really attractive.* It didn't occur to me other people would think that was wrong. Later, I developed a crush on a kid named Taylor. I wrote him a poem and, after building up the courage, gave it to him. We had been good friends, but after he read it, he tore it up in my face, and from then on we never spoke again. After that, I decided not to tell Mitchell—I'd rather never know whether he liked me than lose another friend.

In eighth grade, my mom found out I liked guys when she read my diary. She just handed it back to me and said, "You might not want to let that get into other people's hands." Since she didn't scream or yell, but just quietly accepted it, I decided to tell some friends at school. Everybody was pretty laid back about it, although a couple of guys stopped speaking to me.

I founded my school's Gay-Straight Alliance (GSA) student club in my sophomore year. Outside of that club, no one ever asked me about being gay, and I never talked about it. Because of the way I looked, people either didn't guess or didn't believe it; those who did know just thought I was confused.

Growing up outside the stereotype let me make my own decisions about coming out. It's not so easy for my younger brother: When he walks into a room, you're pretty sure he's gay; needless to say, he's had a much different high school experience. While I didn't get picked on for being gay or any of the typical things for which kids get picked on in high school, my brother got picked on for *everything*. A lot of the worst violence happens to the more feminine boys—regardless of whether or not they're gay—or to the transgender students. But of course, that's something no one likes to talk about in Mission Viejo.

My parents may have been okay with me being gay, but they would not let me date. We fought about it constantly. First they said I could date when I turned seventeen; once I was seventeen, they thought college would be a better time. Their rationale was they didn't want me to get mugged or killed, even in the safest city in America. They didn't want me in a movie theater holding some guy's hand and end up getting attacked. No matter what I said, I could not calm that fear.

The way my dad put it was he didn't mind my *being* gay; he just didn't want me *living* gay—and risking my safety—while in high school. He didn't want me to hide anything—lead the GSA, he said. But no making out with guys, no having guys over. He wanted me to grow up a little bit first, to understand the world we lived in. So I finally gave in and didn't date in high school. I took it with a grain of salt because I knew my life as a gay teen was so much better than that of a lot of my friends.

> **"Even if you can't date and are only looking for somebody to hang out with—just normal high school stuff—it's challenging."**

Even if you can't date and are only looking for somebody to hang out with—just normal high school stuff—it's challenging. You may not feel comfortable at the parties or clubs all the straight kids are going to. If you don't go to the GSA meetings and meet people, then you hole up in your room and go online, where there are communities for gay kids. A lot of the gay people I knew in high school had friends on MySpace who helped them get by each day. MySpace and the Internet—that's how I met the gay kids in Mission Viejo.

It took a few years, but now my parents and I have an amazing relationship. Of course there were glitches along the way: I had to tell my mom that AIDS couldn't be spread by kissing. Although *Will & Grace* was one of my parents' favorite shows, when the issue hit closer to home, it took them a while

"Allowing someone to use gay as a synonym for 'stupid' is a big deal."

to understand that being gay isn't alien—it's just guys versus girls. These days, my brother is the president of the GSA, and when he puts up event posters, both my parents go to school to help him. Unfortunately, they have to do it late the night before so the posters don't get torn off the walls.

* * *

Although I came out as gay in eighth grade, by sophomore year of high school, it became clear to me that I also like girls. I didn't tell people I was bisexual right away, however, as many of my friends were straight girls, and they preferred me being gay. And although my friends were all very progressive, they just didn't understand bisexuality in guys and didn't want to hear about it. So I waited until most of them had graduated and then came out as bi in my senior year.

Being squeamish about bisexuality is not so uncommon in the gay community either. Some gay people see bisexuality as fence-sitting. When I'd say I'm bi, they'd accuse me of trying to come out of the closet halfway. They thought being bi was trying to appease all of your straight friends and gay friends at the same time. They want you to be totally activist, totally for gay rights, and totally gay.

Mission Viejo is a very white, very privileged community. Gay kids weren't getting beaten up or thrown out of the house. The problem was kids getting called the "f" word. (I don't even like using it.) Some people think it's not a big deal and that we should be

"It's that kind of slow, steady pressure against gay kids that keeps them lying to their parents out of fear or drives them to hurt themselves."

fighting other battles. But allowing someone to use gay as a synonym for "stupid" is a big deal. It doesn't have to be physical violence; verbal abuse is all it takes to send someone home in tears or to make him stop coming to school

coming to school or to experiment with drugs. It's that kind of slow, steady pressure against gay kids that keeps them lying to their parents out of fear or drives them to hurt themselves.

Every time a teacher does nothing, or a principal refuses to take the issue seriously, or a PTA mom just laughs it off, it makes other kinds of attacks against gay people, including violence, that much more acceptable. School should be a safe place, and when you can't go to class because other students are harassing you and the teacher won't do anything about it, there's a serious problem.

> **"When you can't go to class because other students are harassing you and the teacher won't do anything about it, there's a serious problem."**

Sadly, the prejudice we had to fight in Mission Viejo sometimes had more to do with the administration than the students. To celebrate the annual national Day of Silence—used to bring attention to antigay name-calling, bullying, and harassment in schools—our GSA decided to ask students not only to remain silent but also to dress in all black. The principal is very progressive; however, there were a lot of homophobic people on the administrative staff. Rather than simply not wearing black that day, one vice principal wore all white, while another vice principal and her assistant dressed in all pink. While we sat in the middle of the quad wearing black in an effort to demonstrate how many people were participating, the two of them made a big deal of parading around, showing the student body how they disapproved of our fight for equal rights.

There were 120 of us dressed in black by our second annual Day of Silence, while about 30 students dressed in white to oppose us. It's difficult enough to see that some of your fellow students are against what you believe in. But when the adults responsible for your safety make a spectacle of themselves and let the students know they don't support you in your fight against bullying and harassment, that strikes a lot deeper and hurts all the more. The worst part, though, was that one

> **"How can you feel safe at school if you know the person in charge of protecting you doesn't believe you should be safe from harassment or attack?"**

of those adults was the vice principal of discipline. How can you feel safe at school if you know the person in charge of protecting you doesn't believe you should be safe from harassment or attack?

JULIA BRINDISI

Student,
Massachusetts College of Art
Age: 19

High school is challenging enough without having to deal with the added struggles of being gay—and it can be much more challenging if you feel you must face things on your own because parents and friends aren't supportive. Julia Brindisi's story makes clear the value of Gay-Straight Alliance (GSA) clubs in schools. And I truly appreciate the efforts by Julia's GSA to reach middle school students. As gay kids come out earlier, in environments like middle school where children have even less emotional maturity than in high school, educating students so that they understand and have compassion for others is vital for everyone and for all our futures.

S ophomore year of high school ended, and the summer of 2005 began. I figured it would be like any other summer. But instead, it was filled with lies and gossip that follow me to this day.

It started with my first girl date. We went to see the animated kids' film *Madagascar*. Her mother drove us early to the theater at the mall. We bought the tickets, and then walked around. We stopped at Arby's, and the blonde chick who took our order asked if we were lesbians. We looked at each other and laughed, shrugging off the question.

After the movie, we sat outside on the grass, talking and then kissing. We only kissed a few times, but it was enough for my mother to see when she came to pick us up. My mother didn't say anything, and it turned out that her seeing me kiss a girl would be the least of my problems that summer.

I battled guilt and insecurity when that girl rejected me and ended all contact between us. Mutual friends explained why my recent fling was avoiding me. She told them I had acted like a "sexual predator," meaning that I had been too aggressive and had not given her a chance to say no. I even heard fictitious stories about how the day had "really" gone. But I had only been pursuing a relationship I felt was mutual.

She managed to change people's opinions of me. Because of this brief relationship, my life became unbearable at times. Many of our mutual friends stopped talking to me.

Later, she changed her mind and tried to rekindle our friendship. I knew I could never allow myself to be friends with her again because she had betrayed my trust. To this day, I have issues trusting people. She became a factor in my depression, a part of the razor blade that almost ended my life—another suicidal gay teenager statistic.

In my social life, I often felt unappreciated and taken advantage of. As other betrayals mounted, I kept mostly to myself. I also felt academic pressure from my parents and hostility between us stemming from our daily miscommunications.

> **"I hadn't even been aware of what the word *gay* meant until seventh grade."**

On top of that was the emotional stress I felt simply because I'm gay. I hadn't even been aware of what the word *gay* meant until seventh grade. Oddly, I never told anyone outright, mostly because I didn't think my thoughts about kissing other girls deviated from societal norms. I didn't even realize I'd have to "come out."

In fact, coming out to my parents turned out to be more of an invasion. They didn't know about the thoughts wandering in and out of my mind. We had never discussed sexuality. I just remember arriving home from school one day and being confronted by my mother with a letter I had thrown in the trash; in it, I had written to my boyfriend that I was bisexual.

After that, communication ended and mistrust set in. I heard a lot of "it's just a phase" and "you're doing it for attention." So when that girl began her campaign of lies and silence, I couldn't turn to my mother for support. And since then I actually have never divulged information about my personal life to my parents because I always feel ashamed or angry when they criticize my decisions. Instead of talking with me directly, my mother still asks questions like, "Are you making a lot of friends? Boys *and* girls?" in a hopeful attempt to find out if my preference for women was indeed "just a phase" now that I'm in college and away from home. It isn't.

> **"I heard a lot of 'it's just a phase' and 'you're doing it for attention.'"**

* * *

In high school, I first came out as bisexual. But by my junior year, I had told most of my friends and my school's GSA club advisor that I was a lesbian. I regularly attended GSA meetings and even became the advisor in my senior year. It became really difficult to walk the halls. I'd constantly hear "that's so gay" or other derogatory terms like *faggot*, *dyke*, and *homo*. I tried to tune it out, or sometimes if I felt comfortable, I'd call the person on it.

Many of my friends felt the same way about homophobic language, but as kids get older, it gets harder to change that behavior. So our GSA started a program for middle schoolers. We distributed a survey about harassment and discrimination to the middle school students and then used the survey results to determine the topics (such as racism, gender roles, social status, and self-esteem) that the GSA would discuss with them. We believe the program caused some students not only to change their behavior but also to open their minds. My high school GSA continues to run this program today.

In the future, I hope that middle school kids *and* high school kids will become more open-minded and speak out when some people refuse other people their rights based on sexual orientation, gender identity, sex, or race.

"The worst thing anyone can do is to do nothing."

Protest against laws you believe are unfair, or try to pass a bill in your state—or even a new policy in your school. The worst thing anyone can do is to do nothing.

PART 4
In the Workplace
Would You Risk Your Career to Be Yourself?

WOULD YOU RISK YOUR CAREER TO BE YOURSELF?

BY LANE HUDSON
Communications Director, Faith in America

I was an overachiever—a campus leader and fraternity president. I also dove headfirst into Democratic politics. By the age of nineteen, in 1996, my involvement yielded a White House internship, a job with a U.S. senator, and my election as a delegate to the Democratic National Convention. Everything seemed to be on track for a career in elective office.

Most of my life, I knew. But for most of my life, I wouldn't acknowledge it to anyone, not even myself. After all, being gay would destroy any chance of holding elective office in a place like South Carolina. In addition, winning an election in the conservative South was rarely done without membership in—and the strong support of—a church. I was raised a Southern Baptist, a faith in which there was no room for homosexuality.

So I lied to my family, my friends, and myself. It was both a subconscious and a calculated decision. I chose a career over my own self-respect.

But Mother Nature always gets her way. Sooner or later, gay people must face their sexuality—and I had to come to terms with mine.

We've all heard the disastrous coming-out stories that ruined careers and relationships. The pressures are intense—certainly for people driven to succeed in highly competitive and very public fields like those in this section, but also for those in professions with a less public face.

And it can also be hard on their parents. Imagine years of believing in your very talented, hardworking children, of providing the support, time, and money to get them the best training and into the best schools, only to see them robbed of opportunities simply because they want to live openly and honestly. Sometimes, out of fear, loving parents may even pressure their children to remain at least partially in the closet rather than assume the "risk" of coming out and possibly jeopardizing their careers.

There was a time when I felt that way, too. I distinctly remember a phone conversation with a college friend who was struggling with coming out soon after leaving college. My advice to him was terrible. In the midst of his personal crisis, the best I could do was tell him he'd have an easier life with a wife and kids—and to turn his back on the difficulties that come with being gay. I spoke from the heart: I myself had decided to take the "traditional" path in life because I believed that was what it would take for me to achieve my political goals. Today, I'm embarrassed by what I told him.

> **"He decided to accept his sexuality and now leads a happy, fulfilling life—professionally and personally."**

Thankfully, for him, Mother Nature overrode my awful advice. He decided to accept his sexuality and now leads a happy, fulfilling life—professionally and personally.

Not long after that, I finally admitted to myself that I was gay and began my coming-out process. I was working as a fundraiser at a boarding school in Virginia. What I remember most from that time were the conversations around the watercooler. We were a close group of colleagues and shared much about our lives. Yet every day, I lied to them; every day, I wanted to tell them, but I didn't. Although I worked in a friendly environment, I didn't have the courage to disclose my sexuality to my coworkers.

Around that time I was elected for the second time to be a delegate to the Democratic National Convention. Ironically, it provided me with a very subtle way to come out—in politics, no less. On the delegate registration form was a section to indicate if you represented a minority constituency. I quietly checked the gay and lesbian box and handed in my form. It felt great.

Recently, a college student I know came to me for advice. He told me that he was being recruited by a federal agency for a job following graduation. He was concerned about taking the job and then having to be in the closet because of the work environment there. He is far from alone in thinking that. In fact, many young gay people feel it necessary to return to the closet after having lived openly and freely during college. Knowing this has led me to become involved with an organization called Out for Work. It provides guidance to out lesbian, gay, bisexual, and transgender college students on how to remain out while transitioning into the workplace.

I'm confident that the advice I offered this time was sound. I suggested that he find a way during the interview process to learn if the work environment was accepting of gays. The rationale stemmed from my own experience. Lying to himself and his coworkers every day around the watercooler is no way to live.

Whether you're a gay college student, an aspiring lesbian politician, a bisexual professional athlete—or the loving parent of one—understand that remaining in the closet can do untold damage. Luckily, we can learn from others who have the courage to tell their stories. Talking is, indeed, one way we can avoid the mental, physical, social, and societal damage that can come from living closeted lives at work and elsewhere.

For more on Out for Work, please visit www.outforwork.org, and see the resource section at the back of this book.

Billy Bean playing for the San Diego Padres

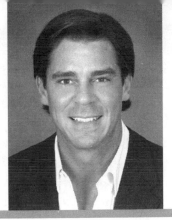

BILLY BEAN
Former Major League Baseball Player

Billy Bean played major league baseball for the Tigers, Dodgers, and Padres from 1987 through 1995, when he walked away from the game because a personal tragedy made it too painful to keep his sexual orientation a secret: His partner had died, and Billy couldn't tell most of the people in his life because he wasn't "out." Four years later, when he came out publicly, his story became front-page news in the *New York Times* and the subject of a *20/20* segment with Diane Sawyer. His desire not to let what happened to him happen to others pushed him to share his story: Billy wrote a book about his experience, *Going the Other Way: Lessons from a Life In and Out of Major League Baseball*, which is being adapted for film. He is the only living former or current major league player to acknowledge his homosexuality.

For parents, his story raises questions: If your child loves sports, and has the talent and dedication to compete professionally, should discrimination keep him or her from it? Or should the cost be a life in which they can't share the truth about themselves with their family, friends, and teammates?

Getting married at age twenty-five, before I accepted my sexual orientation, is something I'll regret for the rest of my life. Had I allowed myself to even consider a sexual encounter with a man before then, I would never have married; my denial caused so much pain and sadness. But in my twenties, I could not reconcile the idea of being gay with being a professional athlete—and I was a professional athlete above all else.

I grew up in Santa Ana, California, in the 1970s, the oldest child in a blended Catholic family of six kids—five of them boys—with a former Marine Corps veteran for a stepfather. The only mentions of homosexuals I recall were occasional faggot jokes. It never dawned on me that I might be one myself. I wasn't effeminate, so my peers didn't torment me. I honestly thought I was heterosexual and was going to marry and have children like everyone else in my world. I don't even remember meeting gay people until I went to college, and I didn't see any similarities between me and them.

One major reason was that I was completely immersed in the world of sports. No one in my family had ever participated in sports, let alone excelled in them. However, from the age of seven, I played baseball, football, basketball, and even ran track. I was the quarterback of the high school football team and was chosen athlete of the year as a senior. I was popular and always had a girlfriend.

When I think back to myself as a teenager, I can see I didn't understand my emotions when it came to my male friends. I certainly felt a huge bond with some of them, especially the ones I played sports with, but I thought of it as part of being teammates, not as sexual attraction. And I was too busy trying to be the most valuable player of every team I played on to focus on much else.

"Homosexuality is not accepted in professional sports."

I'm sure my many years of success on the playing field growing up helped me feel secure and accepted in the hyper-heterosexual environment of professional sports. I certainly didn't see any option to be otherwise. To this day (let alone thirty years ago), homosexuality is not accepted in professional sports, whether behind the closed doors of the clubhouses, on the buses with your teammates, in the hotel room when you are traveling with your team—or even on your own time.

You may be questioning how I could not have known for so long. To understand requires insight into what it takes to make it into the world of Major League Baseball: how hard you must train, how intense the competition and pressure are, how much money is at stake—and the demand that you always have "your head in the game." I spent the years from my teens to my twenties working toward that goal. And then, as I arrived on the doorstep of my dream—and two years into my marriage—I began to discover my

> "Once I did, I broke down in tears—because I knew it was real and because I had a wife at home."

homosexuality. Also consider that there was no Internet, no visibility for gay people outside big cities, certainly no role models in professional sports, and no way for a big-league athlete to discuss these issues in a protected, safe environment.

The first time I clearly sensed I might be gay was in 1991, during the off-season. I had been traded from the Detroit Tigers, my first major league team, to the Los Angeles Dodgers, and was back in my home state. I was living with my wife in West Hollywood—a thriving gay community where we ended up by accident: I was an investor in a condominium building there, so when I got back to LA, my agent suggested we move in. Unbeknownst to both of us, the gym my wife signed us up for was a gay gym. I started feeling a peculiar kind of energy at that gym during workouts.

At first, I was frightened by my feelings—but also incredibly thrilled. It didn't bother me when men looked at me. What did bother me, however, was that I knew most of my teammates would never have stood for that type of flirtation.

It took two more years before I acted on my curiosity. Once I did, I broke down in tears—because I knew it was real and because I had a wife at home.

I never told any of my friends I was gay until I left my wife and moved in with my first partner, Sam, at twenty-eight. I didn't tell my family until I was thirty-four. I came out publicly a year later. By then, I had been retired from baseball for four years.

I came close to telling my roommate and good friend Brad Ausmus when we were with the San Diego Padres. I was really struggling at the time, and it was affecting my game. He knew something was wrong, but I was afraid to trust anyone. I am sure Brad would have told me it was something that could be dealt with, reminded me how precious every moment at the big-league level is—and convinced me not to give it away, which is what I did. Such a mistake.

What was I afraid of? If the news had gotten out, it would have been a hurricane of attention and distraction. And although I was already in my late twenties, being gay was still new for me. I was very uncomfortable with it and not mature enough to even contemplate weathering that kind of storm publicly. I hadn't even accepted myself as gay, and given society's attitudes, let alone those in professional sports, that

> **"I was making every effort to keep my life a secret, and in doing so, I made our home life miserable because I treated our relationship like it was a crime."**

takes time. And since I hadn't struggled with this when I was younger, I was still dealing with all the fear, pain, and terror of being exposed.

I was most afraid after I told my wife I was gay, in 1994. I told her because she was beating herself up over why I wouldn't give our relationship another chance. She needed support to get through this, and she told a few very close friends, which I totally understood and wanted for her. However, I knew that if a rumor about me got started, it could be just days before word got around. So then I really felt the need to project I was straight. I overcompensated by dating other women and going to strip clubs with my teammates. I was swirling in fear of being caught for something I barely understood.

All this paralyzed my relationship with my partner, Sam. I was making every effort to keep my life a secret, and in doing so, I made our home life miserable because I treated our relationship like it was a crime. I have tremendous regrets about that—especially because Sam died suddenly in early 1995, and I never got the chance to say the things that might have helped him understand my own homophobia.

My lowest point of all was choosing not to go to Sam's funeral because I couldn't come up with a valid reason to miss a game merely for the funeral of someone I could only say was "a friend." I walked onto the field that day wanting to die. There was no one I could talk to about it. The isolation was overwhelming. I couldn't even talk to my own mom about the death of my partner because she didn't know I was gay. It was devastating.

I'd like to say all the challenges are behind me. But even today, there are times that leave me feeling depressed. Every family holiday, for instance, I'm reminded I'm different. Every time I leave my parents' home, they have a look of sadness on their faces. Even though I know they love me, the change from straight Major League Baseball player married to a pretty girl to a gay man who left baseball for someone who lives far away in Miami Beach remains

"Knowing that I am living truthfully always makes me feel better."

difficult for them. The desire to please others is my greatest gift and greatest flaw. Knowing that I am living truthfully always makes me feel better.

What would have helped me most when all these feelings surfaced was being able to confide in someone. I tried to handle it on my own, and I realize now that I was not strong enough to do that. And that was at twenty-seven. I can only imagine what it's like to come out alone as a teenager. Who would want his or her child to go through that?

I should have trusted my family, or a psychologist, or even my closest friends. But I was so afraid they wouldn't understand me or that they'd reject me. In the end, my friends taught me so much about unconditional love and acceptance.

I can't say the same about my public life and career. We have all seen how the sports community and the media go crazy over a rumor of homosexuality. I was afraid of anyone finding out while I was an active player. I had so much to lose—something I had spent years working for, something I loved, something that brought public recognition and financial reward. It's a lot to give up—especially when you feel in your heart you shouldn't have to. There are no circumstances in which people should have to choose between their sexual orientation and their career—whether they're playing pro ball or running the concession stand.

I wasn't living near my baseball friends when I came out and hadn't been in day-to-day contact for a few years. In newspaper articles and TV interviews, my closest friends were very supportive. A few players used the platform of my story to make sure everyone knew they were "uncomfortable" with the idea of a gay teammate, insinuating that a gay man wouldn't be able to control himself in the locker room around them.

I've used those lame comments as an opportunity to explain to people that, as a gay teammate, I had much *more* self-control than some of those straight guys, as far as personal conduct was concerned. In the ten years I played, not one single person knew I was gay, not even the guys I roomed with for years.

> "As a gay teammate, I had much *more* self-control than some of those straight guys, as far as personal conduct was concerned."

Around a major league clubhouse, as long as you don't rock the boat, everything is fine, but once you do, you become an outcast quickly. In that world, being gay is a sinking ship. There are gay teens today who want to play pro sports and who believe they have to live a lie, no matter how painful, to do it. This must change. Discrimination should not keep them from their dreams. And living dishonestly is too high a price.

Above: Barney Frank (seated second from left), in the summer of 1955 at a Catskills resort with his parents, Sam and Elsie Frank, younger brother David, younger sister Doris (standing at left), and older sister Ann— known to many today as Ann Lewis, a leading Democrat and former communications director for President Clinton.

BARNEY FRANK
Congressman from Massachusetts

Barney Frank has served in Congress for twenty-seven years—and for twenty-one of those years, he has been openly gay. Currently, he is chairman of the House Financial Services Committee, which oversees the banking and housing industries, a particularly important post in today's economic climate. The *New York Times* recently called Barney one of the most powerful members of Congress, noting his ability to build bridges across party lines to help pass legislation. He has also often been cited for his quick wit, his impatience, and his brilliance. I can attest to all three.

While arguing for passage of the Employment Non-Discrimination Act, a bill prohibiting discrimination against employees based on sexual orientation, Barney appealed passionately and personally to his fellow representatives, emphasizing how the bill would help young people: "I used to be someone subject to this prejudice, and, through luck and circumstance, I got to be a big shot. I am now above that prejudice. But I feel an obligation to fifteen-year-olds dreading to go to school because of the torments, to people afraid they will lose their job in a gas station if someone finds out who they love." The next day I called to ask him to participate in this book. He returned my call in his trademark cantankerous tone, but as

I described the book, he asked his aide to hold his calls and told me it was "brilliant—just what the country needs." I was so moved to hear that from someone so renowned for getting things done. And I am so grateful for the chance to get to know him better as he opens his life to us in this chapter.

G ay, lesbian, bisexual, and transgender people, and the large number of others who have joined our fight against prejudice, have made great progress over the past forty years, but we still have more to do. That there is still a phenomenon known as *coming out*—the term applied to honest discussions of gay people's sexuality—is an illustration of this. What is often overlooked is that straight people also have conversations in which their attraction to the opposite sex is discussed, but in their case it is not called coming out—it's called talking.

My own coming out was a three-step process that extended over thirty-four years. (One of the signs of the progress we have made is that younger people have increasingly been able to carry out this process with more speed—and less angst.) My first coming out was to myself, at the age of thirteen, in 1953. A friend commented during horseplay that I seemed to be acting "queer." I'm pretty sure he didn't mean it seriously, but my reaction was one of horror.

This occurred one year before the national icon, President Dwight Eisenhower, promulgated an executive order declaring that those of us who were gay or lesbian were unworthy of serving our own federal government because our alleged degenerate moral character and susceptibility to blackmail made us security risks. (President Bill Clinton, to his credit, explicitly abolished this order, and we no longer face security clearance problems.)

"The notion that I would have chosen to identify with a group that seemed universally despised is as stupid a view as is possible for a rational human being to hold."

At thirteen, however, I could not see the progress that was to come, and I was terrified, depressed, and determined never to tell anybody. The notion that I would have chosen to identify with a group that seemed universally despised is as stupid a view as is possible for a rational human being to hold. While there are aspects of virtually every debate that seem to me reasonable when actual public policy is concerned, the notion that people choose their sexuality falls entirely outside that category.

For the next twenty-six years, I did everything I could to conceal my sexuality; I shared it only when I sought sexual contact. I faced a decision in 1972 when I ran for a seat in the Massachusetts State House—three years after the Stonewall Rebellion in New York City, when the gay rights movement, as it was then called, had begun to surface. Although I was running in a district in downtown Boston that was fairly sophisticated in its social attitudes, it seemed clear to me that if I were honest about my

> **"I soon learned that a vigorous and successful career cannot compensate for a cramped and repressed private life."**

sexuality, I would not get elected, so I opted to remain closeted. I did, however, promise myself that I would not shy away from being an advocate of gay rights, and in December 1972, I became the first state legislator in Massachusetts history to file bills seeking to outlaw prejudice against gay people in employment and to repeal the sodomy laws.

I tried hard to maintain a duality for the next few years, but it was a serious strain. I spent a good deal of time socializing with gay and lesbian people and receiving praise for my role as a gay rights advocate. But I soon learned that a vigorous and successful career cannot compensate for a cramped and repressed private life. In fact, frustrations that come from deprivation in the latter creep into the public part, and can lead to people becoming less effective in their careers.

As I approached my fortieth birthday in 1980, I regretted that I had made a very significant sacrifice of a healthy private life—which I saw so many others enjoying in my political associations with gay men and women—and I decided to join those who were being open about who they were. It had seemed clear to me by 1977 that I was unlikely to get elected to an office beyond the one I then held. While I thought fondly of going to Congress, the incumbent congressman in the district in which I lived, Tip O'Neil, was unlikely to give up the speakership to which he had just been elected, and the prospect of remaining in the Massachusetts legislature while closeted became less and less attractive. I had by that time finished law school. I planned to serve another couple of terms, become a practicing lawyer, and then come out publicly which, given my legislative service and work as a top assistant to the mayor of Boston, would have helped me gain a platform for gay rights advocacy while practicing law as a career.

So I began to come out for the second time. I selected a handful of people whom I believed I could trust with what seemed to me at the time—I'm a little embarrassed now to think about it—an enormously big deal. I told my three siblings and my adult nieces, as well as a handful of close personal and political friends. Two of them were prominent gay leaders, one of whom said he was not at all surprised. When I asked why, he told me that when we spent time together, he always noticed at whom I would look. The other was Steve Endean, then an emerging gay rights leader, who later told me he was greatly disappointed because he had been making a point of noting the number of prominent straight legislators who were advocates of the cause and was finding us one by one confiding in him that he did not have that much straight support after all.

This process went forward slowly and with a great deal of drama as I approached people, sought privacy, and unburdened myself—and at that time, being gay still seemed like a burden.

Then politics and religion intervened. I had become fairly prominent as a liberal state legislator, and one mile from where I lived was the boundary of the district that had been extremely well represented for ten years by Robert Drinan, a liberal Democrat and a Jesuit priest. In 1980, Pope John Paul II, having recently succeeded to the papacy, issued a decree directing all priests to leave elective politics. Although anguished by this, Father Drinan announced he would not run for reelection. I announced my candidacy for his seat shortly thereafter—and the closet door slammed shut once again. I spent from May to November running for Congress.

There then ensued a period that lasted until early 1987 during which I was elected to Congress, reelected after a tough redistricting battle, and resumed the role I had tried to play in the state legislature: that of an elected official concealing his homosexuality while fighting for gay rights. However, there was one difference. When I got to Washington, I decided (partly because I was four hundred miles from my district) that I could live more honestly as a gay man privately, while still being very discreet—to use a nice word for deception—publicly.

Once again, it didn't work. Abraham Lincoln's insight is as relevant to an individual as it was to a country: I could not live half slave and half free, privately free to be a gay man but publicly a slave to the prejudice that would not allow me to acknowledge it or act appropriately. After several years, I realized I had to choose, and in early 1987 I decided to be honest about my sexuality, even if it came at a cost to my career, which at that point seemed very possible.

How to let my constituents know then became the issue. An interesting dance had evolved over the previous couple of years. Increasingly, members of the press found out I was gay, including some gay journalists who were themselves declining to be honest publicly (so there was little chance of them outing me). The reporters wanted me to announce it because they knew it would be a good story. But their ethic then—and essentially still today—was that they would not out someone unless he or she had done something wrong that stemmed from being gay or lesbian. The press wanted to write the story about my being gay but

> **"I could not live half slave and half free, privately free to be a gay man but publicly a slave to the prejudice that would not allow me to acknowledge it or act appropriately."**

did not want to initiate it; I was ready to come out voluntarily, but I also did not want to initiate the story. My view was that I could survive politically by acknowledging that I was gay, but that I would have to minimize it, as was then often the fashion. How could I tell voters that being gay was no big deal if I went to the trouble of announcing it?

A deadlock resulted. Then, wanting to avoid the potential embarrassment of another newspaper breaking the story first, the main newspaper in my district, the *Boston Globe*, decided it would ask.

To my pleasant surprise, Kay Longcope, a distinguished lesbian reporter and the first out journalist at the *Globe*, arrived in Washington to ask me the question. I had very carefully—and very nervously—prepared, and had my answer ready.

"Are you gay?" Longcope asked me with her tape recorder running in my DC office.

"Yes," I replied. "So what?"

The article appeared in the *Globe* on May 30, and that day I marched in the 1987 Memorial Day march in South Attleboro, Massachusetts, my first public appearance as a gay man.

A number of my liberal colleagues and personal friends had urged me not to come out, and Tip O'Neil had even cautioned his staff to be ready to deal with media inquiries because "Barney Frank is going to come out of the room." Their argument was that by acknowledging being gay, I would diminish my ability to work with them on a number of issues important to them, to me, and to the country—that I would become a one-issue candidate. I could not refute them because I was not certain that they were incorrect. I did tell them that I simply could not live any longer in the anguished, self-denying situation in which I became more and more active publicly and more and more cramped privately.

> "I simply could not live any longer in the anguished, self-denying situation in which I became more and more active publicly and more and more cramped privately."

Indeed, while they did not know it, it was in trying to deal with those pressures that I had behaved recklessly by engaging with a hustler. And one of the advantages of my coming out publicly in 1987 is that when that hustler made a series of accusations against me in 1989, it helped some of my straight friends understand why, two years prior, I had decided to come out voluntarily: I had understood how unwisely I had behaved in trying to reconcile my public and private selves.

In the twenty years since then, being gay has had no negative impact on my career—it has, in fact, been somewhat helpful. I am better able to do a job that includes a good deal of interpersonal relationships now that my work life is balanced by a satisfying private life. And as a liberal Democrat, I have the strong support of my political allies, unlike the hostility facing gay Republicans from within their own party.

I now chair the Committee on Financial Services in the House of Representatives. The only time my being gay comes up is when I mention it—and I mention it because I don't want the people with whom I deal, including those at the highest levels of world finance, to forget that I am one of those people against whom prejudice is still a factor. As I said on the floor of the House during the debate on the bill to ban discrimination in employment based on sexual orientation, I'm a big shot now, and I don't have to worry about being mistreated.

But I remember the terror of fearing that people would find out about my sexuality and the mistreatment that I knew would result. Being protected against that mistreatment now must not mean that I forget what I faced then—what millions of Americans still face. So I am happy to say that the third time I came out was the charm, and it has put me in a position to carry on the fight against this dreadful prejudice more effectively than I ever thought I could.

Above: John Amaechi (third from left), pre-NBA days, in England

JOHN AMAECHI
Former NBA Basketball Player

I'm rarely speechless, but it's hard to fully articulate my admiration for John Amae-chi and what he has done with his life. John is the first NBA basketball player to come out publicly, and since doing so in 2007, three years after leaving the NBA, he has been a full-time role model for gay kids everywhere.

We learn in this chapter about the unspoken discrimination in sports and how debilitating it can be. I hope athletically gifted kids and adults will read this   not only the gay ones, to see that they are not alone, but also the straight ones, to learn how accepting their gay teammates would allow these outstanding athletes to make even stronger contributions to their teams.

John is also much more than one of six male professional athletes to come out. He is fully committed to helping kids, and especially gay kids struggling to find safe and caring environments. He is a spokesperson for the Human Rights Campaign's Coming Out Project and supports many other groups including GLSEN and The Trevor Project. In England, he started the ABC Foundation and its Amaechi Basket-ball Centre to further his belief that "no child should go un-coached: in life or in sport." Read more in John's best-selling autobiography, *Man in the Middle*.

I didn't pick up a basketball until I was seventeen, but from then on I didn't stop till I reached the NBA. It took six years from my first practice to starting for the Cleveland Cavaliers—a long road in a short time for a boy from Manchester, England.

My road to accepting my sexual orientation took much longer. I first realized I was gay when I was nine or ten, but I never used the word and my name in the same sentence, even in my head, until I was at least twenty-three. Growing up, no one else ever said anything about it to me. All they ever talked about was my height—six feet ten inches—and my color.

I was born in Boston, in 1970, to a Nigerian father and English mother. My parents divorced when I was four, and I moved with my mother and two younger sisters to England. At eighteen, I came back to America alone to play basketball, attending senior year of high school in Ohio. I played college basketball at Vanderbilt University and then won a basketball scholarship to Penn State.

I can trace my first same-sex attraction to my primary-school friend, Paul, who lived on our street. I remember telling my mother, "I like Paul. I like him a lot." Then I added, "I more than like Paul." My mom didn't say anything, although it may have been what prompted her to ask one of my sisters several years later if I were gay. I never got to tell my mom myself; she passed away young, at fifty, a year before I made it into the NBA. But I have no doubt what her response would have been. In fact, my sister had asked my mom if it would matter if I were gay, and mom had said no.

I did date girls in secondary school. Well, not many . . . maybe two. I asked one of them out simply because she was the other "brown" person in school, and kids said, "Aren't you supposed to be together because you're both brown?" She called me the day after our date and said, "Let's not do that again." Then I went out with one of my favorite teacher's daughters, and that didn't go well either. After that, I knew instinctively partnering with a woman was not in my future.

> "I did what many gay people do—denied the pain of my isolation and focused on other things."

For the rest of school, I had no social life. Certainly none in terms of other gay people—I didn't know any. One of my sisters later told me she thought I was asexual because she never saw me be attracted to anyone. Instead, I did what many gay people do—denied the pain of my isolation and focused on other things. It started with academics. I made a chart of all the people in my school I had to beat academically and compared our scores weekly.

At night in my bed I'd make myself focus on contentment. *What's the point in trying to be happy?* I'd tell myself. *Let's try not to be completely miserable.* My lowered expectations started early.

The first gay person I met was my sister's friend Johnny from theater class. How exotic he was. I said to myself, *Ah, so that's a gay person.* I couldn't relate to him, partly because he was an actor and I definitely wasn't. But what struck me was his comfort level. He radiated confidence. I can still picture my sister saying, "He's gay," and the guy didn't flinch. Just hearing the word *gay* in those days hurt me physically. It was like being punched.

> **"Just hearing the word *gay* in those days hurt me physically. It was like being punched."**

* * *

I started playing basketball because a scout approached me on the street in Manchester and asked if I wanted to play. I'm still not sure why I said yes. I had no particular interest in sports. But it quickly turned out to have a big benefit: The number one reaction to seeing someone my size is to laugh—and whether it's a nervous reaction or otherwise, the impact on me is the same. However, from my first day in the gym, that great embracing atmosphere made me feel less like a freak. I went from being this six-foot-ten-inch-tall person that everyone stared at to a valuable commodity. Despite the fact that I had absolutely no skills, people looked at me and said, "I want him on my team." From that moment on, there was nothing else in my life.

It wasn't until I came to this country that being gay became a constant distraction. I knew right away I could never be out and win a spot in the NBA. At college, the incongruence in my life was overwhelming. On many occasions, I'd be under the shower for thirty minutes telling myself, *I cannot be this person. I'm John Amaechi. I'm captain of a Big Ten basketball team. I cannot be this person.*

It's devastating every time you have to censor yourself. You see your team-mates checking out a female volleyball player in the gym with abandon. But you can't even look at another man's face too long. And while some of it may be your own paranoia, a lot of it is legitimate. I can still hear, "Why are you looking at him for that long?"

"I knew right away I could never be out and win a spot in the NBA."

People have a finite amount of psychic energy, in the scientific sense. If you want to be elite, every tiny percentage has to be devoted to your performance. So maybe you don't take the energy you need to hide who you are from your "performance" area. Maybe you take it from your "social happiness" area instead. And you tell yourself, forget about that.

But it's tough over a long period of time. And to have a successful sports career, you have to keep it up. After playing with the Cavaliers for a year, they didn't re-sign me, so I played in Europe for three years while attempting to return to the NBA. It wasn't until 2001, at age thirty-one, that I signed a ten-million-dollar contract with the Utah Jazz. I had been in the closet twenty years.

* * *

People say professional sports are particularly homophobic. But it's an excuse for a society with a horrible blemish to assign blame to one segment that's both small and notorious for being stupid. Sports does not inform society. Society informs sports. Athletes live up to the expectations we have of them.

You also hear about the issue of trust. But that's the ultimate double bind. When I came out, one of the most powerful players in basketball, Cleveland Cavalier forward Lebron James, said of professional sports teams, "We spend so much time together, we're like family. You take showers together; you're on the bus; you talk about things. With teammates, you have to be trustworthy. If you're gay and you're not admitting that you are, you're not trustworthy. It's the locker room code. It's a trust factor."

But where is his reassurance to those of us on the other side? Where's that trust factor? Does he say, "If you did come out to me, I would embrace you as part of my team"? Because one word from a player like Lebron ends a career.

He's that powerful. All he has to say is "I'm not playing with that guy," and it's over. So any gay player on his team right now isn't coming out.

Why would someone? There's so much to lose. People focus on the money, on losing endorsements. But it's not only about that, or losing your job, or even your love of the game. It's your whole identity. Imagine walking through airports or down the street and having people want to be you. Now imagine choosing to go from that to what it will be like the day after you announce you're gay. Say you're a kid from a one-parent family in the Bronx who made it from nothing. Everything you've achieved disappears, and suddenly you're just a big gay guy. The psychological and emotional gulf is so wide; it's like losing yourself. You evaporate in a second.

To come out as an active player today, you'd have to be superb, indispensable to your team. And the problem isn't just with your fifteen teammates. It's also with the owners, fans, and society at

> **"The psychological and emotional gulf is so wide; it's like losing yourself."**

large. Even now, most of my teammates talk about me fondly, but some won't talk to me. And the ones who do, prefer that I don't mention they're still my friends because it makes them uncomfortable. It puts them in a position of having to take sides. And one thing athletes don't do well is take sides, especially when it's political. They can't bite the hand that feeds them.

* * *

Even when I wasn't out publicly, many of my teammates knew I was gay. My friends hung out in the stands and family room with my teammates' wives and girlfriends. And all my friends were gay. Soon after college I had decided I wouldn't have any friends who didn't know I was gay—and in my world, that pretty much meant having only gay friends, and some were not the most butch looking. But my teammates just didn't talk about it. They wouldn't ask me what I did on the weekend so they wouldn't run the risk that I'd tell them. It was "don't ask/don't tell."

There are hundreds of professional sports people in this position. People know. They see them with their "manager" all the time, and they see the one time they slip up and put their hand in the small of his back. But on a cerebral level, they also know they're all teammates.

I'm always asked about the locker room. Yes, there's been a homoerotic element to sports since Homer. But the whole idea that gay people in the locker room will somehow launch themselves at people is absurd. It's a workplace issue. The analogy in an office would be that I'm in the cubicle next to you and I'm going to launch myself over the partition and rape you.

Of course, nudity in the locker room compounds the fears. But note that the media is allowed in the locker room just ten minutes after a basketball game. I always made it a point to be showered and changed before they arrived. But not everyone does. Everything is contextual; there's a difference between work and a romantic situation.

Although I've only recently come out in this country, I've been out for a decade in England. There is a different attitude there. I was the first Englishman to play in the NBA and was considered a good role model for the country. I believe people were aware of what a distraction it could be in this country if they said, "He's a good basketball player. Oh, and he's gay as well." Even today, the fact that I'm a PhD candidate and have been practicing psychology for four years is always less important in the scheme of things. People say, "You're the gay guy who played basketball." Why should that one aspect of your life—the fact that you are gay—be the main thing people use to identify you after all you've achieved and all you are as a person?

> "But the whole idea that gay people in the locker room will somehow launch themselves at people is absurd."

In this country, images of gay people have been limited for so long. And while I do not for a second think that Jack from *Will & Grace* is not a legitimate gay role model, if people only think of Jack, that's damaging. In 2007, I was speaking to a group of people in New York, and a woman came up to me afterwards and said, "Thank you for doing this because before I met you I didn't realize black people could be gay." Now that's a tragedy.

I retired in 2004 and came out three years later. I didn't expect my story to be headline news, but it was. Most people were supportive. However, among the thousands of e-mails I received were a number of death threats. I remain glad that I chose to come out as it has helped create dialogue about being gay in sports and society. I hope this dialogue will help kids realize they aren't alone.

TAMMY BALDWIN
Congresswoman from Wisconsin

This year marks Congresswoman Tammy Baldwin's tenth year in the House of Representatives. In 1998, she became both the first woman in Wisconsin elected to the U.S. Congress and the first person to win a House seat as an openly gay nonincumbent. Over the years, Tammy has not only worked to achieve equality for all Americans through legislation. She has also made her efforts personal by bringing her partner of twelve years, Lauren Azar, to congressional events, providing her fellow policy makers with an understanding of the need for acceptance in a way they can't miss. Tammy is a true role model for teens and their parents, reminding them that kids can be themselves and succeed in a very public arena. In many ways, her honesty, integrity, and courage make her a role model for us all.

My interest in public service was apparent to me much earlier than my sexual orientation. I can date it back to middle school, in my hometown of Madison, Wisconsin, where I first ran for student council in 1974. My love for it continued through high school and college, when I realized

I wanted a career in politics. I began asking myself: Would I run for public office? Would I become a lobbyist?

About the same time, I had a dramatic awakening. In my junior year of college, I fell in love with a woman. It hit me like a ton of bricks. I remember thinking, *No wonder there weren't any sparks and it didn't go any further with those guys!* Like my girlfriends, I had dated guys in high school. And they were lovely guys. In fact, I recently got together with probably my most serious boyfriend in high school, and I still adore him—but not in the sense of marriage.

> **"I remember thinking, *No wonder there weren't any sparks and it didn't go any further with those guys!"***

Although I was thrilled to be in a relationship that finally felt right, I kept thinking about its effect on my future career. I didn't know any gay politicians. I didn't even know any gay adults. I was absolutely certain I'd eventually have to make a choice.

In the supportive atmosphere of Smith College, a women's college in Massachusetts, my girlfriend and I began coming out to friends. We quickly learned there was an active lesbian community on campus. That was one big difference between realizing I was gay in college versus high school: It was much easier to meet gay people my own age.

Another difference was that documentaries about the gay liberation movement were first appearing. I don't know if I'd have been able to see them when I was in high school without my family finding out. And it was important for me to see them because they helped me create a context for my new self. I didn't have a gay family to join; so what was I becoming a part of?

While I was thinking about my political future, I was lucky to be learning about gay heroes like Harvey Milk, Frank Kameny, and Del Martin and Phyllis Lyon. It gave me instant role models—not people I could actually talk with but whose stories helped me realize my world wasn't ending.

At Smith, I felt safe. However, I knew after graduation I'd head home to Wisconsin for law school and to be closer to my recently widowed eighty-year-old grandmother. Even though home is liberal Madison, I was worried. My first girlfriend had a tough time with initial rejection by her family, and watching that scared me. Actually, the more I think about it, I remember it terrified me. I hadn't yet told my grandmother, mother, or friends from high school. I kept thinking: *This is big. It's life altering. Sure, I've read about those heroic figures. But what makes me think I can do what they did?*

Growing up in my grandparents' home, I don't remember any discussions about being gay. Had I been raised in a family that felt women should not be successful, smart, and ambitious, there probably would have been some serious rebellion on my part that might have led to me figuring out and asserting who I am earlier. But my family was quite the opposite. My aunt, for example, followed in my grandfather's footsteps and became a biophysicist at a time when women really didn't get PhDs in that type of work. She blazed a trail in an incredibly male-dominated field, even more than the field I chose, although I'm clearly in a male-dominated field.

My first year back in Madison, I asked each of my dear friends from high school out to dinner, then geared myself up to tell them. I remember one friend being particularly furious—but not for the reason I feared. She said, "How long ago did this happen and how long has it taken you to tell me? I'm your best friend! Didn't you trust me?"

Because I was now in a place where I'd never been out before, I also spent the year figuring out how to meet other gay people. One of my mother's responses to my coming out was to introduce me to her gay friends who, of course, were ten to twenty years older than me. (My mother was trained as a social worker and had gay colleagues. She is, and always has been, an accepting person.) It was wonderful of her and great to have them as resources—although it wasn't the social circle I was looking for.

My grandmother was less comfortable. She sat with it for a long time. Our circumstances, however, were nothing like a teen coming out to parents upon whom they're dependent and fear will kick them out of the house. In this case, she was increasingly dependent on me. I feel blessed she had plenty of time to get used to the idea. She lived to be ninety-four and got to meet people I dated, including my partner of twelve years, Lauren.

I also spent those years in internal debate over whether I could run for local office. I decided to test the waters by working on local campaigns. Through this, I met real-live role models, including Dick Wagner and Kathleen Nichols of the Dane County Board of Supervisors. An out gay man and an out lesbian had gotten elected in the liberal community of Dane County. I felt my question had been answered. I joined them in working on campaigns and eagerly identified myself to them as gay. Thus, by the time I had the opportunity to run for the Dane County Board myself, it wasn't like I *could* go back in the closet.

I remember a big moment right after that first campaign. When journalists had profiled the candidates, they hadn't asked, "And by the way, what is your sexual orientation?" They simply listed me as a single graduate student. (I was in law school.) However, after I won the election, our largest-circulation paper, the *Wisconsin State Journal*, decided to write a series on the gay community, with a different focus each day: the gay bar scene, gays and religion, gays in politics. I accepted an invitation to be interviewed.

> "Thus, by the time I had the opportunity to run for the Dane County Board myself, it wasn't like I *could* go back in the closet."

I was really concerned about the article. I hadn't hidden being a lesbian, but no matter how out I was before, this article would make it public to about fifty thousand people, the paper's circulation at the time. I worried what it would mean; after all, I had a listed address and phone number.

The article was a turning point. Many people who already knew sent messages like, "I'm so proud of you for doing that. You're going to educate lots of people." Some who didn't know had an issue with it, but they were civilized people. The Conservatives kind of grumped. I only had one "hate call" in the middle of the night. But with so much support, it put the negativity in context.

It was a good warm-up for what was to come. I was the county board's third openly gay member; so that barrier had been broken. But when I was elected to the Wisconsin State Legislature, I was its first openly gay member.

And then I ran for Congress. Wisconsin had never elected a woman before, and no state had ever elected a candidate who was out during their campaign. (Gays and lesbians who served before me came out in office and, in most cases, had been elected several times before addressing the issue with their constituencies.)

That's when I started getting some of the hateful stuff—people protesting and sending vitriolic letters and threats. But I didn't feel like it related to me personally or to my coming-out process. It just proved those creeps are out there.

It did, however, have the potential to affect more than me. Being an out public figure also impacts your partner. When I started in politics, I dated a number of women, and depending on factors like whether they were out to their families, it varied as to what risks they felt they could take.

I met my partner Lauren just before running for Congress, so she came into the situation with her eyes open. I think it gave her a chance to be a bit more open in her large corporate law firm. She wasn't necessarily in the closet, but it wasn't something all 350 lawyers knew. As my political career gained momentum, she became more comfortable talking about our lives. When someone asked, "What did you do this weekend?" she'd say, "I was campaigning with my partner for Congress." It was a natural way for her to bond with her colleagues because she wasn't leaving out big parts of her life in discussions with them.

> **"Wisconsin had never elected a woman before, and no state had ever elected a candidate who was out during their campaign."**

* * *

For me, any challenges pale in comparison to how rewarding it is to hear from young people who appreciate what I do. I will never forget a high school student who wrote me from a small town in southern Illinois. He was following a path similar to mine—public service, class president—and thinking, "I'd love to do this for the rest of my life." Then he came out, and it all came crashing down. He was depressed and suicidal. On the Internet, he saw an article about my election to Congress. And it hit him: "I don't have to give up my dreams. And I don't have to give up my life." He wrote to me, and I called him, and we talked about how he had to go for his dreams because then he could have the same effect on others that I'd had on him. Last I heard from him, he was still very politically involved.

Young people approach me at campaign events; others e-mail. I recently got a note saying, "I worked on your campaign just as I was coming out. I don't know how I would have gotten through it if I hadn't seen so many normal, wonderful, contributing citizens around me who happened to be gay and lesbian, too. It showed me a path."

One way we can make a better future for gay kids is through education—of both the gay and the heterosexual communities. And it should start early in life because kids are coming out earlier.

In the 1970s, although I was in one of the country's most progressive public school systems, there was no curriculum that referenced contributions by gays to America or even noted they were part of society.

"I don't want parents to feel they must tell their children not to be who they are in order to keep them safe."

There still hasn't been enough progress on that front. Yet it could be included in so many ways. We could mention that a famous historical figure was gay or talk about the gay rights movement in discussing other social change movements. We could include it in sex education by at least saying, "These people exist, too." That would tell gay kids they have a place in the rich and diverse history of this country. And it would tell heterosexual students that gay people are accepted and valued. Many parents need this information as much as their kids do because they probably grew up deprived of it.

I grapple with the issue of education in my own work on the Employment Non-Discrimination Act and the struggle to pass a bill that includes protection for transgender people. How do I educate my colleagues about Transgender 101? Many are now comfortable with protecting people based on sexual orientation, but we haven't gone the same distance on transgender issues. When I think of the parents of young children dealing with gender identity issues—something Barbara Walters presented so movingly in a 2007 *20/20* segment—I know we must help ensure that these children are protected as well.

When she learned I was gay, one thing my grandmother felt was afraid. She wasn't sure how much the world had changed and didn't want me to be the experiment to see how far it had gotten. I don't want parents to feel they must tell their children not to be who they are in order to keep them safe. I want them to know that the healthiest thing they can say is, "Be who you are, and we'll work to make the world safer together."

HILARY ROSEN
Political Analyst and Media Consultant

Hilary Rosen is president of OurChart.com, a social networking site for lesbians based on the Showtime TV drama *The L Word*. She is also an on-air political analyst for MSNBC and a consultant in the media and technology field. Previously, Hilary was chairman and CEO of the Recording Industry Association of America, where she served for seventeen years during major crossroads in the industry's transition to the digital age.

Hilary was also a founding member of The Human Rights Campaign, the largest gay civil rights organization, and has been a tireless worker for full and equal rights for the gay community. She is smart, thoughtful, and above all, compassionate—on both a professional and a personal level. Four years ago, when I was hospitalized in Washington, DC, where Hilary lives, she was one of my first visitors and a steady one. I will never forget how she doted on me.

I kissed my friend Catherine in fifth grade. We were playing "date." I really did love her—but not in "that way." At least I was pretty sure I didn't. Years later, though, I'd remember that moment and wonder if it were more than a friendly kiss.

I really wasn't one of those girls who always felt like they didn't fit in. In fact, it was the opposite. I always fit in. I was everybody's friend. In my New Jersey high school in the 1970s, my girlfriends and I used to hang around in gangs—which meant we had lots of friends who were boys, and we all went out together. We didn't think of them as dates.

But starting in eleventh grade—driving age basically—things changed. My friends paired up with boys. And boys became more than a passing topic of conversation; they became a preoccupation. I didn't like it, but I played along. It can't be a coincidence that my longest-term boyfriend in high school also turned out to be gay. I guess we felt safe with each other.

> **"I instantly knew that I was gay. And I was scared to death. What about my plans? What about my career?"**

Then we all went off to college. Even though I planned to major in business, I chose a school in Washington, DC. I really wanted to be a senator, but my mother was a politician—the first woman elected to our city council—and by that point in my young life I had already been through enough of her campaigns to know that I never wanted to actually run for office. I had it all figured out, however: I would become CEO of a Fortune 500 company but participate in politics enough so that I would be appointed to a vacancy in the U.S. Senate.

When I got to college, everything exploded. I fell madly, truly, deeply in love with my freshman roommate—yes, the one assigned to my dorm room. It was a dorm scandal because we also had another roommate, who was freaked out. We said we didn't care because we were in love.

But I did care. I cared a lot. I was in love with this girl, and I instantly knew that I was gay. And I was scared to death. What about my plans? What about my career? How could I be this way? I was ashamed and certain that I would be an outcast in the world I had worked so hard to cultivate.

Those early college years were scattered and painful. I can hardly remember ever doing schoolwork. I was living with my girlfriend while dating boys to try and get the "gay" out of me. And I was exploring the reality of what being gay actually meant. I went to the gay student union meetings and found out that we had no rights and no respect in the world and that politics was a means to

> **"I was living with my girlfriend while dating boys to try and get the 'gay' out of me."**

gain what we needed. Well, that was an environment I certainly knew, but I wasn't sure I was ready to put the two halves of my life together yet.

In my sophomore year, I got a job as an intern on Capitol Hill. It was exhilarating. Despite my original plan to go back home and enter the business world in New York City, Washington politics had me hooked. I stayed after graduation.

Around that time, my girlfriend and I broke up. We'd been together for four years, but there had been so much drama and dating of others in between that I knew it really was just a first love. She left DC, and I became a lobbyist at the tender age of twenty-one.

Although my dating life had gotten pretty advanced by then, I still wasn't out professionally. In 1982, I was the Washington lobbyist for the City of San Francisco with Mayor Dianne

> **"Senator, when Jesse Helms goes to the Senate floor to demonize fags, he is talking about me, too. I am gay."**

Feinstein when the AIDS crisis hit. Feinstein chaired the U.S. Conference of Mayors Task Force on AIDS. My job was to help get federal funds to the issue. But senators like Jesse Helms (R-NC) and Orrin Hatch (R-UT) were making it difficult. I had a good relationship with Senator Hatch because of other issues that my firm worked on, so I went to talk to him. I will never forget that conversation.

"Hilary," he said, "why do you care so much about this issue when it affects just a few homosexuals?"

I replied, "Senator, when Jesse Helms goes to the Senate floor to demonize fags, he is talking about me, too. I am gay."

Senator Hatch look stunned. I was, too. I had never said those words out loud at work.

He hugged me. I went back to my office and came out to my boss, and then called Mayor Feinstein and came out to her, too.

Senator Hatch ended up helping us rein in Jesse Helms on a few of those amendments. (I think Senator Ted Kennedy gets more credit for his help, though, than I do.) But that first step I took in Senator Hatch's office was the most enormous relief.

PART 5
What I Know Now
On Losing a Child

The late Anna Wakefield, above, and her mother, Mary Lou Wallner, opposite

MARY LOU WALLNER
Founder, TEACH Ministries

I t started with a phone call late on a Friday night in February 1997. The call was from my ex-husband, informing me that our twenty-nine-year-old daughter, Anna, had committed suicide. She had been found late that afternoon after hanging from the bar in her closet for fifteen hours.

As we drove the 550 miles to the town where Anna had lived and died to plan and attend her funeral, I said to my husband, Bob, that I did not want Anna's death to be in vain. I had no idea what I could do, however, because there was one major complicating factor: Anna was a Christian and a lesbian. And I was a fundamentalist Christian who had been taught all my life that homosexuality was a sin.

I learned of Anna's homosexuality in a "coming-out" letter she wrote to us from college in December 1988. Here is an excerpt from the letter I sent her a few weeks later in response:

> Undoubtedly, the most difficult part of your letter was the gay thing. I will never accept that in you. I feel it's a terrible waste, besides being spiritually and morally wrong. For

a reason I don't quite fathom, I have a harder time dealing with that issue than almost anything in the world. I do
and will continue to love you, but I will always hate that,
and will pray every day that you will change your mind and
attitude.

The years after our letter exchange were stormy at best. I didn't want her
to be a lesbian, and I continued to firmly believe it was a choice she'd made.

What made Anna's death even more difficult was that in August 1996—
eight years after she had first come out to us and just six months before she
died—I received an angry letter from her, cutting off all contact with me.
She told me that I was her mother only in a biological way, that I had done
colossal damage to her soul with my sham-
ing words, and that she did not want to, and
did not have to, forgive me. I was at a loss. I
sought counsel from family and friends, and
they all told me to respect Anna's wishes and give her the space she was asking
for. So I did.

"I did not want Anna's death to be in vain."

* * *

What do I wish I'd done? What would I do now? Grab my toothbrush, credit
card, and car keys, jump in the car, drive to where she lives, and tell her I love
her no matter what. I did not do that, and now I never can.

I had so much to learn. We really don't learn unless we're ready, especially
when it comes to this particular subject. We must want to search and understand. If we don't, no amount of information thrust upon us will penetrate
our hearts. I would give anything to go back in time with an open heart. But
while Anna was alive, I was unteachable.

"What do I wish I'd done? Grab my toothbrush, credit card, and car keys, jump in the car, drive to where she lives, and tell her I love her no matter what."

After Anna took her life, I
needed some answers. I began to
read everything I could get my
hands on. I read books about grief,
grace, suicide, and even homosexuality. Somehow, I had to try to
understand what had happened

to Anna that caused her so much emotional pain that suicide was her only answer.

"What if I had condemned her in my heart, and sometimes to her face, without reason?"

One book I read was Mel White's autobiography, *Stranger at the Gate: To Be Gay and Christian in America*. As I read, I began to wonder: What if Anna hadn't chosen to be a lesbian? What if I had condemned her in my heart, and sometimes to her face, without reason?

I decided to e-mail Mel to tell him Anna's story and let him know his book had made me take a hard look at the topic of homosexuality. He e-mailed me back with words full of compassion for the grief I was now experiencing and the pain Anna had suffered as a gay Christian rejected by her church and her family.

A few months later, in October 1999, Mel convinced us to come to Lynchburg, Virginia, to meet with his newly formed organization, Soulforce, and tell my story to two hundred lesbian, gay, bisexual, and transgender people. I had only five minutes to share it. As I spoke of Anna's tragic death, I watched people in the audience weeping openly, and I struggled to keep my own tears under control. Bob and I were astounded at the number of people who approached us afterward and said, "You just told my story, only I haven't gotten as far as the suicide part—yet."

I began to wonder if what I'd been taught all my life in church was true. Soon after we got home from Lynchburg, I e-mailed Mel to thank him for paying our way to this life-changing weekend. He e-mailed back just three words: Do your homework! And so we did.

"I began to wonder if what I'd been taught all my life In church was true."

In about a year's time after reading everything we could get our hands on, talking to people on both sides of the issue, studying the "clobber passages" (a handful of Bible verses that seem to condemn homosexuality), and praying to be shown God's truth—our beliefs were revolutionized. We began to understand that we must never take Bible verses out of the context and the culture of the day in which they were written. We came to understand that several passages in the Bible speak of same-gender sex. But in every instance, the Bible is talking about heterosexuals who, filled with lust, became sexual perverts. The Bible says nothing about innate homosexuality as we know it today, or about people of the same gender living in loving, committed, monogamous relationships. We discovered that homosexuality is not a choice and, therefore, cannot be a sin.

"We were finding out what it was like to be the object of the church's hatred for gay people."

In 2002, my husband and I formed TEACH Ministries. (TEACH is an acronym for To Educate About the Consequences of Homophobia.) We began traveling around the country to tell our story to anyone who would listen. We felt that if telling it could save just one life, it would be worth it.

* * *

Ten years after Anna's death, *People* magazine featured our story in its November 19, 2007, issue. We never dreamed we'd get hundreds of e-mails in response—or that some would be nasty and downright hateful. After all, almost all the groups to which I'd spoken in the past had been friendly. Not so with all *People* magazine readers. While most were positive, the negative e-mails really rocked me back on my heels. This was something new for us.

One person wrote, "Christians should love the person but not their sin. It appears *People* magazine hunted down the most left-wing nuts to agree with you in your drive to make homosexual behavior become accepted. Perhaps your daughter's death is an indictment of the homosexual lifestyle? Never thought of that? You just assumed it was because people weren't tolerant enough, right? Shame on you." We were finding out what it was like to be the object of the church's hatred for gay people. Having once been much less accepting, it was very unsettling.

Being one of five families featured in the award-winning documentary *For the Bible Tells Me So* has also had a tremendous impact on us, as it has had on many others. About homosexuality and Christianity, it has appeared in theaters across the country and is now being shown in educational institutions, churches, and community centers worldwide. It has really made a difference in the lives of many Christian families with gay children.

Are you wondering how to prevent what happened to my family from happening to others? The answer is simple. Get to know gay men and lesbians. Do your homework, as we did. If you don't, vital and valuable members of our world will continue to be at risk—of religious bigotry, hate crimes, and suicide.

For more on Mary Lou and Bob Wallner's TEACH Ministries, visit its website at www.teach-ministries.org, as well as that of For the Bible Tells Me So, *www.forthebibletellsmeso.org.*

The late Sean Kennedy, above, and with his mother,
Elke Kennedy, on his prom night, opposite

ELKE KENNEDY
Founder, Sean's Last Wish

The phone woke me out of a sound sleep. I glanced at the clock; it was 4:30 a.m. I had a bad feeling in my stomach that got worse when I heard the voice at the other end. Someone from Greenville Hospital told me that something had happened to my son Sean, and I needed to get there as fast as possible. I asked if Sean was okay, but the person would only say that I should come right away.

I jumped out of bed, threw on some clothes, and woke my husband. So many thoughts were going through my mind. He must be okay, right? What could have happened?

As I drove to the hospital the sinking feeling in my stomach got worse, but I tried to stay calm. My husband also reassured me. I called my ex-husband, Sean's dad, to tell him something had happened and that I was on my way to the hospital.

At the hospital, I was met by several of Sean's friends. They were crying, and I could only get bits and pieces of what had happened. I started to think it might be worse than I had imagined. I told the nurse at the ER desk who I was, and she said I couldn't see Sean yet because they were still running tests. They brought all of us to a separate waiting room, and a pastor came to talk with us. That's when I knew it was really serious.

I noticed one of Sean's friends had blood on her jeans. She told me that she was the one who had found him outside Brew's, a local bar, held him until the ambulance came, and rode with him to the hospital. We cried together, and I tried to console her. I told her I was sure Sean would be okay. He just had to be.

When I finally got to see my son, my knees buckled. He was lying flat on his back, stitches on his upper lip, blood on his hair and neck, hooked up to a respirator. As I stood there holding his hand, he felt so cold. I wanted to hug him, to keep him warm. I kissed him, telling him I was there and that I loved him so much and to please wake up. I remember praying.

A doctor came in and explained that the tests had revealed Sean had severe brain damage and his injuries were not survivable. *What does this mean?* I thought. *That my baby is gone?* I screamed inside and out: *That cannot be; he cannot be gone.* I sank to my knees. My husband lifted me up, and I stood over Sean's bed asking God to let me take his place. He hadn't gotten the chance to live his life.

The next seventeen hours were the toughest. I had to call my older son, who was on vacation, and my daughter, who had just started a job in Germany five days earlier. My son got home in about five hours; my daughter could not get back until Friday, two days later, and never got to say good-bye.

About sixty of Sean's friends and family waited with us at the hospital. They told stories about how they loved Sean and how he had been there for them.

As the day wore on, we learned more about the events of the previous evening. We found out that Sean had been attacked by someone who hated gay people—the last word my son heard was *faggot*. He was the victim of a hate crime—he lost his life for being gay, for being himself and being happy.

At 11:20 p.m. on May 16, 2007, my beautiful Sean was pronounced brain dead. My baby was gone forever. I would never be able to speak with him again, to tell him I love him.

I remembered the last time we spoke. We had an argument about him picking up after himself and turning off lights. It seemed so trivial now.

And then I thought about how, two weeks earlier, Sean had come into my room and given me a huge hug. "You can never die because I could never live without you," he said. I told him that I would probably die before him because that's how life is—children survive their parents. Little did I know.

I left Sean's room and went to the waiting room to tell everyone that Sean had passed on but that he would never be gone from our hearts as long as we remember him. I offered each of his friends the chance to see him one more time. Two at a time, for the next two and a half hours, the nurses and my husband took his friends back to say their good-byes.

Then I made the most difficult call of all—to Sean's sister in Germany to tell her that her brother had just died. I wanted to be there, to hold her; I knew she was all alone. I wish I could have waited till she got home, but I didn't want her to find out over the Internet or from the news. Next to losing Sean, that was hardest for me.

As a mother you have goals, dreams, and hopes for your children before they are even born. I remember when I was carrying Sean that I dreamed of him being a leader—kind, considerate, nonjudgmental, and compassionate about life and other people. But most of all I wanted him to feel loved, to be happy about who he was, and to stand up for what he believed. Years later, when he had first started living his life as openly gay, I had worried about others' intolerance of him. But by then he had become the caring, nonjudgmental person I had dreamed of. And I thought: *How could anybody hate him?*

* * *

On May 16, 2007, at about 3:45 a.m., Sean was leaving a bar in our hometown of Greenville, South Carolina. Three boys sat in a car outside the front door, and one of them called Sean over and asked him for a cigarette. Sean gave him one and was walking away when the guy in the back seat, Stephen Moller, got out of the car, approached my son, and called him "faggot." Then he punched Sean so hard he broke Sean's facial bones and separated his brain from his brain stem. Sean fell backward onto the pavement, and his brain ricocheted in his head.

Sean's murderer got back into the car and left my son to die.

A little later he left a message on the phone of one of the girls Sean knew: "You tell your faggot friend that when he wakes up he owes me $500 for my broken hand."

The prosecutors claimed they could not prove malicious intent on Moller's part, so he was not indicted for murder, which carries a minimum sentence of thirty years to life in South Carolina. Instead, he was indicted for the only other charge applicable in the case, involuntary manslaughter, which carries a sentence of zero to five years. Rather than the maximum sentence of five years, Moller received a five-year suspended service reduced to three year (with credit for the seven months he served in jail before he was released on bond); this means he will only have spent ten months in prison when he becomes eligible for parole. If granted he will be on probation three years. He was also sentenced to anger management classes, ordered to take alcohol and drug counseling and random drug testing, and given 30 days of community service.

As a parent, you live in dread of that 4:30 a.m. call. You look for a safe community in which to raise your children. I thought Greenville was such a place, but I was wrong.

* * *

Sean could never sit still when he heard music. He used to sing "Mr. Jones" to me at the top of his lungs. He could pick up any instrument and play any song he heard on the radio by ear. He was drum major in high school and recruited people to keep the band alive: It went from ten members at the beginning of the school year to over twenty by year's end because of his enthusiasm. One of the members he recruited, who had never thought of being in the band, is now going to the University of Southern California on a band scholarship.

Many evenings, I'd come home to find his friends sleeping on my living room floor. Later, I would find out that he had just befriended many of them that very day. One young man had been thrown out of his Christian university—and his parents' home. Sean found him sitting on the curb, brought him home, listened to him, and gave him food and a change of clothes. The night Sean died, this same young man told me he might not be here today if it hadn't been for Sean's kindness.

After his death, I found out just how many people Sean had touched through his kindness. There were over seven hundred people at his memorial service. He was proud of who he was and stood up for what he believed in. He had reached all the dreams and hopes this mother could ask for, and he had accomplished this in only twenty years. I am so proud to be his mother!

Sean wanted to go to Las Vegas for his twenty first birthday. He wanted to be a Web designer. He wanted to travel—especially to visit his grandmother's grave in Germany. But most of all he wanted equal rights for everybody: from a young age he disliked that some people were treated badly by other people, and he wanted to change that.

Sean knew at an early age that he was different, although he did not let others know until he was about seventeen. One day, after he had just told a few of his friends that he was gay, he found the word *fag* carved into the side of his truck. He was mad and it shook him up, but it was then that he decided that he would not live in fear.

After that, he told me that he was gay. He said, "Mom, if you don't want to love me anymore, I'll understand." I told him there was nothing he could ever do to make me stop loving him.

My son's murder was a hate crime—he lost his life for being gay, for being himself. But there is no hate crimes statute in South Carolina. Within days of Sean's death, I decided to start a foundation. Sean's Last Wish helps get hate crimes legislation introduced and educates the public about hate and violence and the gaps in existing laws, which I found out in South Carolina are greater than I ever imagined.

I have traveled over twenty five thousand miles since his death, speaking at Gay Pride celebrations, universities, and other events in the Carolinas, Georgia, New York, and California. I have met thousands—young people and adults—who have told me stories of being disowned by their parents for being gay. Many have not spoken to their parents in years. Some ask me if I'll be their "mom" because they wish their mom would love and accept them like I loved and accepted Sean. How any mother could discard her child is beyond me. The job of a mother is to love unconditionally.

Here is my message to parents: Don't worry about what the neighbors might say or what your church tells you. Follow your heart. These are your children. Love them, stand by their side, and support them so they can be happy and live life.

I would give anything to have my son back to talk with, hold, and tell him I love him one more time. My son is gone—but your children are still here. What would you do if you got the phone call I got? You might not have time to let them know you love them. Then there are only regrets. Tell them you love them and are there for them right now.

After Sean's death we were no longer welcome at our church. Church friends stopped calling—they didn't want to take sides! We do not belong to any church now. I have been told numerous times by people calling themselves Christians that my son is in hell and that I will go to hell because I love him and I fight for equal rights for all human beings. Although it hurts terribly when people say these things to me, it is nothing compared to the pain of losing my son.

The God I know and love tells us to love one another and not judge. I am glad I have my faith and my personal relationship with God. That is what has helped me through the last year.

Everyone has a right to his or her religious beliefs. But we all have an equal duty to work for the dignity of all human beings. Equal rights are guaranteed to us by our Constitution. And no one has the right to force his or her beliefs on others—especially when those beliefs support violence against others.

My son had a love for life and an irresistible smile to go with his generous personality. He never judged and was always there to help. Sean will live on in our hearts. His last gift to us was the gift of life: By donating his organs, he was able to help five people who are all doing well today.

Please don't blindly follow what people tell you. Research for yourself, and no matter what, be true to your children. Love them every day while you have them.

We all have to stand together to stop the harm. No mother should ever have to bury her child. No mother should ever have to lose her child to hate and violence. No mother should have to fight for justice for her child.

PART 6
The Sin Question

LOOKING TO THE PAST
FOR THE FUTURE

BY MITCHELL GOLD

Here is a crucial question that some religious communities will have to resolve to overcome the harmful division that has become associated with the issue of sexual orientation—a question that will soon move to the forefront of how people of faith address sexual orientation in America: Is having or expressing affection toward a member of the same sex a sin?

To understand the question, let's look to—and learn from—the past. A Southern Baptist minister from Georgia, Dr. David Gushee wrote a thought-provoking book, *Righteous Gentiles of the Holocaust*, in which he discusses why so many people who called themselves Christians either took part in the extermination of six million Jews during the Holocaust or stood by while it took place—a behavior he views as not much better than that of the perpetrators'.

After Hitler came to power, what enabled him to carry out such brutality? Dr. Gushee believes it was the Christian churches' long history of preaching that Jews were sinners and killers of Christ.

A member of the First Baptist Church in Decatur, Georgia, Dr. Gushee has served in various ministries, including several years as a co-pastor of a Jackson, Georgia, Baptist church and as an interim pastor in a Presbyterian congregation. His credentials have included many years of service on the Christian Ethics Study Commission of the Baptist World Alliance as well as a leadership role in helping Baptist colleges and intellectuals articulate their visions for the twenty-first century. He is currently the distinguished university professor of Christian ethics at McAfee School of Theology at Mercer University. An author of nine books, he is also a contributing editor for *Christianity Today*.

Dr. Gushee is still trying to figure out how same-sex orientation relates to sin. In an article for the *Associated Baptist Press* on May 1, 2008, entitled "On Homosexuality: Whose Narrative Do We Believe?" he wrote the following:

> Either homosexual behavior is by definition sinful, or it is not. If it is sinful by definition, then presumably it must be resisted like any other sin. If it is not sinful by definition, then the homosexuality issue is a liberation/justice struggle for a victimized group. Probably the right answer to this question will be very clear to everyone (that is, to 99% of all reasonable Christian human beings) in 100 years, as the proper positions on slavery and Nazism and civil rights and Apartheid are to modern-day Christians. But in real time, right now, it is tearing churches and denominations apart here and around the world.

Dr. Gushee is not an advocate for equal civil rights for lesbian, gay, bisexual, and transgender people; he is not yet sure what position to take. He belongs to a denomination that forbids gays from being out members of its churches or—needless to say—in the clergy. Dr. Gushee is not like the few clergy (compared with the number of clergy in America) who have taken a moral stand against the legal and spiritual discrimination gay people face today.

My hope is that after reading this book, Dr. Gushee and others like him will come to recognize that being gay is not a sin, and that our gay brothers and sisters are entitled not to special rights, but merely to the full set of rights enjoyed by other Americans. Think deeply about the damage that will be incurred if we have to wait another hundred years: the suicides and horrible depression that you have read about in this book. Search for the right answer within yourselves to guide your behavior today.

Women are not inferior to men. Jews are not Christ killers deserving of extermination. The Bible does not support the enslavement of African-Americans. And being gay is not a sin.

I am not a Christian theologian; I am one of the oppressed people oppressed by those claiming to be "Christians"—I use Dr. Gushee's quotes around "Christians" the same way that he has. In his book, he goes on to write, "The Holocaust was not merely an event in Christian history but in fact a nauseating Christian moral failure. What makes this moral failure all the worse is that it has never been adequately addressed by those who bear the name of Christ."

I've thought a long time about his use of the word *nauseating*. It's a familiar feeling: Whenever I think about the people I know who have lived through the agony of thinking they are sinners because of something they heard in their church or family—Jarrod Parker, Irene Monroe, Jared Horsford, Mel White, Bishop Gene Robinson, and others in this book—I do get physically ill. I'm brought to tears and have knots in my stomach. The pain and agony of what they have gone through is nothing less than debilitating.

Dr. Gushee concludes:

> We study the Righteous Gentiles because we want to nurture the kind of people who . . . would want to create communities of Christian people—communities of Muslims, Buddhists, Jews, secularists, human beings—who are prepared to risk all to stand with victims rather than hide in neutrality or join in victimization. We return to the past to learn from our predecessors, people who spent years in an unimaginably intense moral crucible. Those who melted under this heat, and especially those who withstood it, have much to teach us. If we can learn something about the nature of a morally discerning and courageous way of life, and about what may be done to nurture such virtues today, then our study will have been well worth this effort.

Of course, I am not comparing the extermination of six million Jews to the emotional and physical harm that has been done to gay people. But I am comparing the root causes of both. That's the critical point.

Some religious teachings have set the stage so Americans go to the voting booth and vote to bring real harm to people of all ages, and the future will have them saying they didn't know. This book has been written so all will know the real pain and harm that are caused by playing the sin card.

Dr. Gushee, today, like others, struggles with whether or not he will become a "righteous heterosexual" and join this struggle for justice for me and the millions of other gay human beings. I hope as you read the following chapters it becomes abundantly clear which side of history you should choose to stand on. Today, become part of what history will record as righteous heterosexuals.

HOMOSEXUALITY IS NOT A SIN

BY JIMMY CREECH
Former Pastor,
United Methodist Church

Over thirty years ago, Jimmy Creech came to a crossroads. He was a reverend in the United Methodist Church, and one of his congregants, Adam, told him that he was gay. Jimmy was taken by surprise, as this man did not fit any stereotype he had known; Adam was a successful businessperson and upstanding member of the church. Jimmy decided to learn more about homosexuality. He studied the Bible and also immersed himself in the science that progress had brought. That path of discovery has made him the supporter of gay rights he is today.

D eclaring same-gender sexual intimacy to be sinful has been conventional teaching in Christian churches since the thirteenth century—not as long as some would claim. This came to be because the church declared all forms of sexual intimacy without the potential for human conception—including intimacy between men and women—to be sinful. The spiritual, emotional, and social consequences for gay people have been horrific.

Homosexuality as we understand it today was not known in the thirteenth century. Sexual orientation—including homosexuality, heterosexuality, and bisexuality—was "discovered" in the late nineteenth century as an essential component of human personality by the emerging science of human psychology. Today, the human sciences recognize that all sexual orientations occur naturally and describe them as normal and healthy. Unfortunately, religion has continued to classify homosexuality and bisexuality as sinful.

Sin is among the most powerful words in the English language. While its biblical meaning is "separation from God," it is commonly used to refer to behavior considered objectionable, even hated, by God. No self-respecting person of moral character wants to sin or be known as a sinner. To be labeled a sinner is to be rejected by God and society.

When someone says "homosexuality is sinful," or "it's a sin to be gay or lesbian," the focus is usually on behavior. But in the minds and hearts of lesbian and gay youths, being gay is not necessarily about being sexually active. It's about who they are: their feelings, thoughts, and desires; their very being; what they know to be natural, normal, and right.

Being gay is not about behavior; it's about relationships. It's about whom an adult loves, marries, and creates a family with. Behavior is something one does on occasion; sexual orientation is someone's inescapable identity. A gay person who is not sexually active is still gay. Sexual orientation is as fundamental and constant as one's DNA. Unlike behavior, which one can choose to stop, no one can stop being gay or lesbian—any more than someone could choose to stop being straight.

To label as sin a person's sexual orientation is an act of spiritual violence. It defines the personal core, the very essence of a young person's identity, as sinful. Believing you're a sinner because you're lesbian, gay, bisexual, or transgender creates severe emotional and mental anguish, especially for young people. Not knowing whom to trust or talk with about it, and feeling alone with the struggle to be who you are, creates a deeply personal crisis. Low self-esteem, self-hatred, and fear of exposure often result in ruined lives, broken families, depression, and, much too often, suicide.

Sexual orientation is not a moral category. Being gay is no less moral than being nongay. Sexual love between two people is healthy and moral, regardless of their genders. When there's abuse, exploitation, or disrespect, sexual behavior between two people is unhealthy and immoral, regardless of their genders.

As it has in other areas of human experience, religion has lagged behind science in accepting and embracing the human reality of lesbian, gay, bisexual, and transgender people. Once, religion deemed women inferior to men. Once, religion deemed interracial marriage sinful. Human experience and scientific understanding over time changed cultural attitudes from disapproval to acceptance in regard to women and race; religion then followed suit.

Given the greater experiential and scientific understanding and acceptance of people who are gay, it's time for religion to stop teaching that homosexuality is a sin. The need for this change is urgent. Religious teachings must be as responsible to experiential and scientific knowledge as to theological tradition. Any understanding of God is diminished when human experience and scientific truth are denied.

Some religious groups have made this change: the Episcopal Church, USA; the United Church of Christ; the Unitarian Universalist Association of Congregations; the United Church of Canada; the Anglican Church of Canada; the Moravian Church; the Methodist Church of Great Britain; the Friends General Conference; Conservative, Reconstructionist, and Reform Judaism; and the Metropolitan Community Church. In addition, every major Christian denomination has internal organized efforts to change their teachings and policies that exclude and persecute lesbian, gay, bisexual, and transgender people. If you're affiliated with a religious body that hasn't made the change, help make it happen. The lives of lesbian, gay, bisexual, and transgender youth are at stake.

Jimmy Creech is the former executive director of Faith in America. He was an ordained minister for almost thirty years until, in 1999, his credentials of ordination were taken from him when he was found guilty of "disobedience to the Order and Discipline of The United Methodist Church" because he conducted a marriage ceremony for two men. Jimmy lives in Raleigh, North Carolina.

HOMOSEXUALITY, THE BIBLE, AND US

BY REV. DR. H. STEPHEN SHOEMAKER

Rev. Dr. H. Stephen Shoemaker holds a Master of Divinity degree from Union Theological Seminary and a PhD from the Southern Baptist Theological Seminary. He has served as pastor of Crescent Hill Baptist Church in Louisville, Kentucky, and Broadway Baptist Church in Fort Worth, Texas. Dr. Shoemaker is the author of numerous articles and six books; his latest, *Being Christian in an Almost Chosen Nation: Thinking about Faith and Politics*, was published in 2006. He and his wife, Cherrie, have two children, David and Ann.

This sermon was given by Reverend Shoemaker on July 15, 2001, at Myers Park Baptist Church in Charlotte, North Carolina. Founded in 1943, the church is especially family oriented, and its eighteen hundred members of all ages are encouraged to ask questions, debate issues, and seek truth.

Today I want to begin a discussion—not end one—on homosexuality, the Bible, and us. Can we be a biblical people *and* a people who welcome and honor homosexual persons as part of our community? I think so. This sermon is an exercise in biblical interpretation; my hope is for a greater inclusion and welcome of homosexual persons into the church and society. Because it is far easier to read scripture as condemning of homosexual persons, it requires a more careful reading. Human sexuality is a complex reality; the Bible is a complex document. I will try to follow the maxim, "Make it as simple as possible, but not simpler!"

The stakes are high. The issue seems to be dividing the church in America, but it need not. We live in a culture rife with hatred, fear, and discrimination toward homosexual persons. Sports talk radio station 610 AM makes frequent fun of gay people. There is a high incidence of teenage and young adult suicide pro-

"Search for the right answer within yourselves to guide your behavior today."

pelled by a crisis in sexual identity. The youth told me this week that the term *gay* has now mutated in current slang to be the general adjective that means "something negative, stupid, or weird": "That's so gay!" Such is how viciousness gets embedded in language.

Carlyle Marney set out the terms for this conversation in 1966, thirty-five years ago.[1] Three of them.

1. "We will have to become, and become known as, a community of responsible involvedness . . . We must adopt a 'we-ness.'" Straight and gay persons are more alike than different. We are talking about ourselves in our sexual vitalities and responsibilities, not us and them.
2. "We will have to become, and become known as, a community of the guilty and of guilt—real guilt . . . For aren't we all harmed harmers?" None of us can pretend innocence. We have all been wounded, and we all have, in various ways, wounded others. There is a created goodness and belovedness we have as God's children, but we are also harmed harmers, wounded wounders, all of us.
3. "The Christian community has to become, and become known as, the community of grace." We are called to be a community of compassion that embodies the unconditional love of God and the

forgiveness of sins. To use Marney's words, the "homosexually committed person has not fallen from grace. He (she) never heard of it."

I would add a fourth statement: The church is a community of the New Creation in the midst of the old creation. The message of our gospel is God loves you exactly as you are, and it is from where you are that you are invited to build with us the banquet of the kingdom and manifest the New Creation.

I.

Today we tackle the biblical passages used to condemn and exclude homosexual persons. I also offer the New Testament passages that in my mind speak to their deeper inclusion and acceptance.

We covenant in this church to exercise a "critical examination of scripture" and to be "open to all new light." Jesus said that the Holy Spirit would continue to teach us. I believe the Spirit is guiding us to a new understanding about homosexuality, much as the Spirit led the church to revise its biblical interpretations about slavery in the nineteenth century.

There are risks in tackling this topic, but there are greater opportunities for good. The first is that it is sometimes in the most difficult of issues and life experiences that we are touched by the radicality of the grace of God revealed in Jesus. The second is that this issue may help us all as we seek to live out our mysterious, wondrous, powerful, unruly, complicated, and conflicted sexual lives in ways that move toward sexual healing and sexual responsibility. So let us plunge bravely ahead.

II.

I discuss here the five biblical passages that address homosexual conduct. I say conduct rather than *homosexuality* because the biblical writers had no conception of anything like homosexual orientation.

Text number one is from Genesis 19, the story of Sodom. Two angels in the guise of men come to visit Lot's house. All the men of Sodom gather at Lot's house and issue this ominous demand:

> Where are the men who came to you tonight? Bring them out to
> us, that we may know them (19:5).

What the men have in mind is rape—gang rape. Lot refuses and offers them instead his daughters, which reveals the low estate of women at the time. The men insist on Lot's release of the guests. The angels strike them blind, and later the city is destroyed.

The sin here is not homosexuality, but rape. Later scripture identifies the sins of Sodom variously as inhospitality to strangers, injustice, greed, lack of care for the poor, and general immorality (see Wisdom 19:13, Ezekiel 16:48–9, Jeremiah 23:14, Matthew 10:5–15, Jude 7). It is we who have forced a focus on homosexuality.

"Today, become part of what history will record as righteous heterosexuals."

Text number two is from Leviticus, 18:22 and 20:13:

> You shall not lie with a male as with a woman; it is an abomination (*toevah*) . . . If a man lies with a male as with a woman both of them have committed an abomination (*toevah*); they shall be put to death.

These verses are from the holiness code, which had hundreds of rules about cleanness and uncleanness. Homosexual conduct between men is forbidden as *toevah*, but if you take a careful look at the whole code, you'll see that it forbids a wide range of conduct, some of which we still consider destructive and immoral, such as incest and adultery. Some we now consider morally neutral—for example, sex during a woman's monthly flow. Some we would never consider *toevah*, like eating barbecued ribs—that is, unless your cholesterol is high.

Jews and Christians alike take these passages and determine which parts still hold moral force and which do not. Our communities tend to agree on the Ten Commandments, but not on all the multiplications of these commandments, nor on the penalties imposed. In Numbers, a man who picks up sticks on the Sabbath is put to death (Numbers 15:32–36). In Deuteronomy, a son is to be put to death for disobeying his parents (Deuteronomy 21:18–21).

The challenge is to make our moral discernments about these laws thoughtfully and as consistently as possible. I use two main criteria in my own interpretation of scripture. The first is from Augustine: Does my interpretation increase the love of God and neighbor, or decrease it? The second is to use Jesus, the Word made flesh, as a key to interpretation: What seems consistent with who he was, how he lived, and what he taught?

And we all seek the help of the Spirit of God as we interpret scripture. As Paul said, "The letter kills, but the Spirit brings life."

We all tend to be selective literalists. We can only hope to interpret consistently and thoughtfully and in ways that bring life and healing.

III.

Those are the Old Testament texts. There are three New Testament texts (I hope you are noticing how few there are).

The first is I Corinthians 6:9–10, in which Paul describes appropriate conduct for Christians. He begins the chapter by saying Christians should not take other Christians to court. No lawsuits between Christian brothers and sisters! Then in verses 9 and 10, he lists behaviors not fit for the kingdom of God: the immoral (*pornoi*), idolaters, adulterers, male prostitutes (*malakoi*), homosexual offenders (*arsenokoitai*), thieves, the greedy, drunkards, slanderers, and swindlers.

Note our inconsistencies. Do we ever have discussions about letting greedy people join the church, or about greedy people becoming deacons, or about greedy people being married in the church? Do we exclude alcoholics, slanderers, and swindlers?

But we also need to look at the two Greek words here often associated with homosexuality. *Malakoi* literally means "soft"; *arsenokoitai* joins two words: "men" and "bed." We have tended through the years to translate these words in line with our current prejudices. I think they are most accurately translated as "male prostitutes" and "homosexual offenders." They, I think, refer to the most prevalent forms of homosexual conduct in the Greek/Roman/Hellenistic world: the use of young males and feminized men as prostitutes and the older man–younger boy form of sexual behavior called pederasty. We are talking here of exploitative, abusive, and promiscuous forms of sexual conduct. The biblical writers could have had no conception of homosexuality as an orientation, or of a lifelong committed and monogamous same-sex relationship.

The second New Testament text is I Timothy 1:9–10. Here is another list of behaviors presented as contrary to Christian doctrine and practice:

"men-slayers, immoral persons (*pornoi*), homosexual offenders (*arsenokoitai*), men-stealers (think kidnappers and slave traders), liars, perjurers . . ."

Again, I would translate the word as "homosexual offenders"—emphasis on the word *offender*—describing exploitative forms of homosexual conduct.

The third New Testament text is Romans 1:18–2:1. Paul is describing what happens when we worship ourselves, the creature, rather than God the Creator. Idolatry takes many forms. Paul groups them into three. The phrase "God gave them up" introduces the three groups.

1. "God gave them up in the desires of their heart to uncleanness (*akatharsian*), to the dishonoring of their bodies among themselves." This is a general description of sexual immorality.

2. "God gave them up to dishonorable passions. Their women exchanged natural relations (*physin*) for unnatural (*para physin*), and their men likewise gave up natural relations (*physin*) with women and were consumed with passion for one another." This refers, I believe, to the patterns of exploitative and abusive homosexual conduct I have described above. We may ask, "What does 'against nature' mean to a same-sex-oriented person?"

3. "God gave them up to an unfit mind to do unseemly things." In this group are those who engaged in "*pornoi*, 'immorality,' and *poneria*, 'evil,'" those "full of covetousness and malice, envy, murder, strife, deceit, evil constructions; gossips, slanderers, God-haters, insolent, proud, boastful, inventors of evil things; disobedient to parents, foolish, faithless, heartless, merciless." (Have we left anyone out?!)

Now Paul turns to the Jews, who had been holding their noses through Paul's description of the first three groups, and says: And so you, my fellow Jews, you, too, "have no excuse when you judge others, for in passing judgment upon the others, you condemn yourselves, for you the judgers do the same things . . ."

This passage is part of a five-chapter-long theological discourse that I summarize in the following five points:

1. The pagan Gentiles are without excuse because they have broken God's laws revealed in nature and conscience (1:18–32).

2. The pious Jews are without excuse because they have become judgers of others while themselves breaking God's law revealed to Moses and Israel (2:1–24).

3. All have sinned and fall short of the glory of God (3:23).

4. But, miracle of miracles, we unrighteous folk have been set right with God by His grace as a gift through the redemption which is in Christ Jesus, whom God put forward as a mercy-seat (3:21–26). The "mercy-seat" is an allusion to the high altar on the Jewish Day of Atonement. The death of Christ has become the Day of Atonement for the whole world, the once-and-for-all forgiveness of sins past, present, and future.

5. In Adam, the old humanity, we all die; in Christ, the New Adam and New Humanity, we all are made alive (5:1–20).

Are you getting the point of the great good news being announced here? We're all in the same boat: of the same belovedness and the same vulnerability, with the same capacity for sin. But God's grace is for all and in all. Sin is strong, but grace is stronger. The old creation is being transformed into a New Creation.

IV.

Those are the biblical passages used by some Christians to condemn homosexual persons. But what did Jesus say about homosexual conduct? If he is our guide to interpretation of scripture, it is important to know what he said.

There's a pamphlet I've seen in a church narthex along with all the other tracts that address one thing or another. The bold title reads: *What Jesus Said about Homosexuality.* You turn the page and find . . . four blank pieces of paper. On the back are the words: *That's right. Nothing!*

Jesus is silent on the subject. Jesus's ethic did not deal with lists of clean and unclean rules. (If this were all the gospel was about, I would not be here today.) His focus was on the heart. And his ethic had a seriously practical purpose: Did it hurt or help people? Moreover, he seemed especially tenderhearted toward those who had made sexual mistakes, perhaps because sexual sinners were trying so hard to love and to be loved. And perhaps because religious people were so fixed in their judgment upon them.

The famous story in the gospel text from John captures Jesus's spirit. Some men drag a woman to him who has been caught in an act of adultery. (Where was the man? It takes two to tango.) They ask him if they should follow the law of Moses and stone her to death. Jesus says, "You who are without sin cast the first stone." He then stoops to write something on the ground. One by one, they all slink away. Jesus turns to the woman and asks, "Where are your accusers?"

"They are gone," she replies.

"Neither do I condemn you," Jesus says. "Go and sin no more."

Here we have a Lord who forgives all our sins and who calls us to a higher moral path. Can we be such a community? A community of morals and mercy? Of character and compassion? Here is the narrow way that leads to life. There are plenty of communities that are one at the expense of the other.

V.

There is one more set of texts. The first is in Acts, where Peter and the church are struggling with what to do with unclean Gentiles who believe in Jesus and want to join up: those of Gentile orientation and Gentile lifestyle.

Peter is struggling with the moral and racial repugnance he feels toward Gentiles, whom he has been taught to consider *toevah*, unclean. In Acts 10, a voice comes to him in a vision and commands him to eat unclean food he has always been commanded to avoid. Peter refuses to eat, but the voice says, "What God has cleansed, you shall not call unclean or common."

At that moment, messengers arrive from Cornelius's house, inviting Peter to his house and telling him the gospel of Jesus. Cornelius is a Gentile; Peter is forbidden by Jewish law to stay with him and eat with him. But the Spirit drives home the point: "Those whom God has cleansed I cannot call common." Peter goes and shares the gospel. Cornelius believes and is baptized. The Holy Spirit falls upon him. And Peter says, "How can I hinder God, whose Spirit has fallen upon them?" (Acts 11:1–18).

This has been my experience over and over for thirty years: I've seen the Spirit of God demonstrably present in gay persons. How can I hinder God?

The last set of texts is from the Apostle Paul. In Galatians 6:15, Paul writes in an unforgettable flourish: "Circumcision means nothing. Uncircumcision means nothing [speaking here of both anatomy and theology]. The only thing that matters is the New Creation!"

The church today seems fixated on battling over old-creation distinctions while God is calling us to something more, something greater: the New Creation. Circumcision means nothing. Uncircumcision means nothing. Jew means nothing. Gentile means nothing. Male means nothing. Female means nothing. Race means nothing. Class means nothing. Gay means nothing. Straight means nothing. The only thing that matters is the New Creation! The New Creation is everything!

In II Corinthians 5, Paul says, "From now on we regard no one from a human point of view"—that is, by race, class, looks, money, sexual orientation, IQ, or percentage of body fat. "For if anyone is in Christ, there is a New Creation. The old is gone; look, everything has become new."

VI.

In our day new light is breaking forth from scripture, from science, and from our own spiritual experience. I think it is saying, "Let us do away with sexual orientation as a moral category. Morality has to do with behavior, not wiring. I may be wrong, you may be wrong, but this is where I stand."

We have an important role to play in a society still filled with hatred and discrimination toward gay persons. This will not be easy, and it may even go against the "conscience" that has been shaped by culture.

In *Huckleberry Finn*, Huck is caught in a moral dilemma between his conscience, shaped by church and culture to accept slavery, and a deeper conscience that has been influenced by his friendship with Jim the slave, owned by Miss Watson. Huck leaves home and is joined by Jim, who is now a runaway slave. Will Huck return him to his owner? Huck writes down a letter to Miss Watson telling her of Jim's whereabouts and feels temporarily better. But he can't escape the dilemma. He looks at Jim and at the letter. This is how Mark Twain captures the scene, in Huck's words:

> I took it up, and held it in my hand. I was a trembling, because I'd got to decide, forever, betwixt two things, and I knowed it. I studied it a minute, sort of holding my breath, and then says to myself: "All right, then, I'll go to hell"—and tore it up.[2]

Huck was willing to go against his culture and church—and go to the hell they told him he'd be sure to end up in—to be true to something truer he'd gotten hold of by benefit of his relationship to Jim.

I think what he got hold of also, or what got hold of him, was the New Creation, the New Creation whose door was opened to us by Jesus Christ.

> If anyone is in Christ, look,
> there is the New Creation
> All this is from God, who
> through Christ reconciled us
> to God's own self and gave to us
> the ministry [service, calling] of reconciliation.

Jesus calls us to follow and become part of the New Creation. Here is the invitation of the gospel: God loves you exactly as you are, and it is from where you are that we invite you to build with us the banquet of the kingdom and manifest the New Creation.

The first step in following Jesus is this: to give as much of yourself as you can to as much of Christ as you know.

As you take that step, there is great adventure ahead: There will be more and more of yourself to give, and more and more of Christ and the kingdom you will discover to give yourself to. The invitation is to all:

> Will you come and follow me if I but call your name?
> Will you go where you don't know and never be the same?
> Will you let my love be shown, will you let my name be known?
> Will you let my life be grown in you and you in me?[3]

Notes
1. Carlyle Marney, "The Christian Community and the Homosexual," *Religion in Life*, (Winter 1966).
2. Mark Twain, *The Adventures of Huckleberry Finn* (Franklin Center: The Franklin Library, 1979), 302.
3. "Will You Come and Follow Me, John Bell?," Hymn composed for the Iona Community.

PART 7
Exposé
A Silent Epidemic of Depression,
Isolation, and Fear

THE UNTOLD STORY

Let me tell you a story—the larger story beyond the ones told in this book's forty essays. It is a story about the epidemic of depression affecting hundreds of thousands of gay, lesbian, bisexual, and transgender teenagers. They experience needless—and horrible—loneliness, isolation, despair, and feelings of worthlessness. Why? Because their families, friends, churches, schoolmates, or teachers have been dismissive of gay people in their presence, have refused to accept them for who they are, or have been outright hostile. For them, every day is a crisis. Every day. Some attempt suicide. Too many succeed.

The title of this book is not overstated. *Crisis* is an apt description for what it's like to go through life lying to the people you love and respect most: your parents, siblings, spiritual leaders, best friends. Imagine what it's like to fear the bullies at school will find out your deepest, darkest secret—or what they'll do now that they know. Imagine what it's like to go through adolescence knowing your parents believe you're sinful or sick or wicked. Imagine what it's like to have your church shun you or your entire family. I wish these were made-up situations from novels that took place in some faraway place, but they're not. They're all stories from this book. American stories.

I can tell you what it feels like from personal experience, too: It's like a slow-motion nervous breakdown. And the thought of yet another gay teen going through the kind of crisis that I knew all too well often brings tears to my eyes. So I put this book together for the same reason I started my not-for-profit organization a few years back—to help many different groups of people understand the harm they might be causing. The name of that organization was carefully chosen: I called it Faith in America because, as a proud American, I do have faith in America—faith that as people understand, they will change their behavior. I hold out hope that the people causing the pain will take the suffering they cause to heart and work toward ending it. It could be that easy.

I'd like to address five specific groups of people: antigay religious groups, school personnel, parents, politicians, and the media.

To Antigay Religious Groups

In Part 1 of the book you read over and over again about the debilitating effects words like *sin* and *abomination* have had when a minister, rabbi, or parent used them in front of a gay youth. I have watched good, well-meaning people cause great harm to others in that way.

In the past, people have misused their Bible to justify slavery; deny women, people of color, and minority religious groups full and equal rights; prevent people of one race from marrying people of another. A scant twenty-five years ago preachers like Jerry Falwell railed that those who died of AIDS deserved what they got. Most people now acknowledge these things were wrong and examples of horribly misguided religious teachings. Just over a decade ago the Southern Baptist Convention publicly apologized to African-Americans for its central role in the perpetuation of slavery and segregation.

Yet that same organization is now behind groups that offer to "cure" gay people, a completely irresponsible—and dangerous—idea that has repeatedly been denounced and rejected by the American Medical Association, American Academy of Pediatrics, National Association of School Psychologists, American Psychological Association, American Psychiatric Association, American School

Health Association, American Counseling Association, National Association of Social Workers, and many, many others. All have stated repeatedly that one's sexual orientation is not an illness—and therefore does not need to be "cured." It is a dangerous idea because it tells kids it is not okay to be who they are, lowering their self-esteem at a critical time in their lives.

These are not fringe organizations (as some irresponsible extremists might claim). They are the organizations that help us live healthier, longer lives. You depend on their members for your day-to-day medical care and to keep your children healthy. The idea of trying to cure gay people is so far out of the mainstream that the National Parent Teachers Association (PTA) has refused to allow a group that purports to help students "convert" from gay to straight to set up shop at its annual convention, although Parents and Friends of Lesbians and Gays (PFLAG), a support group for gay kids and their parents, has been welcomed regularly.

If you're straight, ask yourself if you honestly think you could change your sexual orientation. This is not a smart-aleck question. It's an important one, and I ask it earnestly. When did you decide you were heterosexual? With enough therapy, or prayer, or practice, do you think you could learn to be gay? Of course not! Being straight—or gay or bisexual—is an innate, immutable characteristic.

I asked you to read this book with the purpose of healing your own family or our larger American family. The greatest, most satisfying love is that which we give to those in need. Today, all teenagers, and especially gay teenagers, are in need.

One more thing. Understand that even though you yourself may not be preaching hatred, the consequences of all this talk about sinfulness promotes hateful actions. In 2007 there was a 24 percent increase over 2006 in reported violence against gay men, lesbians, bisexuals, and transgender people in the United States. (The actual statistics are higher.) The number of murders more than doubled: from ten in 2006 to twenty-one in 2007—the most in any year since the turn of the century, according to the National Coalition of Anti-Violence Programs, an umbrella group of the country's gay antiviolence groups.

Some of the victims were not yet twenty-one. You may have heard of Matthew Shepard, murdered in Laramie, Wyoming, in 1998; his mother,

Judy, started the Matthew Shepard Foundation and has worked tirelessly to help prevent such tragedies from happening to others. Victims whose stories are perhaps less well known include fifteen-year-old Sakia Gunn, killed at a Newark, New Jersey, bus stop in 2003, and Sean Kennedy, murdered outside a bar in Greenville, South Carolina, in 2007. (His mother, Elke Kennedy, and stepbrother, Jarrod Parker, wrote chapters for this book.)

Sadly, many of the perpetrators have been under twenty-one as well. In 2007, Roberto Duncanson, twenty, was stabbed to death in Brooklyn, New York, by a seventeen-year-old who didn't like the way Roberto was looking at him. In 2008, Lawrence King, a fifteen-year-old eighth grader, was gunned down in his classroom in E. O. Greene Junior High School in Oxnard, California, by a fourteen-year-old classmate known to bully and harass King because he sometimes wore makeup and jewelry to school.

Many of the perpetrators saw their crimes as justifiable *because their victims were gay*. Religious messages about gay people are being used to poison people's minds, inspiring them to kill, something you may associate more with the Middle East than America. But if connecting religion and murder sounds far-fetched to you, it shouldn't. Some of the murderers are actually proud of their crimes and have cited Bible verses in their defense. In some jurisdictions, they have even gotten more lenient sentences because their victims were gay.

And according to Dallas Drake, principal researcher for the Center for Homicide Research, suicide and homicide are opposite sides of the same coin. "Of course it's not politically palatable for anyone to come out and say, 'Kill gay kids,'" he notes. "But by preaching messages that lower the self-esteem of LGBT teenagers, homophobes can get people to do the job themselves."

Not speaking out is the same as being complicit in the violence. Read what some conservative Christian thinkers have written about homosexuality and sin. (A place to start is Part 6 of this book, "The Sin Question"). And please tell your minister, priest, rabbi, or imam to stop preaching hate.

For Teachers, Principals, School Administrators— and Parents

I remember when school safety meant a crossing guard at the busy intersection near the elementary school playground. In these post-Columbine days, all parents are rightly concerned about whether their children will come home safe from school and how they will be treated while they're there.

Most school principals are aware of the seriousness of bullying at their schools but continue to underestimate how it affects gay kids. And it is serious. We know how serious, thanks to *The National School Climate Survey* by the Gay, Lesbian, and Straight Education Network (GLSEN), which has documented the experiences of gay students in American high schools for nearly ten years.

More than three-quarters of students hear such derogatory remarks as "faggot" or "dyke" frequently at school, and nearly nine out of ten reported hearing the phrase "that's so gay"—meaning "stupid" or "worthless"—frequently as well. Imagine the outrage there would be if ethnic, racial, or religious epithets were tossed around so cavalierly.

Over one-third of students have experienced physical harassment at school on the basis of their sexual orientation, and more than one-quarter on the basis of their gender expression. Nearly one in five has been physically assaulted.

Gay students were five times more likely to report skipping school because of safety concerns than their peers. The high school dropout rate for gay teens is several times higher than for their heterosexual peers. Imagine feeling physically endangered at your place of work all day long. Wouldn't you want to get out of there?

As you might expect, the worse the harassment, the worse students did in school. Those who experienced the most frequent physical harassment were more likely to report they did not plan to go to college. Overall, gay students were twice as likely as the general population of students to report they were not planning to pursue any post-secondary education.

The good news is that we know how to solve these problems. Students in schools with a Gay-Straight Alliance (GSA) club were less likely to feel unsafe and less likely to miss school. Having a comprehensive anti-bullying policy that specifically addressed sexual orientation and gender identity was related to lower rates of harassment and higher rates of intervention by school staff when incidents occurred.

Eleven states and the District of Columbia have comprehensive anti-bullying laws that specifically address sexual orientation (only seven of these laws mention gender identity).* Having such policies makes a huge difference: The laws give teachers and administrators a clear mandate on how to handle situations as they arise, and the schools in these states have significantly lower rates of harassment. The rest of the states afford much less protection to gay students—whether they have generic anti-bullying laws or no laws at all.

GLSEN is not some radical organization. Dedicated to improving school safety for *all* students, its research and publications have been endorsed by many mainstream organizations. In 2006, it worked shoulder to shoulder with the Christian Educators Association International, the self-described alternative to the National Education Association and American Federation of Teachers, to hammer out *Public Schools and Sexual Orientation: A First Amendment Framework for Finding Common Ground.* This first-of-its-kind publication aimed at both school officials and parents sought to use the First Amendment "to establish guidelines for how public schools should guard the rights of all students in creating a safe learning environment."

Among the report's recommendations? "Take seriously complaints of name-calling, harassment and discrimination regardless of the reason. Investigate the complaint and intervene directly when it has merit, making clear that such behavior is unacceptable on the public school campus. The public school environment cannot be a hostile place to study or work."

Educators must take full responsibility for the safety and acceptance of *all* their students, gay and straight alike. The National Education Association agrees, stating: "[F] or students who are struggling with their sexual orientation or gender identification, every school district and educational institution should provide counseling services and programs that deal with high suicide and dropout rates . . . These services and programs shall be staffed by a trained professional."

The best way to do that is to adopt a written zero-tolerance policy on bullying and homophobic language at your school. And push for such laws in your town, city, and state. Then make sure those laws are followed—GLSEN

*In addition to the District of Columbia, the eleven states with anti-bullying laws that address sexual orientation are California, Iowa, Maine, Maryland, Minnesota, New Jersey, Vermont, Connecticut, Massachusetts, Washington, and Wisconsin. (The policies in the last four states, however, are not transgender inclusive.)

can help you with that as well. And don't just get out of the way of the establishment of gay-straight alliances—work toward their creation.

And Especially to Parents

This book has brought together stories by people of different backgrounds, many of whom are by any standards successful—even famous—today. Some were always driven to prosper and prevail. Others had to overcome great odds, including their own self-doubts. Nearly all were at one point almost derailed by the fear that those they loved most might turn their backs on them because of who they were. The success stories in this book come both because of, and in spite of, that adversity. For some, the adversity manifested itself outwardly; for others, it became inner torment. And then there are some who had it easier than others: *those whose parents were loving and supportive from the start.*

Don't be fooled by your overachieving children. And don't be afraid to ask the ones who withdraw silently what is troubling them. Whatever your child's sexual orientation, treat it with respect. It's their creator's gift to them, a natural and wonderful part of their being.

Most of all, make sure they know they can confide in you. If they happen to be gay, help them on their journey. But don't wait for them to come to you: by then it may be too late. Let them know you are ready to talk to them about it when they are ready to talk to you about it. Teach them to love, cherish, and above all respect their chosen mate.

And become active. The violence that took fifteen-year-old Lawrence King's life did not just affect him, after all. It affected every other child in that classroom who witnessed it—and every other child in that junior high school, even the ones whose parents are appalled by the idea of antigay slurs. Do you really want your kid's school to be next? Do you want your children going to classes in an environment where that kind of behavior is tolerated or acceptable, *even if it's not leveled at them?*

Join GLSEN, which can help you get an anti-bullying policy inclusive of gay and transgender kids put in place and help set up a GSA club at your child's school. Educators believe in their value—more than half of secondary school teachers nationally believe that having a GSA club helps create a safer school.

Lobby your state legislators to make such a policy the law in your state. If your child is gay, join your local PFLAG chapter—there are over five hundred nationwide with over two hundred thousand members, as well as sister organizations in countries all over the world. All those moms and dads can't be wrong.

Your kids will always be your kids, and they need their parents to ensure that they have all the rights—and responsibilities—guaranteed to all Americans under the Constitution.

For Politicians

The Declaration of Independence says, "all men are created equal, that they are endowed by their creator with certain unalienable rights, that among these are life, liberty, and the pursuit of happiness." We've fixed certain problems in that equation in our nation's history along the way—we've included women and black people, for example. But the best this country has ever done for its gay citizens on a national level is agree to count the crimes against us—and the federal government wouldn't even do that without a fight (and it still doesn't do a very good job).

The federal government says you can't be fired because you're black, or a born-again Christian, or a woman—but that it's just fine if you're gay. Gay people have no explicit federal protections in this country, let alone the right to serve in the military or to get married. They are regularly denied public accommodations and have their children taken away from them. The U.S. Census won't even count them.

Too many politicians are not leaders but, rather, organizers of followers. It is sometimes disheartening to see the way our political system works: the vicious cycle of getting elected only to immediately start running again for reelection. It seems like politicians take action only if it will get them reelected.

There are some politicians who do believe in full and equal rights for gay people but who simply don't have the backbone to lead—to stand up and say what they believe, to elucidate the issues, thereby changing our country for the better. And then there are the politicians who are bigots, acting from fear and ignorance about who gay people are—and from their misguided and ill-informed religious beliefs. And, perhaps most distressingly, there are also politicians who are using civil rights for gay people as a tool for their own advancement.

I'd like to think that all such politicians simply don't understand the harm they cause by their actions. After they read this book, I hope they will think about the despair these teenagers felt as they grappled with their already complicated adolescence. Imagine what a gay fourteen-year-old feels like when he learns that when he is an adult, he will not be protected in the workplace, not assured nondiscrimination in housing, and not allowed to marry the person he loves. What signal does that send to him? It says, *you are second class and unworthy*. I hope every night, when these politicians lay their heads on their pillows, they have trouble sleeping for knowing the pain they cause, when instead they could be leading and be part of a magnificent solution.

There are, of course, those few politicians who do lead. For them I hope this book provides more reinforcement that what they do is good and just. And may they have sweet dreams as they sleep through the night.

For the Media

I empathize with the pressure news organizations are under to be more profitable, and the never-ending reduction in staffing. With the advent of twenty-four-hour news channels, everything began to move more quickly. The longer you spend on one story, the greater the possibility all your hard work will be overshadowed by new, late-breaking news. But this can't be the excuse for the lack of critical, investigative journalism about the harm caused to gay teens.

In his book *The Assault on Reason*, Al Gore discusses how the media neglected its responsibilities leading up to the Iraq War and how, through more adversarial questioning of government officials, this costly war could have been prevented.

When fundamentalist religious groups and politicians attack the gay community, your reporting is largely uninformed. You unquestioningly report their claim to "family values" in their crusade against marriage equality. But gay folks have families, too, and are valued by their own families as well. Now that you have read this book, please consider how a more analytical approach to groups on both sides of the issue will ultimately yield a better story.

You also cause harm by choosing what *not* to report. Here are some story ideas:

1. Marriage
In light of recent court decisions about marriage equality in California and New York, what are Christian ministers preaching about gay people? Why do gay people want to get married? And what are American "family values" in the twenty-first century?

2. Christianity, Tolerance, and Homosexuality
What local Christian ministers from more conservative denominations are breaking with tradition and refusing to teach that being gay is sinful?

3. Hate Crimes
The FBI began tracking hate crimes against gay people in 1990. (To date, this is the only gay-inclusive legislation to pass both houses of Congress.) Since 1997, there have been 181 murders in which victims were targeted because they were gay—a number disproportionate to the gay population. The number of felony assaults is similarly skewed. What precipitated the most recent incidents in the city or state you cover? More importantly, what is being done to end such violence? If your state has no hate crimes statute, what is preventing the legislature from passing one?

4. Gay People of Faith
Religious denominations from Orthodox Jews to Jehovah's Witnesses to Muslims have gay organizations so people can pursue their faith while being true to their sexual identities—even when the teachings of the former conflict with the latter. The Resources Section on page 358 provides a list of a number of these groups. How do these people of faith interpret their religious texts?

5. Gays in the Military
U.S. military policy is still "don't ask, don't tell," but everyone knows gay people serve. Ask gay veterans just back from Iraq—and those with whom they served—how this policy affected them and the effectiveness of our armed services.

6. Homelessness

A recent study suggests as many as 60 percent of homeless youth may be lesbian, gay, bisexual, and transgender. And the leading cause of homelessness among all teens is parental conflict. Who are the parents of the homeless kids in your area, and why do they say their kids are living on the street? How does that compare with what their kids say?

7. School Safety

Do schools in your area have a gay-inclusive anti-bullying policy? Such policies enhance the safety of *all* children. If not, who is standing in the way? And has your school board endorsed the formation of GSA clubs in schools? If so, how have these clubs impacted students, teachers, and administrators?

8. Employment

Most Americans don't know that in thirty states it is legal to fire someone because he or she is gay; in thirty-eight states, it is legal to fire someone because he or she is transgender. The federal Employment Non-Discrimination Act (ENDA) would end all that. In 2007 it passed the House but died in the Senate. Yet most Americans believe job discrimination based on sexual orientation is wrong. Ask your audience if they disagree with the senators who voted against ENDA.

And, since this is a presidential election year, here are questions you might ask our national candidates:

1. How do you reconcile the separation of church and state with your opposition to marriage rights for lesbians and gay men?
2. If passed by Congress, would you sign an employment non-discrimination act that includes protections for gay, lesbian, bisexual, and transgender Americans?
3. What will you do to help stop the epidemic of depression for hundreds of thousands of gay teenagers?

Please don't ignore this ongoing, significant mental health crisis. You can literally save lives by simply reporting the facts.

Resources

ORGANIZATIONS TO CALL

In addition to the issues of depression and suicide that affect gay teenagers, there are also other risk factors. They face higher rates of homelessness and substance abuse than their peers; homelessness among gay youth is epidemic in some cities. They are more likely to be sexually assaulted or contract HIV. So-called ex-gay ministries have decisively shifted their focus in recent years—to young people. The children of gay and lesbian parents—whether they themselves are gay or not—often have their lives turned upside down by restrictions on parenting, foster parenting, and adoption because laws vary from state to state. And gay youth face increased harassment and alienation at school—a problem that doesn't necessarily stop when they go to college.

Fortunately, whether you are a lonely teenager or a loving parent, you do not have to deal with these issues alone. Many wonderful organizations stand ready to offer guidance and support.

This list is by no means comprehensive; it mainly focuses on national organizations that provide services specifically for young people and includes a separate listing of websites for many faith-based groups. Any one of these organizations can put you in touch with a local chapter near you or a group in your area.

Advocates for Youth

2000 M Street NW, Suite 750
Washington, DC 20036
(202) 419-3420
www.advocatesforyouth.org

Advocates for Youth creates programs and advocates for policies that help all young people make informed and responsible decisions about their reproductive and sexual health. Its website includes a wealth of information aimed at gay, lesbian, bisexual, transgender, and questioning kids, as well as at parents and educators. It also has great links to other resources of all kinds.

Atticus Circle

Seven Straight Nights For Equal Rights
515 Congress, Suite 1320, Austin, TX 78701
512-450-5188
info@AtticusCircle.org
www.atticuscircle.org
www.sevenstraightnights.org

Atticus Circle educates and mobilizes fair-minded straight people to help advance equal rights for lesbian, gay, bisexual, and transgender (LGBT) partners, parents, and their children. In conjunction with Soulforce, Atticus has created Seven Straight Nights for Equal Rights, a week of vigils led by straight allies to support civil rights for LGBT Americans, held each year around the country. See their websites for dates for Seven Straight Nights.

Beyond Ex-Gay

e-mail: bxg@beyondexgay.com
www.beyondexgay.com

Beyond Ex-Gay is an online community and resource for people "who have survived ex-gay experiences" such as reparative therapy. Those behind the site believe that "healing comes through community and through sharing our stories and experiences." A fledgling yet important group, it has a website that includes first-person accounts from over twenty people of a variety of religious backgrounds who endured attempts to be "cured." It also includes links to groups of gay orthodox and fundamentalist Jews, Christians, and Muslims that are too small to have well-established Web presences themselves.

COLAGE

1550 Bryant Street, Suite 830
San Francisco, CA 94103
(415) 861-5437
www.colage.org

Sometimes teenagers are affected by homophobia not because they are gay, but because their parents are. COLAGE is a national movement of youth and adults with one or more gay parents. It has chapters in thirty-one states and Washington, DC, as well as Canada, the UK, and Sweden. Its website provides an online community where visitors can connect with others facing similar issues, as well as books and pamphlets for the whole family.

Faith in America (FIA)

PO Box 1176
Hudson, NC 28638
(888) 913-2484
www.faithinamerica.info

The mission of FIA is the emancipation of gay people from bigotry disguised as religious truth. Started by Mitchell Gold, FIA works with churches and other organizations across the country to publicly expose religion-based bigotry against gay people and to inform the public how women, people of color, and people of minority religions have been mistreated similarly by religion in the past.

If you don't like what your church is saying about you, your child, or gay people in general, or if it no longer accepts you because you are or a family member is gay, FIA can offer you information on how to talk to clergy about the harm it is doing. FIA also offers opportunities to help get that message out so that gay people of faith nationwide can fully participate in their religious communities.

Gay, Lesbian and Straight Education Network (GLSEN)

90 Broad Street, 2nd Floor
New York, NY 10004
(212) 727-0135
www.glsen.org

GLSEN is the leading national education organization focused on ensuring safe schools for all students. If you would like to start—or are having trouble starting—a Gay-Straight Alliance (GSA) club in your school, GLSEN can help. You can download a resource guide directly from its website. The website also offers a treasure trove of books and videos for and about gay youth, their parents, and their teachers.

An important GLSEN project is the annual National Day of Silence, with which students bring attention to anti-LGBT name-calling, bullying, and harassment in schools by taking a daylong vow of silence. And GLSEN is also a partner, along with almost fifty other organizations, in No Name-Calling Week, a program aimed at grades five through eight that strives to end bullying in communities and schools.

GLSEN also focuses on convincing education leaders and policy makers of the urgent need to address anti-LGBT behavior and bias—including bullying—in our schools by advocating for safe-schools laws and policies that specifically include sexual orientation and gender identity and with training for administrators, principals, and educators. GLSEN founder Kevin Jennings has written the introduction to the "School and Social Discrimination" section of this book.

Gay-Straight Alliance Network

160 Fourteenth Street
San Francisco, CA 94103
(415) 552-4229
www.gsanetwork.org

Looking for step-by-step instructions on how to start a Gay-Straight Alliance (GSA) club in your junior high or high school? These people are experts. Their website also offers a listing of every GSA in California, a registration form to get yours listed, and even information for "super-rad straight allies." Although not a national group, the information here is well worth a visit from out-of-staters.

GLBT National Help Center

2261 Market Street, PMB #296
San Francisco, CA 94114
(415) 355-0003 (administration only)
www.glnh.org

GLBT Hotline

(888) 843-4564
(888) THE-GLNH
e-mail: glnh@GLBTNationalHelpCenter.org

GLBT National Youth Talkline

(800) 246-7743
(800) 246-PRIDE

The GLBT National Help Center (along with its GLBT Hotline and national Youth Talkline) is an outgrowth of the Gay & Lesbian National Hotline. The center now offers a second hotline aimed exclusively at young people that provides peer counseling. Both help people end the isolation that many feel by providing a safe environment on the phone (or via e-mail) to discuss issues people can't talk about anywhere else. The website also provides a good database of national gay organizations and publications.

Human Rights Campaign (HRC)

1640 Rhode Island Avenue NW
Washington, DC 20036
(202) 628-4160
www.hrc.org

The largest national gay, lesbian, bisexual, and transgender civil rights organization, HRC offers a wealth of resources on everything affecting the LGBT community, including information for "straight allies," non-gay people supportive of their gay family, friends, and coworkers.

HRC's Coming Out Project encourages gay Americans to live openly by providing resources that empower them to talk about their lives. (The Snapshot Project, www.hrcsnap shot.org, offers a lighthearted approach to starting that dialogue.)

One of the contributors to this book, former NBA player John Amaechi, is a spokesperson for the Coming Out Project. Another contributor, Candace Gingrich, sister of Newt Gingrich, works in HRC's Youth & Campus Outreach Program, helping to empower the next generation of LGBT leaders.

In addition, the HRC Religion and Faith Program amplifies the voices of clergy who support gay equality while also guiding people of faith in talking about gay issues from a religious perspective.

Joe Solmonese, president of HRC, contributed his story to this book.

Matthew Shepard Foundation

301 Thelma #512
Casper, WY 82609
(307) 237-6167
www.matthewshepard.org

Matthew Shepard was murdered at age 21, and his parents, Judy and Dennis Shepard, have created an organization to help stop the hate that resulted in their son's death. See the "Matthew's Place" section of the website for youth-oriented news, podcasts, state-by-state resources, and even jewelry and clothing in support of safety and equality for all.

For information on organizations that advocate for victims of anti-gay and anti-AIDS violence, harassment, domestic violence, or sexual assault, you can contact the **National Coalition of Anti-Violence Projects (NCAVP)**, a coalition of gay and gay-friendly groups, via its website: www.ncavp.org.

National Gay and Lesbian Task Force

1325 Massachusetts Avenue NW, Suite 600
Washington, DC 20005
(202) 393-5177
www.thetaskforce.org

The task force trains gay leaders, equipping state and local organizations with the skills they need to defeat antigay referenda and advance pro gay legislation. Its annual Creating Change conference is one of the largest meetings of LGBT leaders anywhere; many of the forums focus on youth-related organizing and training. Publications by its Policy Institute, on topics ranging from homelessness among gay youth to violence in public schools, are excellent resources for the media and politicians. The National Religious Roundtable is an interfaith network of leaders from pro-gay faith, spiritual, and religious organizations.

Out for Work

1325 Massachusetts Avenue NW, Suite 700
Washington, DC 20005
(866) 571-LGBT
www.outforwork.com

Out for Work prepares LGBT college students as they make the transition from the world of academia to the workplace. Its programs culminate in a national conference in Washington, DC, every September. The conference features keynote speakers from Fortune 500 companies, noted panelists addressing critical employment issues, and an impressive career fair.

Parents and Friends of Lesbians and Gays (PFLAG)

1726 M Street NW, Suite 400
Washington, DC 20036
(202) 467-8180
www.pflag.org

Approximately one in four families has an immediate family member who is lesbian, gay, bisexual, or transgender. PFLAG has supported families navigating the coming-out process and beyond for the past thirty-five years. The mom of a gay son started PFLAG after marching alongside him in the 1972 gay pride parade in New York City. So many young gay men and women came up to her and begged her to speak to *their* parents that she decided to start an organization. Today PFLAG has over five hundred chapters nationwide. Executive Director Jody Huckaby contributed his story to this book.

Point Foundation

5757 Wilshire Boulevard, Suite 370
Los Angeles, CA 90036
(323) 933-1234
www.pointfoundation.org

Point Foundation provides scholarships, mentorship, and leadership training for students of merit who have been marginalized due to sexual orientation, gender identity, or gender expression. Scholarships are available to both college and graduate students. Scholars are also matched with mentors—university presidents, professors, artists, journalists, doctors, lawyers, businessmen and women, philanthropists—in their academic field of interest. Jorge Valencia, executive director of the Point Foundation, contributed his story to this book.

The Human Rights Campaign also maintains a list of more than 150 scholarships for high school and college students: http://www.hrc.org/issues/youth_and_campus_activism.asp.

Safe Schools Coalition

1612–109th Avenue SE
Bellevue, WA 98004
(206) 632-0662 ext. 49
www.safeschoolscoalition.org

The Safe Schools Coalition is a good first stop for journalists, educators, legislators, or parents concerned with how to make public schools safer. Its mission is to help schools become safe places by reducing bias-based bullying and violence and helping schools better meet the needs of LGBT students and those students with LGBT parents. The Safe Schools Coalition conducts workshops for educators and community groups on coming out, on its "bully-proof curriculum," and on antigay harassment and violence in schools.

Soulforce

PO Box 3195
Lynchburg, VA 24503
(434) 384-7696
info@soulforce.org
www.soulforce.org

The mission of Soulforce is to cut off homophobia at its source: religious bigotry. Soulforce uses a dynamic take-it-to-the-streets style of activism modeled on the principles of Gandhi and Martin Luther King, Jr., to connect the dots between antigay religious dogma and the resulting attacks on the lives and civil liberties of LGBT Americans.

Its annual "equality rides" send openly gay students around the country to talk with officials at the religious and military schools that currently uphold antigay policies. It was cofounded by Mel White, who contributed his story to this book.

The Trevor Project

9056 Santa Monica Boulevard, Suite 208
West Hollywood, CA 90069
Helpline: (866) 488-7386 (4-U-TREVOR)
Information: (310) 271-8845
www.thetrevorproject.org

The Trevor Project operates the only nationwide 24-7 crisis and suicide prevention helpline for gay and questioning youth. It has responded to more than one hundred thousand calls since it went into operation. Named for the protagonist of a film about gay teen suicide that won the Academy Award for best live-action short in 1994, it also offers a website that provides young people with an opportunity to e-mail questions anonymously; there are educational materials available for download as well. Charles Robbins, its executive director, authored the introduction to the "Family and Community Rejection" section of this book.

Truth Wins Out

PO Box 25491
Brooklyn, NY 11202
www.truthwinsout.org

This organization is a think tank run by journalist Wayne Besen, who has been doggedly pursuing the misleading and damaging claims of reparative therapy for years, debunking the ex-gay myth and providing accurate information about the lives of gay people.

Youth Resource

2000 M Street NW, Suite 750
Washington, DC 20036
Phone: (202) 419-3420 ext. 30
www.youthresource.com

This website is a project of Advocates for Youth, an organization listed on page 352. It is aimed directly at gay, lesbian, bisexual, transgender, and questioning young people. On it, they can find information on health, advocacy, "queer living," and news, as well as original work by site readers. It features information on issues ranging from HIV prevention to same-sex marriage written by and for other young gay people.

RELIGIOUS ORGANIZATIONS

Some churches, synagogues, and mosques have turned their backs on gay people, but gay people of faith have not given up their religious beliefs. There are so many organizations for gay believers that we cannot list them all. It is heartening indeed.

To find a welcoming Christian congregation of any denomination, visit GayChurch.org, an international directory of "gay- and lesbian-friendly Christian churches throughout the world." The churches in the Metropolitan Community Church* network (www.mcchurch. org) are among the most gay friendly—they are run by and for gay people (although, of course, all are welcome), and you can find one pretty much wherever in the United States—or the world—you are.

For religious issues specific to the transgender community, start with TransFaith Online, an ecumenical site: http://www.transfaithonline.org.

The following is a partial listing of national organizations. Most should be able to refer you to a congregation in your area. (A few smaller organizations have been included because there are far fewer groups for non-Christians.)

Affirmation (Methodist): www.umaffirm.org

Affirmation (Mormon)*: www.affirmation.org
Like the Church of Latter Day Saints itself, Affirmation is a large, worldwide organization with chapters across the United States as well as in Europe, Australia, South Africa, and South Korea.

---

* *These groups have special services or ministries specifically for young people.*

al-Fatiha (Muslim)*: www.al-fatiha.org
A U.S.-based international organization with two chapters here (New York and Atlanta), al-Fatiha sponsors annual conferences and provides asylum support. Its human rights advocacy includes interfaith work. A member of al-Fatiha works with PFLAG to sensitize that organization to issues specific to Muslim families.

Association of Welcoming and Affirming Baptists: www.wabaptists.org

Brethren Mennonite Council for LGBT Interests*: www.bmclgbt.org

A Common Bond (Jehovah's Witness): www.gayxjw.org
Comprised both of people who "were, [and] still are, associated with the church," A Common Bond is a resource for active as well as "recovering" Jehovah's Witnesses.

Dignity (Catholic): www.dignityusa.org

Emergence International (Christian Scientist): www.emergence-international.org

Friends for Lesbian, Gay, Bisexual, Transgender and Queer Concerns (Quaker): flgbtqc.quaker.org

Gay and Lesbian Acceptance (Community of Christ): galaweb.org

Gay Bible Christians (Pentecostal): www.gaybiblechristians.org
"Don't let bad Christians keep you from a good God." There are a growing number of gay Pentecostal churches across the United States. Some have broken away from the Metropolitan Community Church, whose theology some members found too liberal. Start with this site or that of the Apostolic Restoration Mission (apostolicrestorationmission.4t.com) to find them.

Gay, Lesbian and Affirming Disciples Alliance (Disciples of Christ): www.gladalliance.org

The Gay and Lesbian Vaishnava Association (Hindu): www.galva108.org

The Gay & Lesbian Yeshiva Day School Alumni Association (Orthodox Jews): members.aol.com/orthogays
"Yes, it's possible to be gay and *frum*."

Integrity (Episcopal): www.integrityusa.org

JQ Youth (Orthodox Jews): www.jqyouth.org
A social/support group of *frum* and formerly *frum* gay Jews under thirty. In addition to monthly meetings and informal get-togethers, JQ hosts an anonymous online discussion group.

Keshet Ga'avah/The World Congress of GLBT Jews: www.glbtjews.org

Kinship (Seventh Day Adventist): www.sdakinship.org

Lutherans Concerned North America: www.lcna.org

More Light (Presbyterian): www.mlp.org

Rainbow Baptists: www.rainbowbaptists.org

Salaam Canada (Muslim): salaamcanada.com

* *These groups have special services or ministries specifically for young people.*

United Church of Christ Coalition for LGBT Concerns*: www.ucccoalition.org

Unitarian Universalists: www.uua.org

One of the most welcoming Protestant denominations, the Unitarian Universalist Association of Congregations has a special Office of Bisexual, Lesbian, Gay, and Transgender Concerns that operates on a national level.

* *These groups have special services or ministries specifically for young people.*

FUNDRAISING

The Rainbow Endowment

c/o Friends Center
1501 Cherry Street
Philadelphia, PA 19102
www.rainbowendowment.org

With less than 2 percent of private philanthropic dollars devoted to gay issues, and little coming from government sources, the burden of funding litigation, education, advocacy, and services falls most heavily on the gay community and its friends and families. To that end, the Rainbow Endowment, founded by tennis legend Martina Navratilova, offers the Rainbow Card: a credit card that lets you contribute simply by using it. Every time you use the card, part of the transaction goes directly to the Rainbow Endowment—and then back out to the gay community. Once a year, the Rainbow Endowment invites nonprofits whose work has a national impact on the gay community to submit requests for funding. Since 1996, the organization has distributed seventy-eight grants totaling nearly $1.5 million. Please consider applying for a card today. —*Mitchell Gold*

ORGANIZATIONS NOT TO CALL

When I suggest that under no circumstances should you contact the following organizations, I do so very carefully and sincerely. Although many of the names may sound warm and caring, they represent a true danger to gay teens. They offer something called "reparative therapy," which purports to change a person's sexual orientation. Not only has science shown that this is impossible, but the effort to "change" a person has been found to be harmful. I've seen the damage done to too many people. Several of them tell their stories in this book.

Following is a list of national groups. If you are unsure whether a local organization is an affiliate of one of these national groups, check http://www .geocities.com/exgaylinks/NationalLinksAD.html. You can learn more about the dangers of reparative therapy in "What Is Reparative Therapy?" immediately following this list.

American Family Association
Courage Apostolate (*Roman Catholic*)
Desert Stream Ministries/Living Waters

Disciples2 (*Mormon*)

Evergreen International (*Mormon*)

Exodus Global Alliance

Exodus International

Exodus Youth

Family Research Council

Focus on the Family

Free to Be Me

Genesis Counseling Services

Higher Path Life Coaching

Homosexuals Anonymous

International Healing Foundation

Jews Offering New Alternatives to Homosexuality (JONAH)

Love in Action

Love Won Out (Focus on the Family)

National Association for Research and Therapy of Homosexuality (NARTH)

New Direction for Life Ministries (*Canada*)

One by One (*Presbyterian*)

Parents and Friends Ministries

Parents and Friends of Ex-Gays (PFOX)

People Can Change

Stephen Bennett Ministries (SBM)

The Way Out (*Southern Baptist*)

WHAT IS REPARATIVE THERAPY?

Frank discussions between parents and children about sex can, of course, be challenging no matter what their sexual orientation. And many people find their sexuality a source of conflict for many different reasons—societal, familial, and religious attitudes toward sex among them. However, for young gay people striving to be open and honest with their loved ones, dealing with sexuality can be particularly problematic because of a sense of conflict between who they know they are and who they've been taught they should be.

Traditional sources of guidance and support like clergy and therapists can help work through such conflicts—but only if they start from a place where one's sexuality is accepted as a healthy element of a larger whole. When therapy is provided by organizations whose basic tenets are unreceptive to the idea of homosexuality, it puts gay people in an untenable position.

How a person feels about his or her sexual orientation is certainly a valid topic for therapy; sexual orientation itself, however, is not a changeable characteristic that can be "treated." Most people are straight; others are gay; still others fall somewhere in between. But we are who we are. A person's orientation cannot be changed through behavior modification, aversion therapy, psychoanalysis, prayer, or religious counseling.

Reparative therapy is a term used to describe an extensive and damaging process known by many other names, including *conversion therapy, sexual reorientation therapy, sexual identity therapy, gender identity therapy, gender affirmative therapy*, and *context specific therapy*. Some of the chapters in this book provide accounts of people who put themselves through it or were forced to undergo it.

Reparative therapy has been widely discredited as not only ineffective but also outright harmful. While some organizations offering such "cures" are straightforward in their nonetheless false claims, others lure patients and families in at their most vulnerable time by appearing to be gay-friendly— Free to Be Me is particularly dangerous in this regard—or by masquerading as therapies for sexual addiction, a problem among gay and straight people alike. Many "ex-gay" ministries are in fact associated with right-wing political movements that also seek to roll back the civil rights gained by gay people since the 1970s (so much for "love the sinner, hate the sin . . .").

All major national mental health organizations have officially expressed concerns about therapies promoted to modify sexual orientation, as have their sister organizations in Western Europe and Canada. Reparative therapy is actively opposed by the American Medical Association, the American Psychological Association, the National Association of Social Workers, the American Academy of Pediatrics, and the American Psychiatric Association, which "opposes any psychiatric treatment, such as 'reparative' or 'conversion' therapy that is based upon the assumption that homosexuality per se is a mental disorder or based upon a prior assumption that the patient should change his/her homosexual orientation."

These are not fly-by-night groups. They are the groups whose members have been behind finding treatments for the most serious health concerns of the twentieth century—polio, tuberculosis, diabetes, depression, AIDS—and are facing down the biggest public health threats of the twenty-first century. According to the American Psychological Association,

> There has been no scientifically adequate research to show that therapy aimed at changing sexual orientation . . . is safe or effective. Furthermore, it seems likely that the promotion of change

therapies reinforces stereotypes and contributes to a negative climate for lesbian, gay, and bisexual persons. This appears to be especially likely for lesbian, gay, and bisexual individuals who grow up in more conservative religious settings.

The Royal College of Psychiatrists, Great Britain's answer to the American Psychiatric Association, goes even further:

> [T]hey may be misunderstood by therapists who regard their homosexuality as the root cause of any presenting problem such as depression or anxiety. Unfortunately, therapists who behave in this way are likely to cause considerable distress. A small minority of therapists will even go so far as to attempt to change their client's sexual orientation. This can be deeply damaging. Although there is now a number of therapists and organisation[s] in the USA and in the UK that claim that therapy can help homosexuals to become heterosexual, there is no evidence that such change is possible.

Certainly there have been enough "relapses" of people prominent in the "ex-gay" movement to have proven this by now. (Michael Bussee, the cofounder of Exodus International, who has since married his life partner and become an outspoken critic of the ex-gay movement, and John Paulk, the former leader of Love Won Out, who resigned after being photographed exiting a gay bar in Washington, DC, are but two examples.) Such therapies do not change the sexual orientation people are born with and cannot ever do so.

The road to hell can indeed be well intentioned: Well-meaning people often try to rid themselves or their children of something they believe is an illness or the source of their unhappiness. Of course, being gay is not an illness and it is not the problem. The problem is people's attitudes *about* being gay (a core theme of this book) and how those attitudes have made people feel about themselves. Is it so shocking to learn that the reparative therapy movement itself can actually trace its roots to Nazi Germany, a regime that not only imprisoned gay men but also has the dubious distinction of inventing the idea of curing gay people?

Rather than resolving conflicts, reparative therapy programs create new ones by falsely promising gay people who are unhappy with their sexual orientation that they can become heterosexual. When gay men and women find that they can't change, they end up with feelings of guilt and failure that lead to depression, loss of friends and social support, addictive behaviors, and substance abuse. Some force themselves into marriages that then fail—sometimes after having children. Some who have sought relief in reparative therapy have actually become suicidal instead.

A good therapist, counselor, psychologist, psychiatrist, or clergyperson should be able to treat the whole person or the whole family. I consider myself truly lucky because when I was in college, on the verge of a nervous breakdown and thinking constantly about suicide, I went to a therapist who probably saved my life. On my first visit, I finally actually said the words to him: "I'm gay but I want to change." And he told me—and I will never forget his words—"Oh, it's okay that you're gay. Many people are. I can't help you change that, but I can help you live with it."

According to the American Psychological Association, the goal of therapy for someone troubled about same-sex attraction should be to "help that person actively cope with social prejudices against homosexuality, successfully resolve issues associated with and resulting from internal conflicts, and actively lead a happy and satisfying life"—not to fix what is not broken. Prayer and spirituality can and should be a part of that process when appropriate, but neither prayer nor therapy can be or should be expected to change someone's sexual orientation.

Some of the groups listed under "Organizations Not to Call" offer counseling provided by genuine therapists (MSWs) or psychologists (PhDs); many, however, are staffed by unlicensed or lay counselors. Whoever their practitioners, not only are their principles antithetical to established medical, psychological, psychiatric, and therapeutic practices but also their practitioners lack the acceptance, understanding, and decency necessary to help someone lead a healthy and productive life.

I believe these groups actually prey on vulnerable people—and especially on young people who, because of parental pressure or sheer inexperience, are not in a position to reject what these organizations are peddling. These groups are full of the worst kind of charlatans, offering medicine that is not just fake, but also poisonous.

ACKNOWLEDGMENTS

To begin I would like to thank my sister-in-law, Mindy Drucker Gold, for helping me bring this book to life, which was one of the most difficult tasks I've ever embarked on. She started the book with me because I asked her to. But as she researched and interviewed people with and without me, I could see it changing her life. Today she is doggedly dedicated to protecting all teenagers who need protecting. She has always been a very special sister-in-law to me, a warm and wonderful caring person, but this book took our relationship to a new level. To say I could not have done this without her is a gross understatement. To say that I love her more than all the stars in the galaxy is also a gross understatement.

Brent Childers has been an invaluable help to us. He's been on a journey that I am honored to accompany him on. Never did we ask for some outrageously deep research to be done that he didn't jump on it instantly . . . the day or time had little relevance to him.

Jimmy Creech, Rev. Mel White, Rodney Powell, and Bishop Gene Robinson are my guiding lights, my checks for moral clarity on a regular basis, people in my life who have been so generous with their time and spirit and provided me with invaluable background information for this book. But most of all, they have each inspired me to maintain my faith in America and to believe that when the true harm is exposed, people will act differently.

Bob Williams, my continuing business partner and former life partner for more than fourteen years, has been by my side with the constant encouragement one needs to complete a project like this. He has been especially patient, always available to provide great guidance on the content as well as the graphic elements of the book.

To Al and Tipper Gore: Your intense determination to help educate America about global warming in the face of so much cynicism and inaction has inspired me to continue on my path. Your success in helping to change America's thinking these past years has given me great hope that once again truth will prevail. Thank you.

Also to the following: Peter Petrillo and Eric Norfleet, my business partners with Wafra Investments, who provide me with an environment to do what I want to do most: create a world more comfortable for everyone in many different ways. George Ackerman, our company president, for making sure I got this book done because he values all human life. Eloise Goldman and Lane Hudson for their dedication to making sure as many people as possible are exposed to this book. Charley Holt, Leslie Stoll, Ken Hipp, Lewis Kohnle, Dan Gauthreaux, Garrett Barr, and all the other good people at work who knew to give me the space to write and edit. Thanks to Ben Precup and Nathan Banks for their graphic assistance, and Nan Huegerich for her legal advice. And special thanks to Dan Swift, my gatekeeper, who knew when to open them and close them so I would get this done, and who helped us with whatever was needed, whenever it was needed, with utmost professionalism. All of you have been so invaluable.

To Greenleaf Book Group, who saw the value in this project and worked at record speed to bring it out as soon as possible. Alan Grimes, Lisa Woods, Meg LaBorde, Sheila Parr, Justin Branch, Jay Hodges, Kristen Sears, Ryan Wheeler, and the whole team . . . you are wonderful to work with.

To Andrew Miller, ghostwriter and editor extraordinaire, for his commitment and his much-needed sense of humor, even on deadline. To Duncan Osborne, of *Gay City News*, for sharing his knowledge about reparative therapy and for responding to questions about far-flung subjects quickly and accurately (and always in good humor); and to James Waller for his invaluable insights into the history of religion. To Jorge Valencia, Vince Garcia, and Ginger Voelker for bringing the wonderful Point Foundation Scholars into our lives. And to Kevin Jennings and Benny Vasquez of the Gay, Lesbian and Straight Education Network for introducing us to Julia.

To Tim Scofield, my partner in life . . . who knows (?), maybe we'll be married by the time this book comes out (!) and all of America will accept and value our family. Thank you for putting up with the late-night editing and the emotional roller coaster as I became part of the life of each of the contributors.

To my parents for giving me the strength to be who I am and for passing on some of their best traits to me. My mother has a great sense of humor and a proven ability to write. I'm sorry this book doesn't show that I got her sense of humor—but hopefully she'll see how all those years of correcting my English have paid off and it'll make her proud. My father is deeply emotional in a very loving way. I've got that part of him in me, and I hope it comes through in these pages.

To my brother, Richard, who always watched out for me from the moment my parents brought me home from the hospital . . . to the day I came out to him . . . and well beyond. Don't say anything bad about me because you'll have him to contend with! To both brother Richard and niece Adrianne, special thanks for lending me your wife and mother for a year to do this book. She would not have been able to do it without your love and support. She adores you both as do I.

To my best friends Reed and Paula: since I was fourteen years old, you've given me the luxury of being who I am with no pressure.

To the many people who have encouraged me on this journey, and with special thanks for the support of the other founding members of Faith in America: Judith Light, Jimmy Creech, Garry Kief, Rodney Powell, Bob Williams, Chad Ramsey, Howard Vine, Jim McGreevey, Ken Wilkinson, and Janis Hirsch.

Finally, to all the strong and courageous contributors to this book. I feel like we have become a family, sharing secrets we tried to forget because the pain was so terrible at times. To each of you who shared little-known portions of your life, who allowed yourself to be vulnerable to millions of people, a special thank-you with enormous appreciation.

I hope each of us will have helped to play a significant role in protecting this and future generations.

PHOTO CREDITS

Through the experiences of five Christian American families—including those of Richard Gephardt and Bishop Gene Robinson—we discover how people of faith handle the realization of having a gay child or family member.

Offering healing, clarity, and understanding to anyone caught in the crosshairs of scripture and sexual identity, this landmark film "boldly takes on a loaded topic and examines it both intellectually and emotionally; the result may well leave you blinking away a few tears." (*Seattle Times*) 2007, 98 minutes, color

Created by Dan Karslake, one of the contributors to this book, the award-winning documentary also features several other contributors to CRISIS, including Rev. Irene Monroe, Jimmy Creech, Bruce Bastian, Rev. Dr. Mel White, and Mary Lou Wallner.